BLACK AMERICANS

ETHNIC GROUPS IN AMERICAN LIFE SERIES

Milton M. Gordon, *editor*

GOLDSTEIN/GOLDSCHEIDER   JEWISH AMERICANS: Three Generations
                           in a Jewish Community

PINKNEY   BLACK AMERICANS

The American Negro is a unique crea-
tion; he has no counterpart anywhere
and no predecessors.

JAMES BALDWIN

BLACK

AMERICANS

ALPHONSO PINKNEY

Hunter College

PRENTICE-HALL, INC., ENGLEWOOD CLIFFS, NEW JERSEY

© 1969 by Prentice-Hall, Inc., Englewood Cliffs, New Jersey

Library of Congress Catalog Card No.: 69–10632

Current printing (last digit):

10 9 8 7 6 5 4 3 2 1

Printed in the United States of America

PRENTICE-HALL INTERNATIONAL, INC., *London*
PRENTICE-HALL OF AUSTRALIA, PTY. LTD., *Sydney*
PRENTICE-HALL OF CANADA, LTD., *Toronto*
PRENTICE-HALL OF INDIA PRIVATE LTD., *New Delhi*
PRENTICE-HALL OF JAPAN, INC., *Tokyo*

For My People

Foreword

The problem of how people of diverse racial, religious, and nationality backgrounds can live together peaceably and creatively within the same national society is one of the most crucial issues facing mankind, second in importance only to the overriding problem of international war itself. Indeed, these two problem areas, while not identical, are, from the view point of recurring social processes of group interaction, interrelated at many points. The United States of America, as the classic example of a highly industrialized nation made up of people of diverse ethnic origins, constitutes, both in its history and its current situation, a huge living laboratory for the serious study of various underlying patterns of ethnic interaction—patterns which produced in this country both corroding failure (particularly with respect to the treatment of racial minorities) and certain modified successes which, however, have by no means been free of a residue of unfulfilled personal hopes, psychological scars, and unjustified hardships for those who were not born with the majority sociological characteristics of being white, Protestant, and of Anglo-Saxon cultural origins.

The explosion in the 1960's of the Negro's or black American's anger and growing revolt against centuries of white prejudice and discrimination have shocked the nation out of an attitude of mass complacency with regard to ethnic group relations. Now, not only social scientists, academic liberals, and well-meaning humanitarians, many of whom had waged valiant battles against racism before, but also millions of other Americans in all walks of life are becoming aware that to devalue another human being simply on the grounds of his race, religion, or national origins, and to act accordingly, is to strike at the very core of his personality and to create a living legacy of personal hatred and social disorganization. All the great religious and ethical traditions had spoken out prophetically against ethnic prejudice (however weak their followers have been in implementation). Now it has become increasingly clear that sheer self-interest and the desire to preserve a viable nation sternly countenance the conclusion that prejudice and discrimination are dubious luxuries which Americans can no longer afford.

We have spoken of the social-scientific knowledge to be derived (and, hopefully, to be creatively used) from intensive study of American ethnic groups. There is another reason to commend such focused scientific attention. The history and the decisive contributions of the various racial, religious, and national origins groups to the warp and woof of American life is not a story that, to say the least, has been overly told in American publication or pedagogy. The important pioneer studies on the Negro of E. Franklin Frazier, John Hope Franklin, and Gunnar Myrdal, and on the white immigrant of Marcus Hansen, Oscar Handlin, and John Higham, all stem from either the present generation or the one immediately preceding it. In the main, American minority ethnic groups have been, by patronizing omission, long deprived of their past in America and of a rightful pride in the nature of their role in the making and shaping of the American nation. It is time for a systematic overview, group by group, of this long neglected portion of the American experience, one that on the one hand avoids filiopietistic banalities and, on the other, does justice to the real and complex nature of the American multiethnic experience.

A final and equally compelling reason for instituting a series of studies of America's ethnic groups at this time is that more adequate theoretical tools for carrying out the respective analyses are currently at hand. In my book, *Assimilation in American Life,* published in 1964, I presented a multidimensional approach to the conceptualization of that omnibus term "assimilation" and endeavored to factor it into its various component processes, at the same time offering certain hypotheses concerning the ways in which these processes were related to each other. Such an approach appears to facilitate dealing with the considerable complexity inherent in the functioning of a pluralistic society. Furthermore, studies of social stratification or social class which have burgeoned to become such an important part of American sociology in the past few decades have made it abundantly clear that the dynamics of ethnic group life, both internally and externally, constantly involve the interplay of class and ethnic considerations. And, lastly, the passage of time, producing a third generation of native-born children of native-born parents even among those ethnic groups who appeared in large numbers in the last great peak of emigration to America in the early part of the twentieth century, has emphasized the need for considering generational change and the sociological and social psychological processes peculiar to each successive generation of ethnic Americans.

For all these reasons, I am proud to function in the capacity of general editor of a series of books which will attempt to provide the American public with a descriptive and analytic overview of its ethnic heritage in the third quarter of the twentieth century from the viewpoint of relevant social science. Each book on a particular ethnic group (and we include the white Protestants as such a sociologically definable entity) is written by an expert in the field of intergroup relations and the social life of the group about which he writes, and in many cases the author derives ethnically himself from that group. It is my hope that the publication of this series will aid substantially in the process of enabling Americans to understand more fully what it means to live in a multi-ethnic society and, concomitantly, what we must do in the future to eliminate the corrosive and devastating phenomena of prejudice and discrimination and to ensure that a pluralistic society can at the same time fulfill its promised destiny of being truly "one nation indivisible."

MILTON M. GORDON

Preface

Relations between black and white Americans have never been amicable, but at few points in history have they been characterized by greater strain than they are at the present time. The history of race relations in the United States has been one in which white people have maintained a position of dominance over black people, relegating them to a lower castelike position in the society. Throughout this long history black people have attempted to liberate themselves from oppression by a variety of means, but these attempts either have been suppressed or have been ignored. In the current crisis black people are making greater demands than they have before, and, while they have made some gains, especially in the last decade, the gap between living standards for black and white Americans is still a vast one.

The present study presents a reasonably complete picture of the status of black people in the United States at the present time. It begins with their first arrival in 1619 and continues up to the present crisis in race relations. Because the history of black people is a complicated one, it has been necessary to sacrifice detail for a recounting of the major events directly relevant to their present status. Life in a racist society for more than 350 years has led to the formation of a vast underclass of citizens in the United States, maintained by differential access to rewards in all social institutions. The oppressed status of black people, then, is a direct result of social arrangements and practices. Therefore, the major emphasis of the present study has been placed on an analysis of the forces in American society which have been responsible for creating and maintaining the subordinate position of black people. Racism in American life is so entrenched and the determination of black Americans for liberation is so great that the present crisis in race relations was inevitable.

Throughout this book the words *black* and *Negro* are used interchangeably. The term *Negro* is used to describe the subjects of this book because it refers to the descendants of the people who arrived from Africa in 1619. It is a term which was invented by white people to apply to black people in the United States; consequently, the black community increasingly disapproves of its use and increasingly prefers the term *black* because it was not designated by white people. Furthermore, it denotes a sense of pride in racial identity.

While this book is a sociological study of black people in the United States, it addresses the general reader as well as the professional student of society. Therefore, lay language has been used throughout. It is hoped that sociological perspective and analysis have not been sacrificed.

Many persons have helped produce this book. Chief among them was Donald L. Noel, who read the entire manuscript. His many suggestions have, in large measure, been incorporated. My secretary, Cecelia Beirne, typed the manuscript several times, displaying amazing patience. Milton Gordon, the editor of the series in which this book appears, contributed many valuable suggestions. Pamela Fischer, the production editor, was especially helpful in solving many of the problems involved in publishing the book. The Hunter College Summer Grants in the Humanities program provided financial assistance.

Whatever virtues this book may have must be shared; its shortcomings are mine alone.

ALPHONSO PINKNEY

Contents

Historians insist that a knowledge of the past is essential for understanding the present. This axiom is especially relevant insofar as black Americans are concerned, for theirs is a unique history. Virtually all aspects of their history are without parallel when compared to those of other minority groups in the United States. The very circumstances which led to their departure from their homeland, the Middle Passage between Africa and the New World, and the institution of slavery which developed on their arrival in what is now the United States are unique to only black Americans out of all U.S. minority groups. The institution of slavery, with all its peculiarities, has left a legacy which continues to play a dominant role in the life of Americans. After nearly three and a half centuries white Americans continue to react to Negroes with a mass irrationality which precludes the complete entrance of blacks into the larger society. Yet it would be difficult to imagine members of a group putting forth more diligent and persistent efforts for acceptance than those put forth by black Americans. A variety of approaches has been attempted throughout the years, and some gains have been made; but a series of historical circumstances has served to preserve the low status of Negroes in the society.

Historical Background

The history of black people in the United States is a complex one, and no attempt to record this detailed sequence of events in one chapter can succeed. However, certain occurrences have greater bearing on the present status of black people in American society than others have. It is to these circumstances that attention is now turned.

SLAVERY

Black people were among the earliest participants in the Spanish explorations of what is now the United States, but the first Negroes to settle on its shores arrived in 1619. In that year a Dutch vessel landed in Jamestown, and the captain sold 20 Negroes to the Virginia settlers. This was 12 years after the establishment in Virginia of the first permanent British colony in America and one year before the *Mayflower* landed the Pilgrims at Plymouth Rock (Massachusetts). Inasmuch as there was no precedent for slavery in English law, these blacks and those who followed for some time had the same legal status as white indentured servants. Their term of service was prescribed by local laws. Throughout much of the 17th century the status of the black man was not at all clearly defined, and the institution of chattel slavery gradually evolved into one in which black people, in part because of their physical differences, were to hold a caste position in society. Like white indentured servants, it was possible for them to gain their freedom after working for a specified number of years or after conversion to Christianity. Their status was that of indentured servant rather than of slave. The ambiguity of this status, combined with the uncertainties attached to the Indian and white indentured servant supply, led to the ultimate relegation of black people to a status of perpetual servitude.[1]

Slavery as practiced in North America was a complex institution. In some respects the practices varied by state, region (Deep South vs. Border South), size of plantation, number of slaves involved, season of the year, and, of course, by the convictions of the individual slaveholders. However, many practices were common throughout the slaveholding states. Furthermore, many of the restrictions imposed on the slaves were also applicable to "free" Negroes in the United States, both in the South and elsewhere in the country. In addition to the general characteristics of slavery in the South, of special relevance to the present discussion are the slaves' loss of their native culture, the attitude of white people toward slaves, the reaction of slaves to their status, and the status of black people who technically were not slaves.

General Characteristics
of Slavery

The first statutory recognition of slavery in North America occurred in Virginia in 1661. This lead was soon followed by the other colonies, and, by the time the colonies gained independence, chattel slavery and a body of law defining the status of slaves had become institutionalized. These laws covered every aspect of the slave's life. In general, slavery in North America developed into the harshest form of social relations ever to exist. The slave received none of the protections of organized society because he was not considered to be a person; rather, he was considered to be property, and only to the extent that a citizen's property must be protected could the slave expect society's consideration. The slaveholder maintained absolute power over his property. He was endowed by law with rights over the slave, and in return he was expected to assume certain obligations toward the slave. "The law required that masters be humane

---

[1] Joseph Boskin, "Race Relations in Seventeenth Century America: The Problem of the Origins of Negro Slavery," *Sociology and Social Research,* Vol. 49 (July 1965), 446–55; John Hope Franklin, *From Slavery to Freedom* (New York: Knopf, 1948), pp. 70–71; Wilbert E. Moore, "Slave Law and the Social Structure," *Journal of Negro History,* Vol. 26 (1941), 171–202.

to their slaves, furnish them adequate food and clothing, and provide care for them during sickness and old age." [2] Therefore slaves were at one and the same time human beings and property, and "throughout the antebellum South the cold language of statutes and judicial decisions made it evident that, legally, the slave was less a person than a thing." [3] In such a status the slaves were denied virtually all rights, both civil and political. Perhaps the most important element in defining the slaves' status was the perpetual nature of slavery; slaves were destined to occupy this status throughout their lives and to transmit it to their children, who in turn transmitted their inherited status to their children. Slavery and Negro became synonymous, and, since slaves were defined as innately inferior, Negroes were defined as inferior beings.

Because slaves were forbidden by law to enter into contractual arrangements, their marriages were not legally binding relationships. Husbands, wives, and children could be separated at the discretion of the slaveholder, as was frequently the case. Thus it was impossible to maintain a stable family system. The slave family had little importance as regards the traditional functions which marriage was expected to perform for those who entered into the relationship. Parents had little to say or do about rearing children or controlling other forces leading to cohesion in family life. The nature of the institution of slavery was such that no family in the usual sense can be said to have existed. Children derived their condition from the status of the mother. The father ". . . was not the head of the family, the holder of property, the provider, the protector." [4] His wife could be undressed and either whipped or violated by the slaveholder or overseer in his presence and in the presence of the children.

Slaves were property which could be sold, traded, or given as gifts, and slave families were frequently dissolved for economic reasons. As Stampp has written, "They were awarded as prizes in lotteries and raffles; they were wagered at gambling tables and horse races. They were, in short, property in fact as well as in law." [5] Female slaves were encouraged to engage in promiscuous relations with other slaves. Although these relations occasionally developed into stable ones, they were more often casual associations entered into for the express purpose of reproduction. In the words of Frazier: "To the slave trader, who had only an economic interest in the slave, the Negro was a mere utility." [6] Clearly no stable

[2] Kenneth M. Stampp, *The Peculiar Institution* (New York: Knopf, 1956), p. 192.
[3] *Ibid.*, p. 193.
[4] *Ibid.*, p. 343.
[5] *Ibid.*, p. 201.
[6] E. Franklin Frazier, *The Negro Family in the United States* (Chicago: The University of Chicago Press, 1966), p. 360.

family system could develop under such circumstances. The permanency of marriage depended on those rare opportunities which slaves had to live and work together within a situation of common experiences and trust.

According to the laws of the antebellum South, slaves had no civil or property rights. "A slave might not make a will, and he could not, by will, inherit anything. Slaves were not to hire themselves out, locate their own employment, establish their own residence, or make contracts for any purpose. . . ." [7] They could not be a party to suits involving free persons. Strict interpretations of laws regulated every aspect of their lives, and the enforcement machinery was such that violation rarely went unpunished. These strict laws were geared toward the behavior of the slaves, but they also clearly regulated the behavior of whites who might interfere with slave discipline. A variety of punishment was meted out to slaves who were found guilty of violating the slave codes, the most frequent being whipping for minor crimes and harsher forms of punishment, including burnings and mutilation, for more serious crimes. The death penalty was common and resulted from such offenses as striking whites.

Stampp views the rigidity of the codes and the harshness of the punishments as serving to instill fear in the slaves. This, he maintains, was accomplished through a series of steps designed by the slaveholders to preserve absolute control over their "human property." The steps were: ". . . accustom him to rigid discipline, demand from him unconditional submission, impress upon him his innate inferiority, train him to adopt the master's code of good behavior, and instill in him a sense of complete dependence." [8]

The work performed by the slaves depended on whether they were on a large plantation or a small farm; whether they were rural or urban; whether the slaveholder specialized in cotton, tobacco, rice, sugar cane, hemp, or other agricultural products; whether they were male or female; whether they were assigned to the slaveholder's house or to his fields; and, of course, the season of the year. Regardless of the foregoing conditions, however, slaves were generally required to work from sunrise until dusk. They usually worked under the supervision of a white overseer, whose job it was to maintain strict discipline. All slaves were required to work, and the slaveholder decided at what age children should go into the fields. In general, by the age of five or six, children were expected to

[7] Arnold A. Sio, "Interpretations of Slavery," *Comparative Studies in Society and History,* Vol. VII (1965), 294.
[8] Stampp, *op. cit.,* p. 148.

follow their parents into the fields. When a slave woman was too old to work in the fields, she was expected to perform domestic tasks for the other slaves, such as caring for small children and preparing food. Old men tended gardens and cared for the animals.

On larger plantations an elaborate division of labor developed. There were skilled craftsmen, such as carpenters, mechanics, and black-smiths; a variety of domestic servants, such as coachmen, housemaids, butlers, cooks, laundresses, etc.; and, of course, there were field hands who cultivated and harvested the crops. In the cities slaves worked in construction and maintenance work, in domestic work, at various crafts such as carpentry and cabinetmaking, in laundries, and in cotton presses.[9] There were few occupational tasks in the antebellum South that slaves did not perform, and, although some slaves managed to evade the 14- to 16-hour day by malingering, the system was such that most of them were forced into a rigorous routine of hard labor.

Because of the division of labor among slaves, status distinctions developed among them. Status was frequently derived from the wealth and extent of holdings of the slaveholder, but the most important distinc-tions were those between domestic slaves and those relegated to field work. The "house slaves" enjoyed higher status that the "field slaves," and they jealously guarded their superior positions. Slaveholders tended to attach greater significance to the appearance of these slaves, and being around the slaveholder's family afforded them the opportunity to assimilate the external forms of behavior which they observed.[10] Slaveholders and their families, who usually preferred mulatto house servants, encouraged the division between "house slaves" and "field slaves" as a means of main-taining control over them.[11]

The living conditions of the slaves were generally in keeping with their almost total lack of status. Most of them lived in small crude huts without the most elementary provisions for sanitation and safety, such as floors, windows, and interior walls. Whole families were frequently crammed into a one-room cabin. According to Stampp, "The common run of slave cabins were cramped, crudely built, scantily furnished, un-painted, and dirty."[12] Cabins were generally without stoves, beds, or other essentials. Writing about his childhood as a plantation slave, Booker T. Washington recalled: "I cannot remember having slept in a

[9] Richard C. Wade, *Slavery in the Cities* (New York: Oxford, 1964), pp. 28–54.

[10] E. Franklin Frazier, *The Negro in the United States* (New York: Macmillan, 1957), p. 55.

[11] See Frederick L. Olmstead, *The Cotton Kingdom,* ed. Arthur M. Schlesinger (New York: Knopf, 1953), p. 184; Stampp, *op. cit.,* pp. 151–53.

[12] Stampp, *op. cit.,* p. 294.

bed until after our family was declared free by the Emancipation Proclamation. Three children—John, my older brother, Amanda, my sister,
and myself—had a pallet on the dirt floor, or, to be more correct, we slept
in and on a bundle of filthy rags laid upon the dirt floor." [13] He reports
that his mother, the plantation cook, prepared food for all the slaves and
whites on the plantation on an open fire in their small cabin. The
crowded conditions under which slaves were forced to live were a constant threat to health and sanity. "One Mississippi planter had 24 huts,
each measuring 16 by 14 feet, for his 150 slaves." [14]

On some of the larger plantations, slaveholders maintained com-
munal kitchens for all slaves, but in general the food provided was the
least expensive possible and no consideration was given to its nutritional
value. "A peck of cornmeal and three or four pounds of salt pork or
bacon comprised the basic weekly allowance of the great majority of
adult slaves." [15]

Living under such adverse conditions, the morbidity and mortality
rates among slaves were high. Such illnesses as malaria, yellow fever,
cholera, pneumonia, tuberculosis, and tetanus were widespread. Infant
and maternal mortality were commonplace. Some of the larger plantations maintained medical doctors for the care of the slaves, but folk
medical practices were usually resorted to. Even when doctors were available, the practice of medicine among the slaves was something short of
scientific. The doctors frequently complained that they were unable to
administer treatment because the slaves were not amenable to the same
medical treatment as white patients. Frances Kemble summarized the
conditions in a slave infirmary on one plantation: "In all, filth, disorder,
and misery abounded; the floor was the only bed, and scanty begrimed
rags of blankets the only covering." [16]

Loss of Native Culture

The Africans who arrived in North America were a diverse people who
represented many cultures. Contrary to popular belief, they were representative of a variety of highly advanced civilizations.[17] These slaves

[13] Booker T. Washington, *Up from Slavery* (New York: Doubleday, 1900), pp. 3–4.
[14] Franklin, *op. cit.*, p. 194.
[15] Stampp, *op. cit.*, p. 282.
[16] Frances A. Kemble, *Journal of a Residence on a Georgia Plantation in 1838–
1839*, ed. John A. Scott (New York: Knopf, 1961), p. 71.
[17] See Lerone Bennett, Jr., *Before the Mayflower* (Baltimore: Penguin Books,
1966); Edwin R. Embree, *Brown Americans* (New York: Viking, 1946); John Hope
Franklin, *op. cit.;* Melville Herskovits, *The Myth of the Negro Past* (New York: Harper,
1941); August Meier and Elliott Rudwick, *From Plantation to Ghetto* (New York: Hill
and Wang, Inc., 1966), pp. 4–22; Charles Silberman, *Crisis in Black and White* (New
York: Random House, 1964), especially Chap. VI.

carried with them to North America a knowledge of the complex cultures they left behind. How much of this original culture was able to survive the brutality of antebellum slavery has been disputed by scholars. There is general agreement, however, that systematic attempts were made to strip these people of their culture. In the first place, slaves were widely scattered on plantations, small farms, and cities throughout the colonies and later throughout the United States. Secondly, slaves arriving in North America were from a diversity of cultural backgrounds. These cultures might have contained many common elements, but they contained even more distinctive characteristics. Furthermore, since young male slaves predominated in the earliest importations, it was virtually impossible for the slaves to recreate the cultures they knew. Frazier summarizes the impact of slavery on the slaves as follows:

> The African family system was destroyed, and the slave was separated from his kinsmen and friends. Moreover, in the United States there was little chance that he could reknit the ties of friendship and old associations. If by chance he encountered fellow slaves with whom he could communicate in his native tongue, he was separated from them. From the very beginning he was forced to learn English in order to obey the commands of his white masters. Whatever memories he might have retained of his native land and native customs became meaningless in the New World.[18]

It is not surprising, therefore, that much of the Old World culture failed to survive. However, the circumstances under which slaves lived did not preclude their retaining some cultural characteristics. For example, Franklin sees African survivals in language, folk tales, music, social organization, and aesthetic endeavors.[19] Other scholars maintain that many more survivals of African cultures were so pervasive that they have remained to the present day.[20]

Clearly, some aspects of African cultures survived in the antebellum South, but the adjustments which these new arrivals were required to make were of such a magnitude that an essentially new way of life developed. Whatever had been a slave's occupation in Africa, he was usually forced to enter farming or domestic service in North America. Slaves were forbidden to practice their traditional religions and were required to practice the religion of their oppressors. Although they were denied formal instruction, they had to learn English. The foods they had eaten in Africa were unavailable on Southern plantations. Family patterns

[18] E. Franklin Frazier, *Black Bourgeoisie* (Glencoe, Ill.: Free Press, 1957), p. 12.
[19] Franklin, *op. cit.*, p. 40.
[20] Herskovits, *op. cit.*; Carter G. Woodson, *The African Background Outlined* (Washington, D.C.: Association Press, 1936).

which they had practiced were not permitted. Given these circumstances, and being denied participation in the culture of the South, it became necessary for the slaves somehow to survive in a world that was both hostile and strange. This struggle for survival forced them to create their own patterns of culture, which represented a mixture of elements brought from Africa and those created by their life experiences in the New World.

Attitudes of White People Toward Slaves

Although the first Africans to arrive in North America were not treated differently from white indentured servants, as the institution of slavery developed, it became synonymous with "Negro." The process was gradual, and some historians attribute it to economic forces,[21] although others see race as the primary motivating factor.[22] Regardless of whether the precipitating factor was economic or a function of racism, the attitudes which ultimately developed toward the slaves, and the behavioral component of these attitudes, led to a system of human bondage without parallel in human history.[23] As Tannenbaum has noted, slavery in North America differed from other systems of human slavery, especially that practiced in Latin America, in that the North American slaves were denied, in law and in practice, moral personalities. He writes: "While the impact of the law did not and could not completely wipe out the fact that the Negro slave was human, it raised a sufficient barrier to make the humanity of the Negro difficult to recognize and legally almost impossible to provide for. This legal definition carried its own moral consequences and made the ultimate redefinition of the Negro as a moral person most difficult." [24] Hence, rather than being reacted to as human beings possessing moral personalities, slaves in North America were considered simply "beasts of the field."

Not all attitudes toward slaves were strongly negative; however, throughout most of the period of slavery the blacks were considered

[21] See, e.g., Stanley Elkins, *Slavery* (Chicago: The University of Chicago Press, 1959); Rayford W. Logan, *The Negro in the United States* (Princeton, N.J.: Van Nostrand, 1957); Stampp, *op. cit.*

[22] Two of the chief proponents of this view are Frank Tannenbaum and Stanley Elkins. See Tannenbaum's *Slave and Citizen* (New York: Knopf, 1946); and Elkins, *op. cit.*, p. 52–89. In a recent work the author puts forth the thesis that slavery in Brazil was not radically different from slavery in North America. See Marvin Harris, *Patterns of Race in the Americas* (New York: Walker and Co., 1964). See also David B. Davis, *The Problem of Slavery in Western Culture* (Ithaca, N.Y.: Cornell, 1966), pp. 223–61; Carl N. Degler, *Out of Our Past* (New York: Harper & Row, 1959).

[23] See Nathan Glazer's "Introduction," to Elkins, *op. cit.*; David B. Davis, *op. cit.*, p. 60.

[24] Tannenbaum, *op. cit.*, p. 103.

uniquely suited for human slavery as a result of certain racial traits which made it impossible for them to adjust to the "civilized" world of the Anglo-Saxons.[25] Hence they were "destined by God" to serve Caucasians because blacks constituted an inferior race. This attitude became dominant and governed the behavior directed toward them. Racial inferiority thus became *the* justification for the institution of slavery in North America. Furthermore, the "free" Negroes were, like the slaves, responded to in similar fashion. Throughout the slave era black people were accorded different treatment from whites, regardless of their degree of achievement. Their status was based on their ascribed, i.e., racial, characteristics.

During the antebellum period slaves came into contact with a variety of white people: slaveholders and their families, overseers who were poor and landless whites, and religious leaders. Although slaveholders differed in their treatment of slaves, they were in general convinced of the innate inferiority of the slaves and treated them accordingly. If the slaves disobeyed orders, they were to be whipped. According to Franklin, "Some planters went so far as to specify the size and type of lash to be used and the number of lashes to be given for specific offenses. Almost none disclaimed whipping as an effective form of punishment, and the excessive use of the lash was one of the most flagrant abuses of the institution." [26]

Slaveholders maintained absolute control over their slaves. As a means of social control, punishment was felt to be most effective. Violation of the norms set by the slaveholder was met with a variety of forms of punishment. Stampp describes some of the more ingenious methods: "A Maryland tobacco grower forced a hand to eat the worms he failed to pick off the tobacco leaves. A Mississippian gave a runaway a wretched time by requiring him to sit at the table and eat his evening meal with the white family. A Louisiana planter humiliated disobedient male field hands by giving them 'women's work' such as washing clothes, by dressing them in women's clothing, and by exhibiting them on a scaffold wearing a red flannel cap." [27]

Frederick Douglass, an ex-slave who became an Abolitionist, writer, and Minister to Haiti, recalled that the first slaveholder on whose plantation he lived frequently engaged in acts of cruelty toward his slaves. For example,

> I have often been awakened at the dawn of day by the most heart-rendering shrieks of an own aunt of mine, whom he used to tie up to a joist, and

[25] Ulrich B. Phillips, *American Negro Slavery* (New York: Appleton, 1918), pp. 342–43.

[26] Franklin, *op. cit.*, p. 192.

[27] Cited in Stampp, *op. cit.*, p. 172.

whip upon her naked back till she was literally covered with blood. No words, no tears, no prayers, from his gory victim, seemed to move his iron heart from its bloody purpose. The louder she screamed, the harder he whipped; and where the blood ran the fastest, there he whipped longest. He would whip her to make her scream, and whip her to make her hush; and not until overcome by fatigue, would he cease to swing the blood-clotted cowskin.[28]

Stampp cites many examples of psychopathic slaveholders who thoroughly enjoyed the practice of inflicting extreme brutality on their slaves.[29]

Because slaves represented an important capital investment in the plantation economy, slaveholders naturally protected their investments, and some reports of the relations between the slaves and the slaveholders indicate ambivalent feelings on the part of the latter. Many of them developed affectionate relations toward their slaves, but this affection was always tempered by antipathy.

On small plantations slaves encountered direct contact with the slaveholders. On larger plantations overseers were hired to maintain discipline among the slaves. Overseers were generally recruited from among the poorer whites, a class not known for its admiration of the slaves. Their treatment of slaves was indicative of the low esteem in which they held these people. On plantations where overseers were employed, cruelty and brutality were institutionalized. Reports of the treatment of slaves by overseers are filled with instances of torture. The overseers were in a peculiar position because they felt exploited by the system, and they tended to displace their frustration onto the slaves. It is reported that fights between slaves and overseers were common, and slaves frequently forced overseers to leave plantations.[30] The brutality of the overseers was indeed widespread, and relations between them and the slaves were rarely amicable.

Although many religious leaders ultimately adopted antislavery positions, most of them perceived of slavery as being divinely sanctioned and thereby a natural condition. Most slaveholders approved of religious training for their slaves, but a series of codes developed whereby religious services were rigidly regulated. One of the most universal of these practices was that Negroes were prohibited from becoming ministers. Services were conducted by white ministers who interpreted their function as one

[28] Frederick Douglass, *Narrative of the Life of Frederick Douglass, an American Slave,* ed. Benjamin Quarles (Cambridge, Mass.: The Belknap Press of Harvard University Press, 1960), p. 29.

[29] Stampp, *op. cit.,* pp. 181–82.

[30] Franklin, *op. cit.,* pp. 192–93.

of teaching the slaves to adjust to their condition of servitude. Frequently, slaves were required to attend the church of the slaveholder. Through the medium of the church, slaveholders sought to maintain slavery intact. As Franklin has written, compelling the Negro slaves to attend church with the slaveholder was "the method the whites employed to keep a closer eye on the slaves." [31] Slaveholders employed ministers who instructed slaves to be obedient and subservient. Bishops and other religious leaders themselves frequently owned slaves. For example, an Episcopal bishop in Louisiana owned 400 slaves.[32] Although slaveholders were generally responsible for the religious life of their slaves and the selection of clergymen to preach to the slaves, they had little difficulty finding allies among the clergy. It was commonplace that the Scriptures were employed to justify slavery, and many books were written in its defense.[33] In general, the clergymen with whom the slaves came into contact were men who used their religion as a means of maintaining the status quo.

Reactions of Slaves

Owners of slaves, supporters of slavery, and believers in the innate inferiority of the Negro justified the institution on a variety of grounds. One such ground was that the slaves, being docile and childlike, approved of their status. They cited the infrequency of serious insurrections and the failure of those which were planned to support their contention that the slaves were indeed happy with their lot in life. Evidence which failed to support their contention was generally ignored. That their beliefs were not rooted in reality is evidenced by the extreme measures which they were forced to resort to in order to maintain slavery. Slave revolts occurred in the earliest records of the period and continued throughout the era. Indeed, evidence indicates that the slave traders in Africa experienced constant resistance to capture from the slaves, and numerous revolts by slaves are reported during the Middle Passage between Africa and the New World.[34] In addition, many thousands of slaves managed, often against extraordinary odds, to escape from chattel slavery. That slaves reacted to their status with constant attempts to alter it meant that

[31] *Ibid.*, p. 199.
[32] *Ibid.*, p. 200.
[33] George D. Armstrong, *The Christian Doctrine of Slavery* (New York: Scribner, 1857); George Fitzhugh, *Cannibals All! Or Slaves Without Masters* (Richmond, Va.: A. Morris, 1857); Fred A. Ross, *Slavery Ordained By God* (Philadelphia: Lippincott, 1857). Both Armstrong and Ross were ministers
[34] See Frazier, *The Negro in the United States*, Chap. V; and Elizabeth Dounan, *Documents Illustrative of the History of the Slave Trade to America*, 4 vols. (Washington, D.C.: Carnegie Institution, 1935).

throughout the period they managed to be "a troublesome property" for slaveholders. Attempts to gain freedom took many forms, two of which were insurrections and fleeing from captivity.

Altogether some 250 slave insurrections and conspiracies are reported to have occurred in the history of American Negro slavery, and, although some of these were more serious than others, the history of slavery in North America is not without widespread popular revolts on the part of slaves.[35] The first such revolt occurred as early as 1663, and such uprisings continued throughout the slavery era. Some revolts were well planned and organized, and others were haphazardly planned.[36] The 250 revolts reported involved numbers estimated as ranging from ten to 50,000 slaves.

Three of the many slave revolts stand out because of the seriousness of the attempts, the number of slaves involved, and the reaction they generated throughout slaveholding North America. In 1800 a slave named Gabriel, a worker on a plantation near Richmond, Virginia, who perceived of himself as having a divine mission, organized the first major slave insurrection in North America. Gabriel is said to have possessed unusual intelligence.[37] For weeks he met on Sundays with fellow slaves at parties and dances. On these occasions he selected special slaves to serve as assistants to work on plans with him. Gabriel picked what he felt to be the most advantageous date for the insurrection. The plan called for the use of few weapons. They were to murder the slaveholders and their families on the nearby plantations. Initially, all whites were to be killed, but, as the revolt spread, landless whites were to be recruited to fight against wealthy landowners. Strategy was mapped for the spread of the revolt and the enlistment of additional slaves into Gabriel's army. Gabriel had been inspired to insurrection by reading the Bible and by the French Revolution. It is reported that ". . . he was said to have planned to buy a piece of silk cloth to have the egalitarian slogan 'Liberty or Death' printed on it." [38] The revolt never materialized because two fellow slaves on the plantation informed on the slave rebels, and the organizers and other participants were killed.

The second major slave insurrection occurred in Charleston, South Carolina, in 1822. Denmark Vesey, an ex-slave who had purchased his freedom with money won in a lottery, planned this insurrection. He was

[35] Herbert Aptheker, *American Negro Slave Revolts* (New York: International Publishers, 1963), p. 162.

[36] For a typology of slave revolts see Marion D. deB. Kilson, "Towards Freedom: An Analysis of Slave Revolts in the United States," *Phylon*, Vol. 25 (Summer 1964), 175–87.

[37] Nicholas Halasz, *The Rattling Chains* (New York: McKay, 1966), pp. 87–97.

[38] *Ibid.*, p. 91.

a gifted carpenter and was said to have been endowed with "exceptional intelligence." [39] In his early years in Charleston he used his shop as a meeting place for black people, and he spent much of his time attempting to strengthen his feelings of self-confidence. He was irritated by complacency among both slaves and free blacks. He became a member of the African Methodist Episcopal Church and, later, a preacher for the purpose of recruiting prospects for the rebellion he was planning. Altogether he spent four years planning his revolt, and slowly he selected those in whom he confided. This insurrection, like that of Gabriel, failed because a "faithful" house servant informed on his fellow slaves. The planners were rounded up; 35 of them were killed and 34 were deported.

The third, and currently the best-known, slave revolt occurred in Southampton County, Virginia, in 1831. The leader of this outbreak was Nat Turner, also an intelligent and talented man.[40] Turner had escaped from slavery but had voluntarily returned because of religious convictions. He became a mystic and frequently buried himself in prayer. He sometimes experienced visions. Through these visions he felt that he had been divinely ordained to lead his people out of bondage. Because of his mysticism, little time and effort went into planning the revolt. Therefore it involved fewer participants than previous revolts, but it became the biggest slave uprising in North America. Armed with an ax and clubs, six men first murdered the plantation owner and his family and then proceeded to nearby houses, killing all through the night. Altogether they murdered 55 whites. By the time the rebellion had been quelled, Turner's troops numbered more than 60. The Army of the United States was finally called to put down the rebellion, and they were joined by other whites who attacked the slaves indiscriminately.

The attack on Harpers Ferry by John Brown, a white man, was an important uprising and no doubt played a major role in the abolition of slavery. However, few slaves joined Brown in his attempt to liberate the slaves. Brown devoted his entire life to the elimination of slavery, and, once he became convinced that moral appeals were of no avail to slaveholders, he concentrated on armed revolt. As with Nat Turner, John Brown's raid on Harpers Ferry was subdued by the armed militia.

Although there were many revolts by the slaves in North America, few of them gained a significant amount of momentum and all of them failed. In no case did they succeed in improving the status of the slaves; rather, they generally brought forth repressive measures. Some reasons for the failure of the slave revolts may be advanced. The very nature of slavery and its effects on the slave were such that successful insurrection

39 *Ibid.*, pp. 116–38.
40 *Ibid.*, Chap. VIII.

was impossible. As Elkins has written, "American slavery operated as a 'closed' system—one in which, for the generality of slaves in their nature as men and women, *sub specie aeternitatis,* contacts with free society could occur only on the most narrowly circumscribed of terms." [41] Such a system had a demoralizing effect on the slaves' personalities, thereby rendering widespread participation in revolts unlikely and, in many cases, unthinkable. As has been mentioned, slaveholders encouraged status differences among slaves as a means of dividing and conquering them. When revolts were being planned, they were most often betrayed by that category of slaves most closely allied to the owner—the house slaves. Because the plantation was a closed system, communication among slaves on the various plantations was impossible. Whenever slaves met, for whatever reason, they were under the constant surveillance of whites. Finally, of crucial importance was the ratio of slaves to whites in North America. Slaves were usually outnumbered, and, where they happened to be in a majority, any slaveholder had the full force of the military at his disposal for the purpose of maintaining order among them. This was the situation after the colonies gained independence, and it was during this period that organized slave revolts were common. Therefore the lack of success of slave revolts cannot be taken as an indication of their acceptance of their status. As Stampp has written, "In truth, no slave uprising ever had a chance of ultimate success, even though it might have cost the master class heavy casualties. The great majority of the disarmed and outnumbered slaves, knowing the futility of rebellion, refused to join in any of the numerous plots. Most slaves had to express their desire for freedom in less dramatic ways." [42]

Recognizing the futility of organized rebellion, most slaves expressed their antipathy for slavery in individual acts. Most frequently these acts took the form of escape from slavery. From the very inception of the institution until its end, runaway slaves posed problems for the slaveholders. The newspapers of the period were full of advertisements in search of slaves who had escaped. The exact number of slaves to escape is not known, but it is estimated that thousands fled each year. Estimates of the total number of escapees in the four decades between 1810 and 1850 run as high as 100,000, with a value of more than $30,000,000.[43] So great was the number of runaway slaves that in 1793 Congress enacted the Fugitive Slave Law, which empowered a slaveholder to seize runaway slaves who had crossed state lines and ultimately return them to the state

41 Elkins, *op. cit.,* pp. 81–82.
42 Stampp, *op. cit.,* p. 140.
43 Franklin, *op. cit.,* pp. 255–56. See also Wilbur H. Siebert, *The Underground Railroad from Slavery to Freedom* (New York: Macmillan, 1898).

from which they fled. The persistence of slaves in risking their lives to escape serves as dramatic evidence of their reaction to their status.

A significant proportion of the slaves to escape were aided in their endeavors by "free" blacks and white Abolitionists. The Underground Railroad is said to have been incorporated in 1804.[44] It was an organized effort to assist slaves attempting to escape. It was operated in defiance of federal fugitive slave laws, and thousands of slaves were able to escape to the North and to Canada through its utilization. So well organized was it that funds for its operation were solicited from philanthropists. Employing several thousand workers, the Underground Railroad operated hundreds of stations in the East and West. The number of slaves to escape through the Underground Railroad is not known, but estimates run into the hundreds of thousands, with an estimated 40,000 passing through Ohio alone.[45] There are recorded instances in which individual "conductors" on the Underground Railroad assisted thousands of black people in their escape from slavery.

Although some slaves successfully accommodated to their status, the persistence of runaway slaves posed continuous problems for slaveholders. So widespread was this phenomenon that a Southern doctor was convinced that Negroes suffered from a "disease of the mind," which he called "drapethomania," which caused them to run away.[46] In reality, however, aside from the general harshness and degradation inherent in the institution of slavery, several of its special features served to motivate slaves to flee.[47] Arbitrary separation of slaves from their families induced many of them to escape. Other slaves resented being moved against their will. Still others reacted to such factors as attempts to work them too severely, fear of punishment, and fear of being sold into the Deep South. The major motivation, however, was a desire to escape from the inhumanity which the institution of slavery imposed on them. The constant fleeing of slaves is hardly compatible with the view of them held by a leading historian of slavery during the first three decades of the 20th century. Ulrich B. Phillips saw the slaves as possessing "a readiness for loyalty of a feudal sort," and he viewed them as a people who were eager to please the slaveholders by working "sturdily for a hard boss." [48] He saw them as a people "who for the most part were by racial quality submissive rather than defiant." [49] The views expressed by Phillips were widely shared among slaveholders and writers of the period.

44 Henrietta Buckmaster, *Let My People Go* (New York: Harper, 1941).
45 Franklin, *op. cit.*, p. 256.
46 Stampp, *op. cit.*, p. 109.
47 *Ibid.*, pp. 109–24.
48 Phillips, *op. cit.*, pp. 291–92.
49 *Ibid.*, pp. 341–42.

The "Free" Blacks

Not all black people in the United States were enslaved prior to the Civil War. Indeed, the population of the so-called free blacks increased steadily from the middle of the 17th century until emancipation. Although they were generally referred to as "free," their status was only slightly higher than that of the slaves and significantly lower than that of their white fellow countrymen. Although their status resembled that of the slaves, they were indeed a people who were neither slave nor free. As one historian of the period has written, "Since the Constitution made no mention of race or color, the states and the federal government separately defined the legal status of free Negroes. Both generally agreed, however, that the Negro constituted an inferior race and that he should occupy a legal position commensurate with his degraded social and economic condition." [50] The population of free Negroes in the United States numbered 59,557 at the time of the first census in 1790, and by the census of 1860 (the last before the Civil War) it had increased to 448,070.[51] They were roughly evenly divided between the South and non-South regions of the country.[52]

Several factors account for the steady increase in the population of free blacks.[53] (1) Manumission of slaves, which had been practiced since the beginning of slavery, continued and became a major factor in the increase in the free black population. (2) Children born to free blacks inherited the status of their parents. (3) Mulatto children born of free black mothers were free. (4) Children of free black and Indian parentage were born free. (5) Mulatto children born to white mothers were free. (6) Slaves continued to escape to freedom. Although the population of free blacks came from several sources, their Negro heritage served to relegate them to a precarious position in society.

Perhaps the most difficult task for the free blacks was that of maintaining their freedom. Franklin describes this condition as follows:

> A white person could claim, however fraudulently, that a Negro was a slave, and there was little the Negro could do about it. There was, moreover, the danger of his being kidnapped, as often happened. The chances of being reduced to servitude or slavery by the courts were also great. A large majority of free Negroes lived in daily fear of losing what freedom

[50] Leon F. Litwack, *North of Slavery* (Chicago: The University of Chicago Press, 1961), p. 30.
[51] U.S. Bureau of the Census, *Negro Population, 1790–1915* (Washington, D.C.: Government Printing Office, 1918).
[52] Meier and Rudwick, *op. cit.*, p. 66.
[53] Frazier, *The Negro in the United States*, p. 59ff.

they had. One slip or ignorance of the law would send them back into the ranks of slaves.[54]

Free blacks were denied many of the rights that white Americans enjoyed. The degree of freedom they enjoyed depended on whether they lived in the South or North, and within these regions it varied from state to state. Their movements were generally restricted, especially in the South, where they were required to carry passes. Most states enacted laws forbidding them to convene meetings unless whites were in attendance. It was especially difficult for them to earn a living. Several states restricted the occupations they could engage in. In spite of these restrictions, the blacks engaged in a number of skilled and professional pursuits. For example, they became druggists, dentists, lawyers, teachers, tailors, carpenters, barbers, shopkeepers, salesmen, and cabinetmakers.

Southern states generally excluded free blacks from the franchise, and most Northern states made it difficult for them to vote. Only one state (Georgia) forbade free Negroes to own property, and many of them amassed great wealth.[55] Indeed, many of the free blacks owned slaves. In general, however, black ownership of slaves differed from white ownership in that the free blacks usually also purchased their slaves' spouses, relatives, or friends. While many of the free blacks attended religious services with whites, in segregated sections of the churches, several all-black congregations and denominations were established during this period. In the South, religious worship, except in the segregated white churches, was difficult for free blacks because it was feared that such services were used to organize insurrections among slaves.

It was difficult for the free blacks to secure education. All Southern states made it virtually impossible, and in the North segregated education was the norm. In spite of the difficulties involved, many Negroes managed to achieve the highest realm of scholarship. Black people were graduated from college as early as 1827.[56] Before the Civil War two colleges, Lincoln University in Pennsylvania and Wilberforce University in Ohio, were established for the education of free blacks.

In general, laws served to maintain the low status of the free blacks, but, where this was not the case, violence was resorted to. Between 1830 and 1850 race riots were widespread throughout the United States. Roaming bands of whites frequently invaded the Negro sections of cities, burning homes and churches and beating and killing the residents. Violence

54 Franklin, *op. cit.*, pp. 215–16.
55 *Ibid.*, pp. 221 23, Phillips, *op. cit.*, pp. 432–36.
56 Logan, *op. cit.*, p. 14.

was resorted to where whites felt that free blacks were competing for jobs, and a common practice among whites was the act of driving free blacks from cities. Rarely were they protected from these acts of violence by law enforcement officials.[57]

Although life for the free blacks was somewhat less circumscribed than for the slaves, they were forced to live within a set of rigidly restricted rules which made it virtually impossible for them to fulfill the obligations of citizenship. Yet the highest degree of civic responsibility was demanded of them, always at the risk of jail or of being reduced to slavery. In spite of the restrictions on their lives and the uncertainties of their status, many notable achievements were registered. Several free blacks distinguished themselves as Abolitionists; many emerged as educators, poets, playwrights, historians, and newspaper editors.

THE CIVIL WAR

By the middle of the 19th century slavery had become a serious problem for the United States at home and in its relations with other countries. Antislavery sentiment within the country reached significant proportions, and, since the British government had already emancipated the slaves in its colonial possessions, relations between the two countries gradually deteriorated. Various proposals for dealing with Negro slaves were discussed, and intersectional strife had reached the point where a bloody confrontation seemed inevitable. The Abolitionists gained ground in their cause of freedom for the slaves, and the slaveholding states maintained their determination to perpetuate the institution. Antislavery societies mushroomed throughout the non-slaveholding states, and the supporters of slavery responded to the challenge by widespread acts of violence.[58] By the time the President-elect, Abraham Lincoln, arrived in Washington in 1861, he had become well acquainted with the institution of slavery through travels in the South. He had expressed opposition to slavery and vowed, on occasion, to put an end to the institution. At other times Lincoln expressed segregationist views. It appears that he was both opposed to the institution of slavery and opposed to racial integration. Upon his assuming the Presidency, the country had already become divided on the issue, and, since seven of the slaveholding states had already seceded from the Union, a civil war was imminent. The Civil War was an all-important development for the slaves, and of special significance were the participation of blacks in the war, the emancipation

[57] Franklin, *op. cit.*, pp. 231–34.
[58] See Carter G. Woodson, *The Negro in Our History* (Washington, D.C.: The Associated Publishers, 1922), especially Chap. XIX.

which it brought about, and the destruction wrought by this armed conflict.

Participation by Blacks

At the beginning of the Civil War, blacks rushed to enlist in the Union Army, but they were rejected. In several instances, after being rebuffed, they organized themselves and trained for service in the expectation that they would ultimately be permitted to participate in a war which they were convinced would end with the freeing of the slaves. In the early stages of the war they were rejected because it was felt that to permit them to fight would endow them with a status comparable to that of white soldiers. Furthermore, Negroes were considered incapable of fighting wars. As Du Bois has pointed out, "Negroes on the whole were considered cowards and inferior beings whose very presence in America was unfortunate." [59] As the war developed, however, army commanders were permitted to use their own discretion about utilizing Negroes. Some commanders insisted on returning runaway slaves to their owners, and others permitted them to fight. As the Union armies moved South, where the war was being fought, blacks rushed to the Union lines.[60] When they were finally permitted to enlist in Union armies, Negroes did so enthusiastically. By the end of the Civil War, approximately 186,000 black troops had been enrolled. These troops took part in 198 battles and suffered 68,000 casualties.[61] It is estimated that 300,000 Negroes were involved in the war effort, including servants, laborers, and spies. The troops were organized into various regiments, including artillery, cavalry, infantry, and engineers. They fought in segregated units and were known as the United States Colored Troops. Most of the Negro troops served under white officers, but Woodson estimated that "Negroes held altogether about 75 commissions in the army during the Civil War." [62] In addition to being segregated, they were paid differentially for their services. "The Enlistment Act of 1862 provided that whites in the rank of private should receive $13 a month and $3.50 for clothing, but Negroes of the same rank were to receive only $7 and $3, respectively." [63] Such discrimination was protested by black troops and by their white commanding officers. During the Civil War Negroes were engaged in combat in every major battle area, and they suffered significantly higher casualty

59 W. E. B. Du Bois, *Black Reconstruction* (New York: Harcourt, Brace, 1935), p. 56.
60 Franklin, *op. cit.*, p. 269.
61 See Logan, *op. cit.*, p. 22; James M. McPherson, *The Negro's Civil War* (New York: Random House, Inc., 1965), p. ix.
62 Woodson, *The Negro in Our History*, p. 374.
63 Franklin, *op. cit.*, p. 287.

rates than did white troops. It is generally conceded that they made significant contributions to the victory of the Union armies.

The Confederate armies, like those of the Union, at first denied Negroes the right to fight in the Civil War, but, unlike the Union armies, the Confederacy was afraid that if blacks were armed, they would rebel. Furthermore, few, if any, blacks expressed willingness to fight for the cause of the Confederacy. One of the major problems faced by this region was the widespread desertion of the slaves to join the ranks of the Union armies. Confederate army units utilized Negroes as cooks and for other menial tasks, and several Confederate soldiers took their Negro servants to war with them.[64] Toward the end of the Civil War, in 1865, the Confederate senate enacted a bill calling for the enlistment of 200,000 black troops who were to be freed if they remained loyal throughout the war. In addition, a bill calling for the conscription of 300,000 additional troops, including Negroes, proved unsuccessful. Few blacks volunteered, and many fled to avoid conscription. Furthermore, by this time the Union armies were virtually assured of victory.

The role of the black soldier in the Civil War has been deprecated. However, one historian of the period summarized their participation as follows: "Without their help, the North could not have won the war as soon as it did, and perhaps it could not have won at all. The Negro was crucial to the whole Union war effort." [65]

The Emancipation

In the midst of the Civil War, on January 1, 1863, President Lincoln proclaimed that "all persons held as slaves within any State, or designated part of the State, the people whereof shall be in rebellion against the United States, shall be then, thenceforward, and forever free." The President made it clear that this action was taken in order to preserve the Union and not to destroy slavery. The newly freed Negroes were asked to refrain from violence and to seek employment at reasonable wages. The Emancipation Proclamation gave impetus to increasing black participation in the ongoing Civil War.

News of the Emancipation Proclamation was received by the slaves with bewilderment. There were nearly 4 million slaves in the South at that time, and life for them had been such that few of them had ever expected to be set free. They did not know what to do. The state of illiteracy which had been perpetuated for most slaves served to complicate their new lives. In many instances they were powerless to protect

---

[64] *Ibid.*, p. 284.
[65] McPherson, *op. cit.*, pp. ix–x. Copyright 1965, Random House, Inc.

themselves against the violence directed toward them by white persons. It is reported: "Many of the slaves immediately left the plantations when they learned that they were free. This was seen as natural since one of the tests of freedom was the ability to move around freely. On the other hand, the attitude of subordination was still strong in some slaves and they were afraid to assert their newly acquired rights." [66] It is perhaps fair to say that emancipation initially came as a shock to the slaves because they were unprepared for it. However, evidence indicates that by and large they welcomed their new status.

The slaveholders and other Southern whites, on the other hand, were not pleased with the disruption of the way of life they had grown to cherish and upon which they were dependent. It is reported that "Some planters held back their former slaves on the plantations by brute force. Armed bands of white men patrolled the country roads to drive back the Negroes wandering about. Dead bodies of murdered Negroes were found on or near highways and byways. . . . A veritable reign of terror prevailed in many parts of the South." [67] Some slaveholders accepted the change in status of the slaves without such vindictiveness, but reluctantly, and others appeared to be relieved that they could now reject a system which had long ago become unpleasant for them.

Destruction Caused by the Civil War

Whatever the causes of the Civil War, the destruction wrought by the conflict was vast. When the Confederate Army surrendered in 1865, it signaled the end to the costliest war in which the United States had ever engaged and, indeed, the bloodiest civil war in human history.[68] Its end marked a victory for the Abolitionists and for the Negroes, for it ended a system of human slavery which had persisted for almost 250 years. However, since the war had been fought in the South, the area had suffered widespread destruction. Southerners had become engaged in a bloody war which they stood little chance of winning in order to maintain the institution which they had grown to cherish. With the end of the war came widespread social disorganization among the whites as well as among the slaves. This social disorganization was matched by massive physical destruction. "Fields were laid waste, cities burned, bridges and roads destroyed. Even most of the woefully inadequate factories were

---

66 Frazier, *The Negro in the United States,* p. 111.

67 Quoted in Du Bois, *op. cit,,* p. 671.

68 See Francis B. Simkins, *A History of the South* (New York: Knopf, 1959), p. 243.

leveled. . . . And if the Union forces did not loot quite as many smoke-houses and pantries as they were blamed for, what they did do emphasized the helplessness of the once proud Confederates." [69]

One reporter, traveling in the South immediately after the Civil War, recorded the physical destruction of that region. Arriving in Richmond, Virginia, he reported:

> All up and down, as far as the eye could reach, the business portion of the city bordering on the river lay in ruins. Beds of cinders, cellars half filled with bricks and rubbish, broken and blackened walls, impassable streets deluged with debris, here a granite-front still standing and there the iron fragments of crushed machinery—such was the scene which extended over 30 entire squares and parts of other squares. [70]

Of Atlanta, Georgia, he wrote: "Every business block in Atlanta was burned, except one. The railroad machine shops, the foundries, the immense rolling mill, the tent, pistol, gun carriage, shot-and-shell factories and storehouses of the Confederacy had disappeared in flames and explosions. Half a mile of the principal street was destroyed." [71]

Such descriptions as these could be matched for each of the principal cities of the Confederacy, and losses of lives were staggering. The South had suffered a humiliating defeat by a superior power. Added to this military defeat was the destruction of a way of life, the most serious aspect of which was the liberation of the slaves, a situation which posed social, economic, and political problems of enormous magnitude. Although General Robert E. Lee accepted the terms of the surrender imposed by General Ulysses S. Grant, Southerners were determined that defeat in battle would not significantly alter their relations with the newly freed slaves. They considered the Negroes to be free but were convinced of their inferiority, and they were also convinced that, given time, Southerners would decide their status to their own satisfaction.

THE RECONSTRUCTION

The efforts to rehabilitate the South and the role of black people in these efforts loom as two of the most controversial aspects of American history. Since economic, political, and social life were disrupted by the Civil War, problems posed by the Reconstruction were not limited to the South, nor was their outcome determined solely by the role played

[69] John Hope Franklin, *Reconstruction After the Civil War* (Chicago: The University of Chicago Press, 1961), p. 2.
[70] John T. Trowbridge, *The Desolate South: 1865–1866* (New York: Meredith Press; and Boston: Little, Brown, 1956), pp. 84–85.
[71] *Ibid.,* p. 238.

by the nearly 4 million ex-slaves. It is primarily to the role of the Negro in the Reconstruction and to the effects of this period on the present status of black people in the United States that attention is now directed.

Presidential Reconstruction

The year following the Civil War was an especially difficult one for the newly freed blacks. President Lincoln had envisioned the Reconstruction as a function of the office of the President, but his assassination in April 1865 put an end to the plans he had formulated. The South was in a state of almost total disorganization, and Lincoln's successor, President Andrew Johnson, appeared to be less concerned about Negro rights than about other aspects of reconstruction.[72] Meanwhile, the condition of the black people gradually deteriorated. Violence on the part of Southern whites grew more intense, and, as one historian has written, "It seems as though in 1866 every Southerner began to murder or beat Negroes." [73] The President was indifferent to the treatment of black people because his conception of democracy did not include the blacks. The Southerners who had waged a war to keep blacks enslaved proceeded to pass a series of laws which became known as Black Codes. These laws were specifically designed to restrict the rights of Negroes. As Du Bois has written, they represented an attempt ". . . on the part of the Southern states to make Negroes slaves in everything but name." [74] The Black Codes varied from state to state, but, in general, they dealt with virtually every aspect of the lives of ex-slaves, and furthermore they were designed to take advantage of the precarious position of the ex-slaves. These codes covered such diverse features as whether Negroes could enter certain states, the conditions under which they were allowed to work, their rights to own and dispose of property, conditions under which they could hold public assemblies, the ownership of firearms, vagrancy, and a variety of other matters. In some states any white person could arrest a Negro. In Opelousas, Louisiana, one ordinance provided that "No Negro or freedman shall be allowed to come within the limits of the town of Opelousas without special permission from his employer, specifying the object of his visit and the time necessary for the accomplishment of the same." It continued, "Every Negro freedman who shall be found on the streets of Opelousas after ten o'clock at night without a written pass or permit from his employer, shall be imprisoned and compelled to work five days on the public streets or pay a fine of five dollars." [75]

72 Simkins, *op. cit.,* especially Chap. 17.
73 *Ibid.,* p. 265.
74 Du Bois, *op. cit.,* p. 167.
75 *Ibid.,* p. 177.

The Southern ex-slaveholders enacted such laws for a variety of reasons, one of them being their irritation at the presence of black troops with bayonets stationed in the South. This practice was only slightly more offensive to them than the establishment by Congress, over the veto of the President, of the Bureau of Refugees, Freedmen, and Abandoned Lands, commonly known as the Freedmen's Bureau, in 1865. This agency had as its responsibility aiding refugees and freedmen by "furnishing supplies and medical services, establishing schools, supervising contracts between freedmen and their employers, and managing confiscated or abandoned lands." [76] The Freedmen's Bureau suspended the Black Codes before they became effective. Nevertheless, it became clear to Northern observers, Abolitionists, and Congressmen that the President maintained little interest in protecting the rights of the freedmen. Violence directed against them became widespread. During the summer of 1866, for example, bloody race riots erupted throughout the South, during which time hundreds of black people were killed. Congress therefore voted itself responsibility for Reconstruction.

Radical Reconstruction

Congress established a procedure whereby the South was divided into military districts and the freedmen became wards of the government. Military commanders of each of the five districts were empowered to suspend the functions of civil government when deemed necessary and to call constitutional conventions consisting of delegates selected without regard to race or previous condition of servitude. The South was finally moving toward democratic reconstruction. In 1865 the Thirteenth Amendment to the Constitution, which abolished slavery, had been enacted and ratified, and in 1866 Congress passed, again over the President's veto, the Civil Rights Act of 1866, which made Negroes citizens and gave them the same rights enjoyed by white Americans. This law ultimately became the Fourteenth Amendment to the Constitution, which prohibited states from depriving any person "of life, liberty, or property, without due process of the law," and forbade states from denying Negroes "the equal protection of the laws."

Perhaps the most revolutionary aspect of the Reconstruction was the participation by blacks in the political arena. In the former Confederate states the black people registered to vote in greater numbers than did whites. The series of Reconstruction Acts enacted by Congress between 1866 and 1868 and the Fifteenth Amendment, which became part of the Constitution in 1870, guaranteed them the right to vote. During

[76] Franklin, *Reconstruction After the Civil War*, pp. 36–37.

the first registrations, when delegates were elected to state conventions in 1868, 703,000 black voters registered as compared with only 627,000 white voters.[77] Negroes were in a majority in the South Carolina state convention and made up half of the delegates in Louisiana. In the other states they constituted minorities ranging from 10 percent of the delegates to 19 percent.[78]

During the period of Radical Reconstruction black people participated in politics to a greater extent than in any other period in American history. The masses of Negroes, however, were illiterate and depended on Southern landowners for support. The landowning class capitalized on the traditional anti-Negro prejudices of the poor whites, with whom the Negroes were in competition, and thereby sought to maintain their position of dominance. Ultimately they were successful in these efforts, but the blacks managed to play a significant role in the political life of the South. Although they made up numerical majorities in the population of several states, they never effectively controlled the affairs of any state. They often held important offices, but there was never a Negro governor. There were two lieutenant governors, and several Negroes represented their states in the U.S. Congress.

Many of the Negro leaders in the South were well educated. For example, a Negro state treasurer in South Carolina had been educated in Glasgow and London; one of that state's Negro Representatives in Congress had been educated at Eton College in England; and a Negro who was a state supreme court justice held a law degree from the University of Pennsylvania. Florida's black secretary of state graduated from Dartmouth College. According to one historian, "One of the really remarkable features of the Negro leadership was the small amount of vindictiveness in their words and their actions. There was no bully, no swagger, as they took their places in the state and federal governments traditionally occupied by white planters of the South. The spirit of conciliation pervaded most of the public utterances the Negroes made." [79] In the realm of social relations, black people gave no indication of serious interest in interpersonal relations with white people. Their chief concern was with being accorded a position of equality with Southern whites.

In spite of the constant attempts at counterreconstruction, especially by such avowed white supremacy organizations as the Ku Klux Klan, the Red Shirts, and the Knights of the White Camelia, the newly freed slaves in the South enjoyed a kind and degree of freedom which

[77] Simkins, *op. cit.*, p. 271.
[78] Frazier, *The Negro in the United States*, p. 132.
[79] Franklin, *Reconstruction After the Civil War*, pp. 89–90.

they had not known before and have not known since. Of paramount concern to them was the question of education. In five states black men were elected to the state superintendency of education, and throughout the South both the young and the old flocked to schools. They freely attended places of public accommodation, they voted in large numbers, and they elected intelligent and capable Negroes to public office. In effect, they enjoyed a significant measure of political, economic, and social freedom.

The Compromise of 1877:
Turn Toward Slavery

Throughout the period of Radical Reconstruction attempts were made by ex-Confederates to impede the progress being made toward racial democracy in the South. Conservatives frequently seized power in state governments, and by 1876 they had succeeded in coming to power and effectively destroying Reconstruction programs in eight states.[80] Federal troops had been withdrawn from all but three states. Violence directed against the blacks was widespread. It was clear that the South was determined to maintain white supremacy at all cost. They were effectively assisted in this endeavor by the outcome of the disputed Presidential election of 1876, in which Rutherford B. Hayes was the Republican candidate and Samuel Tilden was the Democratic candidate. This disputed election was settled in Congress by the Compromise of 1877, in which Hayes was finally declared the winner. In effect, the Compromise of 1877 saw the Republican Party (the so-called Party of Emancipation) abandon the Negro to former slaveholders.[81] It was felt by the party leaders to be necessary to avert another civil war. Nevertheless, for all practical purposes this compromise signaled a return toward slavery which was to characterize the relations between blacks and whites in the South for decades to follow. The remaining troops were withdrawn from the South, and the South was accorded complete home rule and other political favors. The most important favor to the Southerners was the promise which the compromise brought in the realm of race relations: "It did assure the dominant whites political autonomy and nonintervention in matters of race policy. . . ."[82]

The leaders of the South promised that the rights of Negroes would be protected, and especially that the newly ratified amendments to the

[80] *Ibid.*, p. 209.

[81] C. Vann Woodward, *Reunion and Reaction* (Boston: Little, Brown, 1951), Chap. 11.

[82] From p. 246 of *Reunion and Reaction* by C. Vann Woodward, copyright 1951 © 1966 by C. Vann Woodward, reprinted by permission of Little, Brown and Company, Publishers.

Constitution would be adhered to. Political leaders in Washington, who were aware of the course the South had been taking since emancipation, appeared to be more interested in political stability than in human rights. Thus virtually all the accomplishments of the Radical Reconstruction were gradually overturned. Black people had been most effective in political life, and the Southern whites were determined to disfranchise them. It was not long before they succeeded. For the Negroes the South proceeded on a backward course. As summarized by Franklin, "Reconstruction was over. The South was back in the Union, with a leadership strikingly like that of the South which had seceded in 1860." [83]

INSTITUTIONALIZED
WHITE SUPREMACY

From 1877 to 1954 virtually all the events pertaining to black people in the United States adversely affected their status. This period of more than seven decades saw profound changes in the society as a whole, but the Negro's status remained relatively fixed. Americans persisted in their prejudiced attitudes toward blacks, and these attitudes were translated into acts of segregation and discrimination in virtually every aspect of life. Where segregation and discrimination were not required by law, they became deeply ingrained in the mores. Such behavior became part of the "American way of life," and few white Americans challenged these sacred practices. Black people, on the other hand, constantly challenged them, especially those which were enacted into law; but they were consistently rebuffed. They had been relegated to a caste position in society, and no black man, no matter what his level of achievement, could expect to be accorded treatment equal to that of a white person.

The Emergence
of "Jim Crow"

With the end of the Reconstruction in the South the restoration of white supremacy was underway. Race became the crucial factor in political, economic, and social life. Although the South was in the vanguard of this movement, it had many allies throughout the country. In 1883, for example, the Supreme Court declared the Civil Rights Act of 1875 unconstitutional. This act made it a crime for a person to deny any citizen equal access to accommodations in inns, public conveyances, theaters, and other places of amusement. Several other judicial rulings of the nation's highest court served to institutionalize white supremacy in the United States. Principal among these was the decision of the Court in the

[83] Franklin, *Reconstruction After the Civil War*, p. 226.

Plessy v. *Ferguson* case in 1896. In this case the Court ruled that separate (i.e., segregated) facilities for blacks and whites were not a violation of the constitutional guarantees of the Thirteenth and Fourteenth Amendments. "If one race be inferior to the other socially, the Constitution of the United States cannot put them upon the same plane," declared the majority opinion.[84] This ruling set the pattern for attitudes toward and treatment of Negroes in the United States that have persisted to the present. It became known as the "separate but equal" ruling of the Supreme Court, and Southerners were more concerned with the separation of blacks than with equality. This decision had been foreshadowed by that in a previous case, *Hall* v. *de Ceur,* in 1877, which stated that "a state could not *prohibit* segregation on a common carrier," and in the case of *Louisville, New Orleans, and Texas Railroad* v. *Mississippi,* in 1880, when the Court ruled that "a state could constitutionally *require* segregation on carriers." [85]

Jim Crow laws had existed in the South since the fall of the Confederacy, but they were quickly repealed by Reconstruction legislatures. However, with the Compromise of 1877 they reappeared, gradually at first, and by 1890 they were mushrooming throughout the South. In the two decades between 1890 and 1910 these laws served to relegate black people to subordinate status in virtually all aspects of life.[86]

Added impetus to the institutionalization of white supremacy was given by the Negro educator Booker T. Washington, who advocated accommodation on the part of black people at a time when accommodation meant continued relegation to a subordinate position in society. He encouraged other Negroes to accept, as he himself had done, the subordinate position of the Negro. "Cast down your bucket where you are," he admonished black people. Washington's position was clearly set forth in a speech he delivered at the Cotton States Exposition in Atlanta, Georgia, in 1895. Among other things, he told his predominantly white audience: "As we have proved our loyalty to you in the past, in nursing your children, watching by the sickbed of your mothers and fathers, and often following them with tear-dimmed eyes to their graves, so in the future, in our humble way, we shall stand by you. . . ." He continued, "In all things that are purely social we can be as separate as the fingers, yet one as the hand in all things essential to mutual progress." [87] Upon com-

---

[84] Logan, *op. cit.,* Document No. 9A.
[85] C. Vann Woodward, *The Strange Career of Jim Crow* (New York: Oxford University Press, 1957), p. 54.
[86] *Ibid.,* pp. 49–95.
[87] Logan, *op. cit.,* Document No. 8.

pletion of his address it is reported that the white audience "came to its feet, yelling" approvingly, while the Negroes in the audience wept.[88] The "Atlanta Compromise" speech, as it became known, assured Americans that the recently mushrooming Jim Crow laws defined the proper form of relations between blacks and whites. Washington was acknowledged as the "leader" of the black population of the United States. The outcome of Washington's program of accommodation to white supremacy was accurately predicted by his most formidable critic, William E. B. Du Bois.[89]

As a leader, Booker T. Washington enjoyed wide popularity among both black and white Americans. He was highly respected by white philanthropists and government officials. As adviser to two Presidents (Theodore Roosevelt and William H. Taft), he is reported to have recommended virtually all appointments of Negroes to high office during their administrations. Washington achieved prominence at a time when relations between black and white Americans were deteriorating, and, although many aspects of his self-help program might have seemed to improve the status of the freedmen, his lack of concern with equal rights for Negroes did not represent an insightful long-range plan.[90]

A wave of terror, stemming from violence directed against Negroes, spread throughout the South. As Frazier has noted, during the Reconstruction Negroes responded to violence by organized action, which often led to race riots, but, because of the precariousness of their position at this time, organized action was rare. Hence whites resorted to lynching and terror as means of containing the blacks. Lynchings in the South increased between 1882 and 1890, and the last decade of the 19th century witnessed a sharp increase. This increase coincided with the many legislative acts in that region which institutionalized the subordinate status of the Negro.[91]

White Americans in the North had apparently lost interest in the welfare of black people. Indeed, many who had championed the cause of the Negro defended the Southern view of race relations. Many periodicals, such as *The Nation, Harper's Weekly*, the *North American Review*, and the *Atlantic Monthly*, carried articles by "Northern liberals and former Abolitionists mouthing the shibboleths of white supremacy regard-

[88] Bennett, *op. cit.*, pp. 228–29.

[89] W. E. B. Du Bois, *The Souls of Black Folk* (Chicago: A. C. McClurg and Co., 1903), especially Chap. III: "Of Mr. Booker T. Washington and Others."

[90] A recent strong defense of Booker T. Washington's leadership is put forth in Howard Brotz, *The Black Jews of Harlem* (New York: Free Press, 1964), pp. 72–83. For a different appraisal see Meier and Rudwick, *op. cit.*, pp. 181–86.

[91] Frazier, *The Negro in the United States*, p. 159.

ing the Negro's innate inferiority, shiftlessness, and hopeless unfitness for full participation in the white man's civilization." [92] Meanwhile, disfranchisement of black people proceeded rapidly, and the number of blacks holding elective offices declined. By the turn of the century the last black Congressman left office, and virtually all black people in the South were disfranchised.

The Black Response

Because of their economic plight and the widespread violence directed against them, many black people sought to improve their status through migration. In 1900 nearly nine-tenths of the Negroes in the United States were in the South, and the vast majority of them lived in the rural areas. The migration took several forms: rural Negroes sought safety in the relative anonymity of cities, Southern Negroes moved North, and many Negroes moved to countries in Africa. Because of their economic plight, the absence of skills, and discrimination elsewhere in the United States, most blacks, of course, remained in the rural South.

The campaign to prove that black people were innately inferior was under way. Southerners led the campaign, but they were by no means alone in this endeavor. Northern newspapers and magazines supported their efforts by running a steady stream of editorials in which Negroes were caricatured as subhuman beings. Meanwhile, a well-fortified group of black intellectuals, led by William E. B. Du Bois, challenged the leadership of Booker T. Washington and organized to protest the subordinate position to which black people had been relegated. Du Bois' response to Washington's teachings was stated as follows:

> . . . so far as Mr. Washington apologizes for injustice, North or South, does not rightly value the privilege of voting, belittles the emasculating effects of caste distinctions, and opposes the higher training of our brighter minds, —so far as he, the South, or the Nation does this,—we must increasingly and firmly oppose them. By every civilized and peaceful method we must strive for the rights which the world accords men.[93]

Despite the widespread campaign to prove the innate inferiority of black people, and despite the efforts of Booker T. Washington in counseling them to accommodate to the status quo, many blacks reached the highest realms of scholarship and organized to protest the many Jim Crow laws being enacted throughout the country. By that time disfranchisement in the South was virtually complete, and a system of rigid

[92] Woodward, *The Strange Career of Jim Crow*, pp. 52–53.
[93] Du Bois, *The Souls of Black Folk*, p. 59.

segregation had been enacted into law. In 1905 these intellectuals met and organized the Niagara Movement, an organization that demanded for blacks the same rights enjoyed by white Americans. This movement convinced numerous white Americans that many black people had rejected the leadership of Booker T. Washington. Furthermore, Washington's program of accommodation appeared to be ineffective in dealing with the widespread anti-Negro mob violence and other acts of white supremacy spreading throughout the United States. Consequently, a group of whites and blacks met in 1909 and organized the National Association for the Advancement of Colored People (NAACP). They adopted a platform calling for the abolition of segregation, equal educational opportunities, the right to vote, and the enforcement of the Fourteenth and Fifteenth Amendments.[94]

World War I
and Its Aftermath

The participation by the United States in World War I did little to improve the status of black people. It did, however, influence their geographic distribution. From 1914 to 1920 an estimated 400,000 to 1,000,000 black people left the South to work in industries of the North.[95] The steady stream of immigrants from Europe had virtually ceased, and blacks in the South were recruited by Northern industries. In addition to economic opportunities, continued lynching and intimidation stimulated the northward migration of Negroes. As these migrants settled in Northern cities, they were forced into segregated neighborhoods. Although continued Southern violence had in part motivated this migration, violence also greeted them in their new locations. For example, a mob of whites in East St. Louis, Illinois, massacred and burned 125 Negroes in 1917. While black troops fought abroad, their civilian counterparts were forced to defend themselves in the streets back home. Lynching continued in the South. A crowd of 3,000 white spectators in Tennessee responded to a newspaper invitation to watch a Negro being burned alive.[96] Violence directed against black people during this period was not limited to civilians; black soldiers in uniform were the subjects of continued violence, including lynching, especially in the South.

Meanwhile, nearly 400,000 Negroes registered for military service in World War I. In characteristic American fashion, they were enrolled in

---

[94] Langston Hughes, *Fight for Freedom* (New York: Berkley Publishing Corporation, 1962).

[95] Franklin, *From Slavery to Freedom*, p. 465; Logan, *op. cit.*, p. 70.

[96] Franklin, *From Slavery to Freedom*, p. 467.

segregated units and usually trained at segregated camps. They served mainly in the Army, being barred from the Marines and utilized in the most menial capacities in the Navy. In the Army they served in nearly all branches except the Aviation Corps. Service in the Army was especially difficult for blacks because they were constantly insulted by white officers. Throughout the war severe clashes between black and white soldiers erupted. Despite these difficulties, they remained loyal, and some 100,000 of them served on overseas duty. Those who served overseas, like those who remained in the United States, were subject to indignities from white soldiers. Nevertheless, many of them performed heroically in battle and received praise for their services from the French.[97]

The year following the end of World War I was an especially difficult one for Negroes. More than 70 black persons, including ten servicemen in uniform, were lynched. The summer of 1919 was called the Red Summer because of the racial violence which took place. From June to September some 25 race riots erupted in American cities, and 14 Negroes were publicly burned alive. The most serious outbreak occurred in Chicago, where 38 persons were killed, 23 of them Negroes. The postwar anti-Negro violence convinced many blacks that it was necessary to defend themselves from these attacks; therefore armed self-defense was widespread, especially in cities.[98]

After the war many blacks remained in Europe, especially in France, where they experienced racial democracy for the first time. Those who returned expected to find changed attitudes in the United States, but they found that white supremacy was still the norm. There had been a deliberate effort to belittle their roles in the war effort, and their scores on the Army intelligence tests were widely interpreted as proving their innate inferiority.

The widespread economic prosperity of the 1920's had little effect on the low status to which black people were relegated. By then much of the country was completely segregated along racial lines, and anti-Negro violence, including lynching, continued unchecked. In response to those conditions, scores of black people in the North and South rallied to the support of Marcus Garvey and the Universal Negro Improvement Association.[99] Garvey was able to build the largest mass movement among blacks in American history. The number of black people who actually became members of the organization is not known; however, estimates

[97] Woodson, *The Negro in Our History,* pp. 526–27.
[98] Franklin, *From Slavery to Freedom,* pp. 471–76.
[99] See Edmund David Cronon, *Black Moses* (Madison, Wis.: The University of Wisconsin Press, 1955).

range up to 6 million.[100] Garvey's popularity was based on his national-istic appeal to poorer Negroes. He advocated pride in blackness and the eventual establishment of a black nation in Africa. Middle-class Negroes, especially the leadership of the NAACP, were his strongest critics, for they envisioned the complete integration of black people in American society. After a persistent stream of rebuffs, however, many black people maintained doubts about this eventuality. As one historian has written in appraisal of Garvey's program: "Its significance lies in the fact that it was the first and only real mass movement among Negroes in the United States and that it indicates the extent to which Negroes entertained doubts concerning the hope for first-class citizenship in the only father-land of which they knew." [101] The Universal Negro Improvement Asso-ciation finally collapsed in 1923, when Garvey was convicted on a charge of using the mails to defraud in raising money for the shipping line which he founded. He was subsequently deported to the West Indies and eventually died in London in 1940.

The post-World War I decade witnessed, in addition to the phe-nomenal growth of the Universal Negro Improvement Association, what has been called a "Negro Renaissance." During the 1920's a number of blacks, especially those in Harlem, were active in publishing books, maga-zines, and newspapers. The theme of the writings and music of this period was an attack on the injustices imposed on Negroes by the larger society. Although black authors had published books prior to this time, it was this period of extraordinary literary activity which convinced the owners of publishing companies that black people were capable of high-caliber literary achievement. Although most of their efforts may be termed social protest, their artistic merit marked them as among the outstanding contributors to American literature and music.

The Depression,
The New Deal,
and World War II

The Great Depression of the 1930's virtually ended the massive mi-gration of Negroes from the South. Although most Americans suffered from the Depression, it was especially difficult for those in low-status occupations, and the overwhelming majority of blacks fell within this category. By the mid-1930's the great masses of blacks were receiving public assistance, and in some sections of the country the figure was as high as 80 percent. When the unemployed and hungry blacks applied

100 *Ibid.*, pp. 205–7.
101 Franklin, *From Slavery to Freedom*, p. 483.

for public assistance, they again met with discrimination. In many sections of the country there was a significant differential between the allocations they received and those received by white Americans.[102]

The government agencies created to deal with problems brought about by the Depression were effective in aiding those poor people who were in greatest need, including a significant proportion of blacks. Whatever assistance was provided by the New Deal generally occurred within a framework of segregation. President Franklin D. Roosevelt appointed what became known as his Black Cabinet to advise him on matters pertaining to the welfare of black people. Many Negroes held high (although primarily symbolic) positions in such agencies as the National Youth Administration and the Department of the Interior. Because of the interest of Roosevelt and of Mrs. Eleanor Roosevelt in the general welfare of the poor, and of Negroes in particular, black people began to shift in large numbers from the Republican Party to the Democratic Party. The northward migration and the residential segregation of blacks in large cities stimulated political rejuvenation for the first time since the Reconstruction. The New Deal policies of the Roosevelt administration ushered in a new conception of the role of government toward citizens. Many of the social welfare measures enacted during this period helped bring the country out of the Depression and have since become firmly established social policy.

In many ways the New Deal signaled a turning point in attitudes toward Negroes.[103] Many of the prominent politicians of this period expressed an interest in the plight of the black population as part of a broader humanitarian interest in the problem of poverty. For example, one individual who expressed great interest in the welfare of black people was Harold L. Ickes, Secretary of the Interior and a former president of a local chapter of the NAACP. In addition, Negro voting strength in Northern cities reached a point where their welfare could not be easily ignored. Furthermore, Negroes organized to protect their interests. In 1933 the Joint Committee on National Recovery, a coalition of Negro rights organizations, was founded to fight discriminatory policies in federal works projects. One of its main accomplishments was exposing differential wages paid to black and white workers.

In general the New Deal benefited black people by creating a favorable climate of opinion for increased civil rights, by increasing the material benefits paid to the unemployed, and by reducing discrimination

[102] Ina C. Brown, *The Story of the American Negro* (New York: Friendship Press, 1957), p. 120; Franklin, *From Slavery to Freedom*, p. 488.

[103] Meier and Rudwick, *op. cit.*, pp. 210–17; Gunnar Myrdal, *An American Dilemma* (New York: Harper, 1944), pp. 1000–1001.

against blacks in employment. However, discrimination continued in federal works projects and in the policies of the Agricultural Adjustment Administration; moreover, segregation was maintained in public accommodations in the South and in housing financed by the Federal Housing Administration.[104]

The rise of industrial unionism, especially the formation of the Congress of Industrial Organizations (CIO), had its impact on race relations during the 1930's. Although separate locals were maintained in the South, the CIO made interracial trade unionism respectable. It gave black and white workers a sense of common interest, and for the first time black and white workers worked together, receiving equal pay for comparable jobs.[105]

As the United States became increasingly involved in the war in Europe, a period of widespread prosperity was enjoyed by most Americans, including Negroes. Again the Southern blacks migrated North by the millions. As they sought employment in the war industries, they were faced with characteristic acts of discrimination. It took the threat of a massive march on Washington by Negroes to force President Roosevelt to issue an executive order barring discrimination against Negroes in industries with government contracts. Since many black people had received technical training during the New Deal administration, they were well prepared to work in industries supporting the war effort.

More than a million black men and women served in the military service during World War II. Approximately 500,000 of them served overseas. As usual, the military services were rigidly segregated, although toward the end of the war a practice of integrating black platoons into white units overseas was established. Widespread violence and discrimination continued, causing black servicemen to question their participation in a war being fought for "four freedoms" by a country which denied them the very principles for which they were fighting on behalf of others. Servicemen in uniform were beaten and murdered by Southern policemen and citizens. Attempts on their part to resist segregation and discrimination resulted in frequent clashes on military installations, both at home and abroad, that sometimes led to race riots. One of the more humiliating practices for black servicemen was that of restaurant owners' serving German prisoners of war in places of public accommodation in the United States while similar service was denied to Negro servicemen.[106]

The continued adherence to white supremacy in the face of widespread participation by Negroes in World War II, as well as the support

---

[104] Meier and Rudwick, *op. cit.,* pp. 212–13; Myrdal, *op. cit.,* pp. 464–66.
[105] Meier and Rudwick, *op. cit.,* p. 213.
[106] Franklin, *From Slavery to Freedom,* pp. 570–73.

of the war effort by black civilians, raised doubts in the minds of many black people about the seriousness of cultural pronouncements of such concepts as "freedom," "justice," and "equality." Meanwhile, as the war was being waged in Europe and Asia, European colonial powers were beginning to lose their black colonies in Africa. At the close of the war the United Nations was established, and the United States became increasingly concerned about its "image" abroad.

During the years immediately following World War II, because of the combination of increased black militancy and changing world conditions, several events occurred which gave black people some hope that their depressed status might somehow be altered. New York State enacted the first state Fair Employment Practices Law in 1945. President Harry S Truman created the first national committee on civil rights in 1946, and in 1948 he issued an executive order banning segregation and discrimination in the armed forces. Meanwhile, the Supreme Court, beginning in 1946, issued a series of decisions outlawing segregation in various aspects of American life, culminating in the decision in 1954 which prohibited racial segregation in public education.

•   •   •

This brief sketch of significant historical events in the lives of Negroes since the first permanent black settlement in North America has focused on those circumstances which are responsible for the present state of race relations in the United States. Black people were enslaved and subjected to a system of bondage with few parallels in human history. Formal slavery ended in a costly war, and a caste system developed which continued to relegate the former slaves and their descendants to a subordinate position in society. By the middle of the 20th century the oppressed status of black people had finally been recognized as a social problem of some magnitude, and there were attempts by both black and white Americans to deal with the problem. These approaches will be discussed in the final chapter. The next several chapters deal with the immediate results of the peculiar history of black people in the United States.

SELECTED BIBLIOGRAPHY

Aptheker, Herbert, *A Documentary History of the Negro People in the United States.* New York: Citadel Press, 1951.

————, *American Negro Slave Revolts*. New York: International Publishers Co., Inc., 1963.

Armstrong, George D., *The Christian Doctrine of Slavery*. New York: Charles Scribner's Sons, 1857.

Bennett, Lerone, Jr., *Before the Mayflower*. Baltimore: Penguin Books, 1966.

Brown, Ina C., *The Story of the American Negro*. New York: Friendship Press, 1957.

Buckmaster, Henrietta, *Let My People Go: The Story of the Underground Railroad and the Growth of the Abolition Movement*. New York: Harper and Brothers, 1941.

Cronon, Edmund David, *Black Moses: The Story of Marcus Garvey and the Universal Negro Improvement Association*. Madison, Wis.: The University of Wisconsin Press, 1955.

Davis, David B., *The Problem of Slavery in Western Culture*. Ithaca, N.Y.: Cornell University Press, 1966.

Degler, Carl N., *Out of Our Past*. New York: Harper & Row, Publishers, 1959.

Douglass, Frederick, *Narrative of the Life of Frederick Douglass, An American Slave* (ed. Benjamin Quarles). Cambridge, Mass.: Harvard University Press, 1960.

Dounan, Elizabeth, *Documents Illustrative of the History of the Slave Trade to America*. Washington, D.C.: Carnegie Institution in Washington, 1935.

Du Bois, W. E. B., *Black Folk, Then and Now*. New York: Henry Holt and Co., 1939.

————, *Black Reconstruction*. New York: Harcourt, Brace and Co., 1935.

————, *The Souls of Black Folk*. Chicago: A. C. McClurg and Co., 1903.

Elkins, Stanley, *Slavery: A Problem in American Institutional and Intellectual Life*. Chicago: University of Chicago Press, 1959.

Embree, Edwin R., *Brown Americans*. New York: The Viking Press, Inc., 1946.

Fitzhugh, George, *Cannibals All! Or Slaves Without Masters*. Richmond, Va.: A. Morris, 1857.

Franklin, John Hope, *From Slavery to Freedom*. New York: Alfred A. Knopf, Inc., 1948.

————, *Reconstruction After the Civil War*. Chicago: The University of Chicago Press, 1961.

Frazier, E. Franklin, *Black Bourgeoisie*. Glencoe, Ill.: Free Press, 1957.

————, *The Negro Family in the United States*. Chicago: The University of Chicago Press, 1966.

————, *The Negro in the United States*. New York: The Macmillan Company, 1957.

Freyre, Gilberto, *The Masters and the Slaves: A Study in the Development of Brazilian Civilization*. New York: Alfred A. Knopf, Inc., 1964.

Genovese, Eugene D., *The Political Economy of Slavery: Studies in the Economy and Society of the Slave South*. New York: Pantheon Books, Inc., 1965.

Grant, Joanne, *Black Protest*. New York: Fawcett World Library, 1968.

Halasz, Nicholas, *The Rattling Chains: Slave Unrest and Revolt in the American South*. New York: David McKay Co., Inc., 1966.

Harris, Marvin, *Patterns of Race in the Americas*. New York: Walker and Co., 1964.

Herskovits, Melville, *The Myth of the Negro Past*. New York: Harper and Brothers, 1941.

Hughes, Langston, *Fight for Freedom: The Story of the NAACP*. New York: Berkley Publishing Corporation, 1962.

Kemble, Frances A., *Journal of a Residence on a Georgia Plantation in 1838–1839* (ed. John A. Scott). New York: Alfred A. Knopf, Inc., 1961.

Litwack, Leon F., *North of Slavery*. Chicago: The University of Chicago Press, 1961.

Logan, Rayford W., *The Negro in the United States*. Princeton, N.J.: D. Van Nostrand Co., Inc., 1957.

McPherson, James M., *The Negro's Civil War*. New York: Random House, Inc., 1965.

Meier, August, and Elliott Rudwick, *From Plantation to Ghetto*. New York: Hill and Wang, Inc., 1966.

Myrdal, Gunnar, *An American Dilemma: The Negro Problem and Modern Democracy*. New York: Harper and Brothers, 1944.

Olmstead, Frederick L., *The Cotton Kingdom* (ed. Arthur M. Schlesinger). New York: Alfred A. Knopf, Inc., 1953.

Phillips, Ulrich B., *American Negro Slavery*. New York: D. Appleton and Co., 1918.

Ross, Fred A., *Slavery Ordained by God*. Philadelphia: J. B. Lippincott Co., 1857.

Siebert, Wilbur H., *The Underground Railroad From Slavery to Freedom*. New York: The Macmillan Company, 1898.

Simkins, Francis B., *A History of the South*. New York: Alfred A. Knopf, Inc., 1959.

Stampp, Kenneth M., *The Peculiar Institution: Slavery in the Ante-Bellum South*. New York: Alfred A. Knopf, Inc., 1956.

Tannenbaum, Frank, *Slave and Citizen: The Negro in the Americas*. New York: Alfred A. Knopf, Inc., 1946.

Trowbridge, John T., *The Desolate South*. New York: Meredith Press, 1956.

U.S. Bureau of the Census, *Negro Population 1790–1915*. Washington, D.C.: Government Printing Office, 1918.

Wade, Richard C., *Slavery in the Cities*. New York: Oxford University Press, Inc., 1964.

Washington, Booker T., *Up From Slavery*. New York: Doubleday & Company, Inc., 1900.

Woodson, Carter G., *The African Background Outlined*. Washington, D.C.: Association Press, 1936.

———, *The Negro in Our History*. Washington, D.C.: Associated Publishers, Inc., 1922.

Woodward, C. Vann, *Reunion and Reaction*. Boston: Little, Brown and Company, 1951.

———, *The Strange Career of Jim Crow*. New York: Oxford University Press, Inc., 1957.

The peculiar history of black Americans is, in part, responsible for their present status. In many ways black Americans, as a group, differ from white Americans. These differences invariably stem from the low status to which they have been relegated in society. In no instance are these differences more pronounced than in population characteristics. In the United States there are several fundamental differences between black and white population characteristics. When black and white Americans share similar socioeconomic status positions in society, they are remarkably similar in fertility and mortality rates, for example, but the over-representation of black people in the lowest status category serves to make for significant group differences between them and their white fellow citizens on population characteristics.

SIZE AND GROWTH

In March 1965, black people made up 10.8 percent of the American population. Their total population of nearly 21 million is exceeded on the world scene by only 24 of the more than 130 independent nation-states and self-governing territories. Only three of the more than 40 independent African states have total populations

Characteristics of the Population[1]

which exceed the number of Negroes in the United States. Within the United States, Negroes are the largest visible minority group. They constitute approximately 95 percent of the "nonwhite" population of the country. The size of the black population is frequently cited as a factor which influences their integration into American society. Since they have been retained in a subordinate position, and since they are responded to as a group, the very magnitude of their numbers may be considered both a handicap and an asset to their advancement in the United States.[2]

At the time of the first population census, in 1790, nearly one out of every five (19.3 percent) Americans was a Negro. Slightly more than 750,000 Negroes were enumerated by that census. With each following census the number increased to the point where, in less than 200 years,

[1] Data on the black population in the United States are sometimes entered as "Negro" and sometimes combined with other "nonwhite" minorities. Since Negroes have made up at least 94 percent of the nonwhite population since the first census, "nonwhite" and "Negro" are frequently used interchangeably.

[2] See Philip M. Hauser, "Demographic Factors in the Integration of the Negro," in Talcott Parsons and Kenneth B. Clark (eds.), *The Negro American* (Boston: Houghton Mifflin, 1966).

nearly 21 million Negroes now reside in the United States. The pattern of growth has been a consistent one, with the percentage of increase being greatest in the earlier years. During the decade from 1800 to 1810, for example, the Negro population increased by 37.5 percent. The decade with the lowest percentage of increase was from 1910 to 1920, when the increase was 6.5 percent. The greatest single historical contributor to the increase in the black population has been the excess of births over deaths (natural increase). Since the first census, immigration has been an insignificant element in black population growth.

TABLE 2–1

THE NEGRO POPULATION OF THE UNITED STATES, 1790–1965

Year	Total U.S. Population	Total Negro Population	Percent of Negro Population
1965	193,818,000	20,944,000	10.8
1960	179,323,175	18,871,831	10.5
1950	150,697,361	15,042,286	10.0
1940	131,669,275	12,865,518	9.8
1930	122,775,046	11,891,143	9.7
1920	105,710,620	10,463,131	9.9
1910	91,972,266	9,797,763	10.7
1900	75,944,575	8,833,994	11.6
1890	62,974,714	7,488,676	11.9
1880	50,155,783	6,580,973	13.1
1870	39,818,449	5,392,172	13.5
1860	31,443,321	4,441,830	14.1
1850	23,191,876	3,638,808	15.7
1840	17,069,453	2,873,648	16.8
1830	12,866,020	2,328,642	18.1
1820	9,638,453	1,771,656	18.4
1810	7,239,881	1,377,808	19.0
1800	5,308,483	1,002,037	18.9
1790	3,929,214	757,208	19.3

Source: Computed from data from the following U.S. Bureau of the Census publications: *Historical Statistics of the United States, Colonial Times to 1957*, Series A 59–70, p. 9, and Series A 17–21, p. 8; *1960 Census of Population, Characteristics of Population, U.S. Summary*, Vol. 1, Part 1, Table 44; *Statistical Abstract of the United States, 1966*, Table 9, p. 11. The 1965 data represent estimates published in *Current Population Reports*, Series P-20, No. 155, "Negro Population: March, 1965," p. 1. The data on the Negro population for 1870 have been adjusted by the Bureau of the Census to account for underenumeration in Southern states.

The proportion of black people in the total population of the United States remained relatively stable up through the census of 1810, when there was a gradual decline which persisted up through the census of 1930. This decline in the proportion of black people in the population resulted mainly from two factors: the decline and ultimate cessation in the importation of slaves, and the increase in the number of white immigrants to the United States. In the decade from 1930 to 1940 there was a gradual increase in the proportion of black people in the population. In 1930 they comprised 9.7 percent of the population, and by 1965 the proportion was 10.8 percent (see Table 2–1).

The growth pattern of the black population may be attributed to two major factors: (1) a consistent increase in numbers from the first census until the present time, and (2) fluctuation as regards proportion of the total population. The proportion was reasonably steady between 1790 and 1830, decreased moderately from 1830 to 1930, and increased gradually since 1930.

FERTILITY

The black population of the United States is increasing at a more rapid rate than the white population. The major element in the Negro population growth rate is the increase in births over deaths. Throughout the present century the birth rate among Negroes has remained consistently higher than the white birth rate. In 1964 the birth rate among nonwhites was 29.1 per 1,000 population, while among whites the rate was 20.0. Since 1920 the nonwhite birth rate has been at least six points greater than the white birth rate (see Table 2–2).

TABLE 2–2

BIRTH RATE PER 1,000 POPULATION IN
THE UNITED STATES, BY COLOR, 1920–1964

Year	Total	White	Nonwhite	Difference
1964	21.0	20.0	29.1	9.1
1960	23.7	22.7	32.1	9.4
1955	25.0	23.8	34.8	11.0
1950	24.1	23.0	33.6	10.6
1945	20.4	19.7	26.5	6.8
1940	19.4	18.6	27.6	9.0
1935	18.7	17.9	25.8	7.9
1930	21.3	20.6	27.5	6.9
1920	27.7	26.9	35.0	8.1

Source: U.S. Bureau of the Census, *Statistical Abstract of the United States, 1966,* Table 49, p. 46.

Another measure of the difference between black and white fertility is the number of children born per 1,000 women between the ages of 15 and 44. Since 1910 the number has been considerably greater for black women than for white women. This difference persisted up to 1950, when it was slight, and in 1960 the difference again became great. For 1910, 1950, and 1960, the number of children born per 1,000 black women was 2,091, 1,572, and 2,003, respectively. Corresponding figures for white women in these years were 1,662, 1,372, and 1,712.[3]

The black fertility rate, like that of whites, is affected by social factors. Blacks and whites who share the same economic status positions, and who share the same residence patterns, show similar fertility patterns. Historically, Negroes have been concentrated in the rural South and have occupied low-status economic positions. Therefore their fertility rate has been higher than that of whites. When they migrate to cities, and when they improve their economic status, the birth rate declines. The economic status has apparently been a more salient variable than whether they lived in rural or urban areas, because within urban areas Negroes have a higher birth rate than do whites.

After World War II the birth rate among Negroes increased rather sharply. This trend continued up to 1960, when it dropped, and the decline has persisted up to 1964. Now that black people are becoming urbanized at an even greater rate than whites, their fertility might be expected to continue to decline. However, because the economic gap between blacks and whites is broadening rather than narrowing, and because the fetal death rate is declining more rapidly among blacks than among white persons, the differential fertility rate may be expected to persist.

HEALTH AND MORTALITY

Reliable statistics on the death rate of black people were not available until about 1900. Although Negroes have a higher death rate than white Americans, the death rate differential is not so great as for births. In 1900 the death rate among Negroes was 25.0 per 1,000 population, while among whites it was 17.0 per 1,000 population. Since that time the gap between whites and blacks has gradually narrowed to the point where, in 1964, the rate for blacks was 9.7 as compared with 9.4 for whites.[4]

[3] U.S. Bureau of the Census, *Census of Population 1960, United States Summary* PC(1)–1C (Washington, D.C.: Government Printing Office, 1961), Table 81.

[4] U.S. Bureau of the Census, *Historical Statistics of the United States, Colonial Times to 1957* (Washington, D.C.: Government Printing Office, 1960), p. 27; U.S. Bureau of the Census, *Statistical Abstract of the United States, 1966* (Washington, D.C.: Government Printing Office, 1966), p. 55.

Negroes still die in greater proportion than whites from diseases which are controllable through the use of modern medical techniques. In 1964, for example, the general mortality rate for blacks was significantly higher than for whites in several categories.[5] Tuberculosis is no longer a major cause of death in the United States, but black people die from tuberculosis at a rate three times that for whites. The death rate from syphilis is three times as great among black people as among whites. Blacks are twice as likely to die from gastritis and infections of the kidney. They are considerably more likely to die from diabetes and pneumonia.

Accidents and homicides cause a considerably greater proportion of deaths among black people than among whites. For every 100,000 black people in the population in 1964, 41 died from accidents other than automobile accidents, while for whites the rate was 28 per 100,000 population. The homicide rate among black people is seven times greater than among whites.

Black mothers die during delivery and from complications of pregnancy at a rate six times greater than do white mothers. For every 100,000 Negroes in the population in 1964, 25 infants died of birth injuries, while among whites the rate was 11.6. While the differential in general mortality rates for blacks and whites is no longer great, black infants have considerably higher mortality rates than do white infants. Since reasonably accurate statistics have been available, the infant mortality rate for black people has been consistently higher than for whites. In 1915, for example, for every 1,000 live births among Negroes, 181 babies died during infancy; the corresponding figure for white babies was 97. This difference has persisted through the years, although between 1920 and 1955 the differences were not so great. Beginning in 1960, however, black babies were again twice as likely to die during infancy as white babies. In 1964 the infant mortality rates for white and black babies, per 1,000 live births in each of these categories, were 22 and 41, respectively (see Table 2-3). There has been a steady reduction in infant mortality rates for both blacks and whites, but the differential between the two has persisted.

A reasonably accurate measure of the health and living standards of a people is their life expectancy. In this regard black Americans have always fared less well than white Americans. In 1900 the life expectancy at birth for Negroes was 33 years, while for whites it was 47.6 years. By 1964 it was 64.1 for blacks and 71 for whites.[6] In both cases the life expectancy at birth has substantially increased, largely because of declin-

[5] U.S. Department of Health, Education, and Welfare, *Vital Statistics of the United States, 1964* (Washington, D.C.: Government Printing Office, 1966), pp. 1-8 — 1-20.

[6] U.S. Bureau of the Census, *Historical Statistics of the United States, Colonial Times to 1957*, p. 25; U.S. Bureau of the Census, *Statistical Abstract of the United States, 1966*, p. 52.

ing infant mortality, and there has been a reduction in the difference between blacks and whites from nearly 15 years to approximately seven years. That white Americans can expect to live longer than black Americans remains a significant indicator of the differences in living standards between these two groups.

In both health standards and mortality rates, black Americans share unequally in the social rewards of American society. The discrepancy between black Americans and their white fellow citizens in this regard is another manifestation of the racist nature of American society.

TABLE 2–3

INFANT MORTALITY RATES PER 1,000 LIVE BIRTHS,
UNITED STATES, BY COLOR, 1915–1964

Year	Total	White	Nonwhite	Difference
1964	24.8	21.6	41.1	19.5
1960	26.0	22.9	43.2	20.3
1955	26.4	23.6	42.8	19.2
1950	29.2	28.6	44.5	15.9
1945	38.3	35.6	57.0	21.4
1940	47.0	43.2	73.8	30.6
1935	55.7	51.9	83.2	31.3
1930	64.6	60.1	99.9	39.8
1925	71.7	68.3	110.8	42.5
1920	85.8	82.1	131.7	49.6
1915	99.9	98.6	181.2	82.6

Source: From 1915–1955, U.S. Bureau of the Census, *Historical Statistics of the United States, Colonial Times to 1957*, Series 101–112, p. 25; from 1960–1964, U.S. Bureau of the Census, *Statistical Abstract of the United States, 1966*, Table 64, p. 55.

AGE AND SEX COMPOSITION

The median age of the black population, like that of the white population, steadily increased in the United States until 1950. In 1850 the median age of Negroes in the United States was 17.3, and by 1950 it had increased to 26.1. In 1960 the median age had decreased to 23.5, and by 1965 the decline had continued to the point where the median age was 21.6.[7] The increase in median age of Negroes resulted from an in-

[7] U.S. Bureau of the Census, "Negro Population: March 1965," *Current Population Reports*, Series P-20, No. 155 (Washington, D.C.: Government Printing Office, 1966), p. 14.

crease in the average length of life and a gradual decrease in the proportion of children. The decrease since 1950 resulted from an increase in the birth rate.

The recent decline in the median age of black people is paralleled by a similar trend among white Americans. The black population, however, is somewhat younger than the white population. There are relatively more young people and fewer old people among Negroes. In 1965, for example, 44.7 percent of the black population was under 18 years of age, compared with 35.5 percent of the white population. On the other hand, among people 65 years of age and over in 1965, 10 percent of the total white population fell into this age category, compared with only 6 percent of the black population.[8] When the Negro populations under 18 and over 65 are combined, one-half of the total Negro population falls within this dependent category; that is, more than half the black population of the United States is either too young or too old for the labor force. With the high unemployment rate for Negroes eligible for the labor force, such a condition poses serious problems of economic support for the black population as a whole.

The age distribution of the black population is not uniform throughout the country. Negroes in the South are somewhat younger than those living elsewhere. For example, in 1965 the median age for blacks in the South was 20.6, while outside the South it was 22.7. The South contains a greater proportion of Negroes in the dependent-children (under 18 years of age) and the dependent-aged (65 years of age and over) categories. Slightly more than 46 percent of the blacks in the South were under 18 years of age in 1965, and 7.3 percent were 65 and over. Comparable figures for non-Southern states were 43.0 and 4.7, respectively. Consequently, in that region of the country, where social welfare services are the least well developed, the need is greatest.

Blacks and whites differ in age distribution on farms and in nonfarm areas. The median age for Negroes living on farms is a mere 17 years, while for whites it is 31.6 years. Furthermore, Negroes living on farms are younger than nonfarm Negroes. The median age for nonfarm Negroes was, in 1965, 22.2 years. This pattern is reversed for white Americans, with the median age being younger in nonfarm regions than on farms. Among black people who live on farms, 54.2 percent are under 18 years of age and 5.6 percent are 65 years of age and over. Among nonfarm Negroes, on the other hand, 43.9 percent were under 18 and 6.2 percent were 65 and over.[9] Again, where social welfare services are the least well developed (i.e., in rural areas), the need is greatest. A higher proportion

8 *Ibid.*, p. 13.
9 *Ibid.*, p. 13.

of Negroes than whites who fall within the dependent-children category are farm residents, while in the dependent-aged category a higher proportion of whites than Negroes are nonfarm residents.

Black females outnumber black males. In 1965 there were more than 850,000 more black females than males in the United States. Furthermore, black females are somewhat older than black males. In 1965, for example, the median age for black males was 20.4, while the median age for black females was 22.7. Among Negroes, 42.9 percent of the females were under 18 years of age, compared with 46.5 percent of the males. Also, 6.4 percent of Negro females were 65 years of age and over, while 5.8 percent of the males were in this age category.[10] Throughout the United States, in all geographical regions, black females tend to be older than black males.

Because of the age differences between black males and black females and the later age of marriage for males, there is a higher proportion of single males than females (31.9 percent and 23.0 percent, respectively). There is also a greater percentage of black males than black females who are married (61.1 percent vs. 59.5 percent). But, among the widowed, a significantly greater proportion of black females fall into this category than black males (13.4 percent vs. 3.9 percent).[11] These figures reflect the greater life expectancy among females than among males.

A higher proportion of black farm residents under the age of 18 are likely to be female (56.2 percent) than male (52.1 percent). On the other hand, among black nonfarm residents, a higher proportion of males than females are under 18 years of age (46 percent vs. 42 percent). Adult males (those 18 years of age and over) are more likely than their female counterparts to live on farms, while adult females are more likely than adult males to live in nonfarm regions.[12]

The black population is younger than the white population, and, although there are substantially more females than males in the Negro population, the males are younger. With the continuing difficulties that Negroes face in securing and maintaining employment, such a population composition is likely to contribute to increased disillusionment and disorder in American cities.

DISTRIBUTION

Black Americans differ from white Americans in their regional and rural-urban distribution in the United States. Furthermore, redistribu-

[10] U.S. Bureau of the Census, *Statistical Abstract of the United States, 1966*, p. 25.
[11] *Ibid.*, p. 25.
[12] U.S. Bureau of the Census, *Current Population Reports*, p. 13.

tion in both these two categories is occurring at a more rapid rate for black Americans than for white Americans.

South–Non-South

Throughout most of American history black people have been heavily concentrated in the agricultural South. At the end of the Civil War more than 92 percent of all Negroes lived in the South. There has been a gradual reduction in the black population in the South since the beginning of the 20th century. At the turn of the century (1900), nine out of ten Negroes in the United States were still in the South. Throughout the present century, however, Negroes have migrated from the South to other regions, principally to the Northeast and to the North-Central states. So widespread has been this migration that, by 1965, only slightly more than half (53.6 percent) the Negroes remained in the South.[13]

Except for the South, where they constitute one-fifth of the population, Negroes represent small proportions in other regions of the country. In the Northeast and North-Central states, 7 percent of the population in 1960 was black, and in the West the blacks constituted only 4 percent of the total population.[14] While the South has experienced a decline in the proportion of Negroes living in that region, each of the other regions has experienced increases (see Table 2–4). The first significant exodus of black people from the South occurred during World War I. This trend has continued, declining somewhat during the Depression of the 1930's and greatly accelerating during World War II. In the two decades following World War II, the proportion of Negroes living in the South declined from more than three-fourths to slightly less than one-half. Altogether 3.3 million blacks left the South between 1940 and 1963.[15] The region with the greatest percentage of increase has been the West. For example, in 1940 slightly more than 1 percent of the Negroes in the United States lived in this region, but by 1965 more than 8 percent lived in these states. The proportion of Negroes in the North-Central states nearly doubled during the same period, from 11 percent to 20.2 percent. The proportion of Negroes in the Northeastern states increased in this period from 10.6 percent to 17.9 percent.

Migration of Negroes from the South has recently decreased. Those

---

[13] As defined by the U.S. Bureau of the Census, the South consists of Alabama, Arkansas, Delaware, the District of Columbia, Florida, Georgia, Kentucky, Louisiana, Maryland, Mississippi, North Carolina, Oklahoma, South Carolina, Tennessee, Texas, Virginia, and West Virginia.

[14] U.S. Bureau of the Census, *Current Population Reports*, p. 1.

[15] U.S. Department of Labor, Bureau of Labor Statistics, *The Negroes in the United States: Their Economic and Social Situation* (Washington, D.C.: Government Printing Office, 1966), p. 2.

TABLE 2–4

NUMBER (IN THOUSANDS) AND PERCENTAGE OF
DISTRIBUTION OF THE NEGRO POPULATION IN
THE UNITED STATES, BY REGION, 1860–1965

Region	1965*		1960		1950		1940		1900		1860	
	Number	Percent	Number	Percent	Number	Percent	Number	Percent	Number	Percent	Number	Percent
United States	20,944	100	18,860	100	15,042	100	12,866	100	8,834	100	4,442	100
Northeast	3,749	17.9	3,028	16.1	2,018	13.4	1,370	10.6	385	4.4	156	3.5
North-Central	4,231	20.2	3,446	18.3	2,228	14.8	1,420	11.0	496	5.6	184	4.1
South	11,226	53.6	11,312	60.0	10,225	68.0	9,905	77.0	7,923	89.7	4,097	92.2
West	1,717	8.2	1,074	5.7	571	3.8	171	1.3	30	0.3	4	0.1

* Data for 1965 are estimates based on a sample conducted by the Bureau of the Census. Therefore the figures do not add up to the total and may differ slightly from those that would have been obtained if a complete census had been taken.

Source: U.S. Bureau of the Census, Census of Population, 1960, General Population Characteristics, United States Summary, PC (1)–1B, pp. 1–164, 1964; U.S. Bureau of the Census, Current Population Reports, Series P-20, No. 155, "Negro Population: March, 1965," 1966.

remaining in that region are heavily concentrated in the Deep South states. In 1960, in five of these states—Alabama, Georgia, Louisiana, Mississippi, and South Carolina—the population was at least one-fourth Negro. In Mississippi Negroes comprised 42 percent of the total population.[16] In the country as a whole, six states—Georgia, Illinois, Louisiana, New York, North Carolina, and Texas—each had more than a million Negroes. Twelve other states had black populations in excess of 500,000 but less than 1,000,000.[17]

The regional redistribution of Negroes generally results from the search for greater economic opportunities. Although they may not earn salaries comparable to white Americans, they can expect to earn significantly more outside the South than in that region. Furthermore, the "North" (i.e., non-South) has generally been more attractive to Negroes because of the relatively lesser degree of institutionalized violence directed against them.

Rural-Urban

The internal redistribution of black people from rural areas to urban centers has been even more dramatic than their exodus from the South. Indeed, those Negroes who leave the South usually settle in urban areas in other regions. Furthermore, within the South the blacks have tended to leave the rural areas and settle in cities. Before the Civil War Negroes were heavily concentrated in the rural sections of the South, but after 1860 they began to migrate to cities. In 1900 slightly more than one in five (22.7 percent) Negroes lived in urban areas. This figure was in contrast to two out of five for the American population as a whole.[18] By 1960, however, nearly three out of every four (73.2 percent) Negroes lived in urban areas, compared to 70 percent of the total population. Negroes have been becoming urbanized at a faster rate than the population as a whole. In the 60 years between 1900 and 1960, the black population has been transformed from a predominantly rural people to a predominantly urban people.

When black people move from the rural South, they settle in the centers of the largest cities. As of 1960, 18 of the largest cities in the United States had black populations of between 100,000 and 1,000,000 (see Table 2–5). These cities varied in the proportion of black people in their population anywhere from 53.9 percent in Washington, D.C., to

---

16 U.S. Bureau of the Census, *Statistical Abstract of the United States, 1966,* Table 26, p. 27.

17 *Ibid.,* Table 26, p. 27.

18 See Conrad Taeuber and Irene Taeuber, *The Changing Population of the United States* (New York: Wiley, 1958), p. 124.

13.5 percent in Los Angeles, California. Of the 21 American cities with populations of at least 500,000, only Boston, Massachusetts; Buffalo, New York; Milwaukee, Wisconsin; San Antonio, Texas; San Diego, California; and Seattle, Washington, had fewer than 100,000 black people.

TABLE 2–5

CITIES IN THE UNITED STATES WITH 100,000 OR MORE NEGROES, 1960

City	Total Population	Negro Population	Percentage of Negro Population
New York, N.Y.	7,781,984	1,087,931	14.0
Chicago, Ill.	3,550,404	812,637	22.9
Philadelphia, Pa.	2,002,512	529,240	26.4
Detroit, Mich.	1,670,144	482,223	28.9
Washington, D.C.	763,956	411,737	53.9
Los Angeles, Calif.	2,479,015	334,916	13.9
Baltimore, Md.	939,024	325,589	34.7
Cleveland, Ohio	876,050	250,818	28.6
New Orleans, La.	627,525	233,514	37.2
Houston, Texas	938,219	215,037	22.9
St. Louis, Mo.	750,026	214,377	28.6
Atlanta, Ga.	478,555	186,464	38.2
Birmingham, Ala.	340,887	135,113	39.6
Cincinnati, Ohio	502,550	108,754	21.6
Dallas, Texas	679,684	129,242	19.0
Memphis, Tenn.	497,524	184,320	37.0
Newark, N.J.	405,220	138,035	34.0
Pittsburgh, Pa.	604,332	100,692	16.7

Source: Compiled from data reported in the U.S. Bureau of the Census, *1960 Census of Population*, Vol. I, *Characteristics of the Population*, 1963.

Today nearly one-half (46.3 percent) of the blacks live outside the South, and, while two-fifths of those who remain in the South live in rural areas, in the North, 96 percent of the Negroes live in cities. If the urbanization rate among black people continues, and if whites continue to flee to the suburbs, in a matter of decades the centers of most large American cities will represent black communities. The pace of this urbanization is rapid. The black population of Los Angeles County, for example, increased by 600 percent between 1940 and 1960, and the black population of Newark, New Jersey, increased from one-third to one-half between 1960 and 1965.[19]

[19] Charles Silberman, *Crisis in Black and White* (New York: Random House, 1964), p. 31.

The widespread redistribution of Negroes, combined with the recent enactment of civil rights legislation, has tended to broaden the focus of race relations from the South to the entire country. Because of the practices of segregation and discrimination throughout the United States, virtually every major city faces serious problems in the areas of *de facto* segregated education, inadequate and segregated housing, and unemployment in black communities. Problems in race relations are being transformed into urban problems, and the problems which were at one time referred to as problems of race relations are increasingly being discussed as the problems of cities.

Through redistribution the black population is becoming more aware of its status relative to that of white Americans. In black communities throughout the United States the residents are organizing themselves and are protesting in a manner which was not possible when they were scattered throughout the rural South. As organized urban residents, their protests are likely to be more effective. Furthermore, they are in a better position to demand that elected officials address themselves to the problems which they face. Recently, these citizens have demonstrated that they are capable of posing problems in large cities with which municipal officials, acting alone, are incapable of dealing. In each of the major uprisings in black communities since 1965 it has been necessary for municipal officials to seek assistance from state governments and from the federal government. (See Chapter IX.)

Finally, the migration of black people alters their status insofar as employment and medical care are concerned. In cities their employment is likely to be upgraded when compared to farm employment in the rural South, and medical care is significantly improved.

●　　●　　●

Black people constitute almost 11 percent of the American population. Within the United States, however, they are not just 21 million citizens out of a total population of 194 million. Rather, they form a minority group which, when compared with the larger population, occupies the lowest status in the society. They have been relegated to a harsh environment not unlike that of the peoples in the so-called developing nations of the world. In many ways they are a nation apart from white Americans. The similarities between Negroes in the United States and peoples in the developing nations, or demographic characteristics, are striking. For example, they have a high birth rate and a declining death rate. Their infant mortality rate is especially high (compared to other Americans), and their life expectancy is low. They continue to die at a disproportionately high rate from diseases that can easily be controlled by modern medical techniques. A high proportion of the black population falls within the dependent-aged and dependent-children categories. They are migrating from rural to urban areas at a rapid rate and are being crowded into special sections of the largest cities in the country. In many regards, then, black Americans resemble the peoples of Africa, Asia, and Latin America. This resemblance has implications for protest movements and other expressions of discontent found among nonwhite peoples throughout the world.

SELECTED BIBLIOGRAPHY

Bouge, Donald J., *The Population of the United States*. New York: Free Press, 1959.

Frazier, E. Franklin, *The Negro in the United States*. New York: The Macmillan Company, 1957.

Hauser, Philip M., "Demographic Factors in the Integration of the Negro," in *The Negro American,* eds. Talcott Parsons and Kenneth Clark. Boston: Houghton Mifflin Company, 1966.

Klineberg, Otto, *Negro Intelligence and Selective Migration*. New York: Columbia University Press, 1935.

Lieberson, Stanley, *Ethnic Patterns in American Cities*. New York: Free Press, 1963.

Pettigrew, Thomas F., *A Profile of the Negro American*. Princeton, N.J.: D. Van Nostrand Co., Inc., 1964.

Taeuber, Conrad, and Irene Taeuber, *The Changing Population of the United States*. New York: John Wiley & Sons, Inc., 1958.

Taeuber, Karl, and Alma Taeuber, *Negroes in Cities*. Chicago: Aldine Publishing Co., 1965.

U.S. Bureau of the Census, *Current Population Reports,* Series P-20, No. 155, "Negro Population: March 1965." Washington, D.C.: Government Printing Office, 1966.

———, *Historical Statistics of the United States, Colonial Times to 1957*. Washington, D.C.: Government Printing Office, 1960.

U.S. Department of Health, Education and Welfare, *Vital Statistics of the United States, 1964*. Washington, D.C.: Government Printing Office, 1966.

U.S. Department of Labor, Bureau of Labor Statistics, *The Negroes in the United States: Their Economic and Social Situation*. Washington, D.C.: Government Printing Office, 1966.

The black community as a distinctive social entity can only be understood within the larger context of the status of black people in American society. Paramount among the factors contributing to its development, continuance, and growth has been the role of racism in American life. Having been systematically excluded from full participation in the larger society, it became necessary for black Americans to develop separate (although frequently parallel) community institutions. The task of developing these institutions was simplified by residential segregation imposed upon Negroes. As with some other minorities, Negroes were never given a choice between developing separate institutions or participating in those of the larger society. They either developed their own segregated institutions or they were forced to exist without them. Since their very survival depended, to some extent, on mutual dependence and aid, they developed within their own communities institutions geared toward their own self-interest and well-being.[1]

In the present chapter primary emphasis is focused on the physical character of the black community and on social stratification. The social institutions which have developed within the black community will be discussed in greater detail in later chapters.

The Black

Community

GROWTH AND
DEVELOPMENT

Until the second half of the 20th century, Negroes were predominantly rural people, concentrated in the South. Although interregional and intraregional redistribution of Negroes has persisted since the turn of the century, so heavy was the concentration of Negroes in the rural South that only in recent years have they become heavily urbanized and reasonably evenly distributed between the South and non-South regions of the country. At the present time the proportion of Negroes living in urban areas exceeds that of the population as a whole living in urban areas. If the present rate of urbanization continues, virtually all Negroes will be urban dwellers by the year 2000.

Whether urban or rural, black people in the United States have always been forced to live with other blacks. Freedom of choice in residence has always been and continues to be an issue about which white

[1] See Hylan Lewis, *Blackways of Kent* (Chapel Hill, N.C.: The University of North Carolina Press, 1955).

Americans maintain strong negative views.[2] White Americans live in communities based on education, income, occupation, and other criteria of status, but Negroes, whatever their status, have always been forced to live with other Negroes. Voluntary associations among black people tend to be limited to those of similar status, but the general residential pattern has been one in which black people of all status levels must live side by side, in the section of the city to which they have been relegated. Residential segregation is as characteristically American as virtually any other aspect of the culture. No matter what the city, the rule is that the "black section of town" is a distinctive one. Kenneth Clark, in discussing the concept "ghetto" as originating among Jews in Europe, has written: "America has contributed to the concept of ghetto the restriction of persons to a special area and the limiting of their freedom of choice on the basis of skin color."[3] The residential segregation of black people is virtually complete, and there is some evidence that, rather than diminishing, it is increasing.

A major trend among the black population in the 20th century has been its increasing urbanization. This process has occurred with the migration of Negroes from rural areas of the South to urban areas of the North and West and from the rural areas of the South to urban centers within that region. The northward migration gained impetus during the second decade of the 20th century and accelerated with the entry of the United States into World War I. With the restrictive immigration laws against Europeans in the 1920's, the northward movement continued, subsiding during the Depression of the 1930's but accelerating again when the United States entered World War II. This regional redistribution and urbanization continued, with more than 3 million black people moving from the South to the North in the period from 1940 to 1960.

All-black neighborhoods develop mainly as a result of racial discrimination. One outgrowth of discrimination is "racial succession," that is, Negroes taking over homes formerly occupied by whites. This phenomenon is especially prevalent outside the South. In Southern cities new housing is built either for Negroes or for whites on a segregated basis. Housing developments are characteristically built in black neighborhoods for blacks and in white neighborhoods for white Americans. In either process, blacks and whites ultimately live in separate neighborhoods, but the difference in regions is that "In most Southern cities, Negroes have

[2] In a recent nationwide poll, more than half of all white Americans indicated that they would object to having a Negro family as next-door neighbors. See William Brink and Louis Harris, *The Negro Revolution in America* (New York: Simon and Shuster, 1964), p. 148.

[3] Kenneth Clark, *Dark Ghetto* (New York: Harper & Row, 1965), p. 11.

continuously been housed in areas set aside for them, whereas in the North, most areas now inhabited by Negroes were formerly occupied by whites." [4]

In addition to residential discrimination, violence and intimidation serve to keep black people within a restricted neighborhood. New York City provides a case in point. In 1900 many Negroes lived in the same neighborhood with working-class white people. This section, known as the Tenderloin, was located in midtown Manhattan. During the summer violence erupted in the neighborhood when a black man was charged with the murder of a white plainclothes policeman. In the ensuing violence, black residents were indiscriminately beaten by mobs of angry white Americans. The police, instead of protecting the blacks, joined the mobs. Hence the Negroes realized the difficulties involved in living peacefully with their white neighbors; they moved north to Harlem at the first opportunity.[5] Anti-Negro violence, resulting from resistance to desegregation in housing, is so widespread throughout the United States that Negroes can, in most cases, expect to live peacefully only when they remain in black neighborhoods. Although there has been some change in recent years, the general pattern still holds.

RURAL BLACK COMMUNITIES

Throughout much of the period following emancipation, a vast majority of black Americans lived in rural areas of the South. However, several rural developments were also to be found in the Northeast and North-Central regions.[6] These communities were generally made up of families of mulatto ex-slaves and of Negroes indigenous to the North. They were located in New Jersey, New York, Ohio, and Michigan. At one point these were thriving communities, held together by family and kinship ties, but with increasing urbanization they have virtually disappeared.

In the rural South black communities have persisted. Although there is some diversity within communities, and from community to community, depending on the region, these residents represent the closest American approximation to a peasant class. They generally work in agriculture, domestic service, and the lowest-paid jobs in industry. Houses

4 Karl E. Taeuber and Alma F. Taeuber, *Negroes in Cities* (Chicago: Aldine, 1965), p. 5.

5 See Gilbert Osofsky, *Harlem: The Making of a Ghetto* (New York: Harper & Row, 1965), pp. 46–50.

6 E. Franklin Frazier, *The Negro in the United States* (New York: Macmillan, 1957), pp. 197–98.

are generally of poor construction, unpainted, in need of repairs, and without indoor sanitary facilities and electricity. They are usually over-crowded, with several children sharing the same bed, often in the same room with other beds for adults or children. One of the civil rights volunteers who spent the summer of 1964 in Mississippi described the community of Itta Bena: "The Negro neighborhood hasn't got a single paved street in it. It's all dirt and gravel roads. The houses vary from beat-up shacks to fairly good-looking cottages. The beat-up places pre-dominate. There are lots of smelly outhouses, and many of the houses have no inside water." [7] Another volunteer described the living arrange-ments in the home of a relatively prosperous independent black farmer with whom he lived during the summer: "In the two-bedroom house in which I live we have 5 small girls, a baby, 3 teen-age girls, the mother and father, one 11-year-old boy, and a grandmother, plus the two of us volunteers. The five children sleep pinwheel fashion in one bed." [8]

The economic conditions of rural blacks are best illustrated by the fact that 80 percent of all nonwhite farm residents had family incomes of less than $3,000 in 1964, and the median income for such families was $1,750.[9] The average family size of Negroes in the South, rural and urban, is 4.56, and 20 percent of the families contain more than seven persons.[10] The rural Southern black man is generally poor and land-less and dependent on the white landowner for both employment and housing.

Rural black communities are physically distinguishable from white communities. On entering virtually any small town, it is possible to distinguish the black section from the white section because the former usually contains unpaved streets, slum housing, and outdoor sanitary facilities. A civil rights volunteer in Mississippi in 1964 describes her impressions on entering the black community in which she was to work: "... then the pavement bellied out and sidewalks disappeared or fell away in broken pieces: Niggertown. Rows of shanties perched on stones and bricks and joined together in precarious asymmetry were interrupted, though not often, by a spacious lawn adorned with [an] air-conditioned

[7] Elizabeth Sutherland, ed., *Letters from Mississippi* (New York: McGraw-Hill, 1965), p. 39.

[8] *Ibid.*, p. 41.

[9] U.S. Department of Labor, Bureau of Labor Statistics, *The Negroes in the United States, Their Economic and Social Situation* (Washington, D.C.: Government Printing Office, 1966), p. 141.

[10] U.S. Bureau of the Census, *Current Population Reports*, Series P-20, No. 155, "Negro Population: March, 1965" (Washington, D.C.: Government Printing Office, 1966), p. 23.

ranch house and a fence. The better-off Negroes had no choice of neighbors. The only other structures with anything of the right angle housed grocery stores with Chinese names and churches." [11]

In rural black communities in the South there is little organizational life except the church and the school. Of these two institutions, the church has played the dominant role. Johnson writes of the influence of the church in the rural South:

> The church has been, and continues to be, the outstanding social institution in the Negro community. It has a far wider function than to bring spiritual inspiration to its communicants. Among rural Negroes the church is still the only institution which provides an effective organization of the group, an approved and tolerated place for social activities, a forum for expression on many issues, an outlet for emotional repressions, and a plan for social living. It is a complex institution meeting a wide variety of needs.[12]

One of the primary functions of the church is that of making the individual's difficulties somehow tolerable. The frustrations inherent in their precarious existence are many, and the constant intimidations and threats of intimidation from rural white Americans add up to a life of hardships. Through the church their lives are made worthwhile, and relief is promised in the afterlife. One of its major functions, then, is providing emotional relief for a difficult life.

Most black people in rural communities are affiliated with either Baptist or Methodist churches, with Baptists outnumbering Methodists. In recent years the church in the rural black community has been in the forefront of the drive for greater civil rights. Individual rural clergymen, under the inspiration and leadership of the late Rev. Martin Luther King, Jr., have played especially important roles in such movements as voter-registration drives and selective-buying campaigns. The civil rights movement was originally organized around such religious principles as nonviolence and the disarming of one's adversary through love.

Education has played an insignificant role in the life of the rural black community. Schools, where available, have generally been housed in old buildings that frequently were originally built for other purposes. The schools have traditionally been rigidly segregated racially. No attempt was made to equalize facilities until the states were threatened by a series of antisegregation decisions by the Supreme Court in the 1950's. Johnson describes what he calls a typical rural Negro school:

[11] Sally Belfrage, *Freedom Summer* (New York: The Viking Press, Inc., 1965), p. 39.

[12] Charles S. Johnson, *Growing Up in the Black Belt* (Washington, D.C.: American Council on Education, 1941), p. 135; Sutherland, *op. cit.*, pp. 50–52.

It is in a dilapidated building, once whitewashed, standing in a rocky field unfit for cultivation. Dust-covered weeds spread a carpet all around, except for an uneven, bare area on one side which looks like a ball field. Behind the school is a small building with a broken, sagging door. As we approach, a nervous middle-aged woman comes to the door of the school. She greets us in a discouraged voice marred by a speech impediment. Escorted inside, we observe that the broken benches are crowded to three times their normal capacity. Only a few battered books are in sight, and we look in vain for maps or charts. We learn that four grades are assembled here.[13]

Until recently teachers have been poorly trained, and compulsory school attendance for black pupils was not enforced. Young children accompanied their parents to work in agriculture during the harvesting season. For all practical purposes, the schools did little in the way of providing education for Negro pupils. Those who managed to receive quality education did so in the face of extraordinary difficulties. Despite the difficulties, studies indicate considerable eagerness on the part of rural black youth for formal education.[14]

Relations between the rural black community and the larger community tend to be economic rather than social or political. Traditionally matters of politics or education were accomplished for the black community by a few black "leaders," whose main function has been to contain the black community. Social relations between the black and white communities on a basis of equality have never existed. Law and custom have decreed that a rigid caste line separate the two communities socially and that no association between blacks and whites, as equals, take place. In matters of economics the black community, with few exceptions, has been totally dependent on the white community for survival. Throughout much of the agricultural region of the South, Negroes have traditionally served as sharecroppers or tenant farmers for white landowners. In this relationship they are totally dependent on the white farmer. In small towns they are usually employed in low-status positions in industry, business, and domestic and public service. A vast majority of the Negro women have traditionally performed domestic services.

Through a variety of techniques rural blacks are kept in a subordinate caste position to white landowners in the rural South. Relatively few landowners control large numbers of Negro tenant farmers. When land is "sold" to Negro tenants, the white landlord profits by taking the land back by illegal means. Virtually all land is thereby held by white farmers. Farm labor is considered to be the work of Negroes. They gen-

13 Johnson, *op. cit.*, p. 104.
14 *Ibid.*, pp. 114–19; John Dollard, *Caste and Class in a Southern Town* (New Haven, Conn.: Yale, 1937), p. 200; Sutherland, *op. cit.*, pp. 90–117.

erally work from sunup to sundown, and even females and children are expected to work long hours to assist in supporting large families. Tenants receive loans in the form of food or cash which must be spent for food. Salary advances and the withholding of loans serve as means of maintaining the subordinate caste position of the black tenants. Intimidation is also an element of economic control. Physical violence in the form of whipping has not been uncommon.[15]

THE URBAN BLACK COMMUNITY

By 1960 the black population of the United States was predominantly (73 percent) urban. Northern and Western Negroes were more highly urbanized (95 percent) than their Southern counterparts, but even in the South three out of every five Negroes lived in urban areas. Even more than his rural counterpart, the urban black man is likely to live in a rigidly segregated section of the city in deteriorated or deteriorating housing. Within the urban areas Negroes are heavily concentrated in central cities with high population densities. Already, 18 of the largest cities in the United States have black populations in excess of 100,000. These cities vary in the proportion of Negroes in the total population anywhere from 14 percent in Los Angeles and New York City to 54 percent in Washington, D.C. In each of the cities the pattern holds: Negroes are moving into the center while whites are moving to the suburbs.

Urban black communities in the North and West differ somewhat from those in the South, especially because Negroes are relative newcomers to these regions, but in one crucial respect they are strikingly similar: Negroes are forced to live in areas with other Negroes. In a recent study Taeuber and Taeuber developed a "segregation index," which was applied to census data for 207 cities in the United States.[16] This index included virtually every city with a population of at least 50,000 and several smaller cities. The segregation index is based on the extent of racial residential segregation in city blocks. If blacks and whites are equally distributed (proportionately) in a block, the segregation index assumes a value of zero, indicating no racial residential segregation. If, on the other extreme, city blocks contain only blacks or only whites, the segregation index assumes a value of 100, indicating complete segregation. For the cities studied the index values ranged from 60.4 (San Jose, California) to 98.1 (Fort Lauderdale, Florida). "Only a few cities had

15 Allison Davis, Burleigh Gardner, and Mary Gardner, *Deep South* (Chicago: The University of Chicago Press, 1941).
16 Taeuber and Taeuber, *op. cit.*, pp. 28–31.

values in the lower range of observed scores—8 cities with values below 70 and 31 cities with values below 79. Half the cities have values above 87.8 and a fourth above 91.7." [17]

Regionally, the South attained the highest degree of racial residential segregation (mean of 90.9), followed by the North-Central states (mean of 87.7), the West (mean 79.3), and the Northeast (mean 79.2). Thus it can be demonstrated that racial segregation in housing is characteristically American, and regional differences are minor. The likelihood is that the rural black who migrates from the South will settle in an urban black slum elsewhere. Likewise, when his children become adults, they too are likely to reside in the black community, for ". . . Negroes are by far the most residentially segregated urban minority group in recent American history. This is evident in the virtually complete exclusion of Negro residents from most new suburban developments of the past 50 years as well as the block-by-block expansion of Negro residential areas in the central portions of many large cities." [18] Unlike the situation among white Americans, Negroes are segregated residentially for racial reasons alone, because poor Negroes and rich Negroes alike are usually confined to the same residential areas. And, unlike some of the earlier immigrant groups, the black migrant to the city, whatever his status, cannot expect to escape from the slums to other sections of the city or to the suburbs.

One of the primary characteristics of urban black areas is the high population densities (number of persons per square mile). In four of the largest American cities or subsections of cities with Negro populations ranging from 335,000 to 813,000 in 1960, in which Negroes constituted from 14 percent to 54 percent of the population, the density of the population reflects the general urban Negro pattern.[19] In Chicago, with a black population of 813,000, Negroes constituted 23 percent of the population. Sixty-six percent of these Negroes, or 15 percent of Chicago's population, lived in black census tracts, which comprised only 8 square miles and 4 percent of the city's land area. In Los Angeles Negroes constituted 14 percent of the population. Some 22 percent of the Negroes, or 3 percent of Los Angeles' total population, lived in an area of 1 square mile and occupied less than 0.5 percent of the city's land area. In the Borough of Manhattan in New York City, where Negroes made up 23 percent of the population, 59 percent of them, or 14 percent of the total population, lived in an area of 2 square miles and occupied 9 percent of

[17] *Ibid.*, p. 34.
[18] *Ibid.*, p. 2.
[19] U.S. Department of Labor, Bureau of Labor Statistics, *The Negroes in the United States . . .*, p. 20.

the borough's land area. In Washington, D.C., where Negroes represented 54 percent of the population, 50 percent of them, or more than 25 percent of the population, lived in an area of 3 square miles and occupied only 5 percent of the city's land area. The population density for each of these Negro census tracts was among the highest in the world: Chicago, 68,000; Los Angeles, 73,000; Manhattan, 118,000; and Washington, D.C., 68,000. These black communities were at least five times as dense as the cities as a whole.

Statistics on housing in the urban black community are as revealing as those on population density. In 1960 slightly less than two-thirds (64 percent) of all urban nonwhites occupied dwelling units defined by the U.S. Bureau of the Census as standard ("slight or no defects, hot and cold running water, and exclusive use of a flush toilet and bathtub or shower within the unit"). The remaining one-third lived in substandard housing. A significantly smaller proportion of the white population lived in substandard housing. Similarly, in 1960, 13 percent of all nonwhite, nonfarm households were defined as seriously overcrowded ("1.51 persons per room"), in contrast to 2 percent among households occupied by white Americans.[20]

Chief among the characteristics of the urban black community are its powerlessness and its dependence on the frequently hostile white community which surrounds it. These enclaves are kept powerless by powerful individuals and institutions in the white community.[21] The dwellings of the urban black community are usually owned by absentee white landlords and institutions, and no attempt is made to maintain the buildings or to provide the customary services to their inhabitants. Residential buildings, for which the occupants are charged high rents, frequently do not provide safe and adequate shelter. Often they are owned by wealthy and politically prominent suburban residents. Community services, such as garbage collection and street cleaning, are provided less frequently than in the white community.

The residents continue to provide a cheap labor supply. Most often they must leave the black community to find employment. Within the community, business establishments, like residential buildings, are owned by whites who live outside the community. The school system is operated and maintained by individuals who live outside the area and who are often unresponsive to the needs of the local residents. Law and order are maintained by a force of policemen who are often hostile and prejudiced.

Such conditions, coupled with the day-to-day frustrations inherent

20 *Ibid.*, pp. 211–12.
21 Clark, *op. cit.*, pp. 11–20; *Youth in the Ghetto* (New York: Harlem Youth Opportunities Unlimited, 1964).

in living in a racist society, contribute to the social pathologies of the black community (see Chapter VI). These communities experience high rates of crime and delinquency, alcoholism, drug addiction, and family disorganization.

In recent years the educational attainment of pupils in the black community has become a center of controversy, stemming from the under-achievement of Negro pupils as compared with white pupils.[22] Teachers tend to place the blame on the homelife of the pupils, whereas parents see the school as the source of the problem. Whatever the source, which is probably a combination of social factors, parents in the black community are pressing their demands for equal educational opportunities for their children.

Existing conditions in the urban black community thus bear many parallels to those in the so-called developing nations. Collectively, the many urban Negro communities in the United States resemble a colonial territory which is seeking to achieve independence from forces beyond its control.

SOCIAL STRATIFICATION

The black community, like the white community which surrounds it, has always maintained a degree of social stratification. During slavery the primary distinctions among the Negro slaves were based on those who worked as house servants and those forced to work as field hands. The house servants were most often mulattoes who represented a favored class in the eyes of the slaveholders. The field hands were the black illiterates who were considered less than human beings. This distinction between slaves was frequently fostered by slaveholders and served as a divisive force between the slaves.

Among the "free" blacks during slavery, several types of distinctions were discernible. As among the slaves, distinctions were made between mulattoes and blacks, with the former enjoying higher status. There were also distinctions between skilled workers and artisans and domestic workers and unskilled laborers. Finally, many of the free Negroes were direct descendants of wealthy white planters. They frequently maintained extensive property holdings and slaves.[23] Although white ancestry was not enough to confer higher social status among the free Negroes, it was frequently associated with greater education and mechanical skill.

[22] U.S. Department of Health, Education, and Welfare, Office of Education, *Equality of Educational Opportunity* (Washington, D.C.: Government Printing Office, 1966).

[23] Frazier, *op. cit.*, pp. 275–76.

After emancipation, class distinctions among Negroes frequently followed the patterns established during slavery: those based on wealth, occupation, "respectability," and skin color. However, another factor assumed prominence. Negroes who had been free before the Civil War distinguished themselves from those who were freed with the emancipation.[24] The restoration of white supremacy, as well as the migrations of the blacks from rural to urban areas and from South to North, had the effect of minimizing class distinctions among Negroes. Yet the black community, like its white counterpart, has continued, through a variety of criteria, to distinguish among its members.

Several studies have focused attention on status distinctions in the black community.[25] In judging one another, black people use many of the conventional social-class criteria utilized by white Americans, such as income, occupation, education, wealth, family background, style of life, refinement, property ownership, organizational affiliations, respectability, and morality. Some criteria, however, such as white ancestry, skin color, and cultural similarity to whites, are peculiar to the Negro community. In recent years black nationalism has made inroads into the black community, especially in urban areas. This development has led to a de-emphasis, if not a cessation, of these characteristics as criteria for status.

The Rural Blacks

Studies of rural black communities reveal the presence of the three social-class levels found in the society at large. In a study of rural Negroes in eight counties in five Southern states, Charles S. Johnson delineated three classes and estimated the percentage of Negroes in each class as follows: upper class, 6 percent; middle class, 12 percent; lower class, 82 percent.[26] The upper-class blacks were those possessing a family social heritage that was known and respected in the community and a high educational and occupational status. These persons were usually medical doctors, schoolteachers, and successful landowners. The middle class consisted of proprietors of small businesses, white-collar workers, schoolteachers, and some skilled artisans. The lower class was composed of unskilled and semiskilled

24 *Ibid.*, pp. 276–78.
25 See, for example, the following: Davis, Gardner, and Gardner, *op. cit.;* Dollard, *op. cit.;* St. Clair Drake and Horace Cayton, *Black Metropolis* (New York: Harcourt, Brace, 1945); W. E. B. Du Bois, *The Philadelphia Negro* (Philadelphia: University of Pennsylvania Press, 1899); E. Franklin Frazier, *Negro Youth at the Crossways* (Washington, D.C.: American Council on Education, 1940); Lewis, *op. cit.;* Hortense Powdermaker, *After Freedom* (New York: Viking, 1939); John Rohrer and Munro S. Edmondson, eds., *The Eighth Generation Grows Up* (New York: Harper, 1960); Robert Warner, *New Haven Negroes* (New Haven, Conn.: Yale, 1940).
26 Johnson, *op. cit.*, p. 77.

workers and domestic workers. Also within this group were found the sharecroppers and tenant farmers.

Dollard also posited the existence of three social classes among Negroes in the small town which he studied in the 1930's, but he concentrated on the middle- and lower-class Negroes.[27] In this community the lower-class Negroes were those individuals with the lowest skill levels, forming the "broad base on which society in this area rests." The middle-class people were mainly teachers and ministers, who attempted to isolate themselves from the lower class and what they considered lower-class values.

Davis, Gardner, and Gardner report that in rural Mississippi social classes were present among Negroes but that the differentiation among classes was slight.[28] In rural Southern communities fewer criteria exist for distinguishing among blacks than are found in urban areas. However, such criteria as education, property ownership, and skin color still constitute a basis for social stratification.

The Urban Blacks

Since the vast majority of black people are urban dwellers, and since the greater complexity of urban life is conducive to greater stratification, it might be expected that somewhat more elaborate stratification may be discerned among blacks in urban areas. Although there are regional differences in stratification among urban Negroes, in general the class distinctions hold in the South and elsewhere. Frazier makes the point that skin color diminishes as a status variable as one progresses from the Deep South to the Border South to the North.[29] In addition, economic opportunities for Negroes have generally been greater in the North than in the South; therefore, greater occupational differentiation has made for some differences in stratification. Finally, compared to the South, the black man in the Northern city is a relative newcomer. Southern Negroes in some ways have a more established system of stratification. It is possible, however, to make some general statements about class distinctions which hold for urban Negroes throughout the United States.

Most of the studies of social stratification among urban Negroes delineate a small upper class, a proportionately small but growing middle class, and a large lower class that encompasses the vast majority of Negroes. The black upper class includes professionals, especially medical doctors, dentists, and lawyers; public administrators; civic leaders; businessmen; educators; and politicians. (These people would be considered

27 Dollard, *op. cit.,* p. 83.
28 Davis, Gardner, and Gardner, *op. cit.,* p. 238.
29 Frazier, *The Negro in the United States,* p. 291.

middle class in terms of their standing in the general society if race were irrelevant.) In describing the upper class Negroes in Chicago, Drake and Cayton have this to say:

> If one wished to ascertain just what people constitute Bronzeville's upper class, it might seem practicable to group together those persons who have the most money, those with the greatest amount of education, those with the "best" family backgrounds, and those who wield the greatest political power—and attach to this group the label UPPER CLASS.[30]

This group, they write, included some 5,000 people in the 1940's, most of whom were medical doctors, lawyers, newspaper editors, civic leaders, and politicians. Their prestige was based on education, professional status, and style of life, rather than on income, although some of them earned as much as $50,000 yearly.

Frazier describes the black upper class in Washington, D.C., which he feels to be typical of other border cities, as comprised of "a relatively large professional class and a clerical group of the same relative size as Chicago and New York. Consequently, those of upper-class status include almost entirely people of professional status, businessmen, and those in clerical occupations." [31]

Upper-class Negroes tend to associate with other upper-class Negroes. Entertaining is done in the home, except for the public events which they sponsor. They are Protestants, usually Congregationalists, Episcopalians, and Presbyterians. They are active in social clubs, especially fraternities and sororities, and they support civil rights activities through the National Association for the Advancement of Colored People (NAACP) or the Urban League.

Middle-class status among Negroes in Chicago, according to Drake and Cayton, is not necessarily limited to those persons of appropriate income and occupation. "Rather, the middle class is marked off from the lower class by a pattern of behavior expressed in stable family and associational relationships, in great concern with 'front' and 'respectability,' and in a drive for 'getting ahead.' All this finds an objective measure in standard of living—the way people spend their money, and in *public behavior*." [32] The middle class in Chicago consisted of a wide variety of occupational categories, including professionals, independent businessmen, clerical workers, service workers, and laborers. Frazier agrees that style of life is the most crucial element in identifying the Negro middle class. He writes, "Because of their fairly secure and adequate incomes, Negroes of middle-class status are able to maintain what they regard as

---

30 Drake and Cayton, *op. cit.*, p. 526.
31 Frazier, *The Negro in the United States*, p. 286.
32 Drake and Cayton, *op. cit.*, pp. 661–62 (italics in the original).

a desirable mode of life. This desirable mode of living includes . . . certain standards of home and family life." [33]

With increasing urbanization there has emerged a rather well-defined middle class among Negroes. In large cities there is a large group of clerical, skilled, and public service workers, in addition to professional workers in virtually every field. Because these occupations provide adequate incomes and economic security, the black middle class has developed stable family lives. There is among the black middle class an overriding concern with "respectability" and a serious desire that their children receive the educational advantages which they were frequently denied.

Middle-class blacks value home ownership and are concerned about maintaining the proper associational relationships necessary for advancing themselves. They are likely to be members of church congregations, including Congregationalist, Episcopalian, and Presbyterian, but, unlike the upper-class Negroes, most middle-class blacks are Methodists and Baptists. Within these two denominations they frequently attend churches which cater to the middle class. Like the upper-class Negroes, the middle class expend considerable time and energy on social clubs and other social organizations, especially fraternities and sororities.

Because of the precariousness of the status of middle-class blacks, their overriding concern is with maintaining respectability. This concern has frequently led to a self-hate characterized by contempt for lower-class Negroes. One writer takes a rather harsh view of the rising Negro middle class and the fantasy world which, he insists, they share with upper-class Negroes. He writes:

> The emphasis upon "social" life or "society" is one of the main props of the world of make believe into which the black bourgeoisie has sought to escape from its inferiority and frustrations in American society. This world of make believe, to be sure, is a reflection of the values of American society, but it lacks the economic basis that would give it roots in the world of reality. In escaping into a world of make believe, middle-class Negroes have rejected both identification with the Negro and his traditional culture. Through delusions of wealth and power they have sought identification with white America, which continues to reject them. But these delusions leave them frustrated because they are unable to escape from the emptiness and futility of their existence.[34]

The lower-class Negro, comprising at least two-thirds of the urban black population, is at the bottom of the class structure in the black com-

[33] Frazier, *The Negro in the United States,* p. 301.
[34] E. Franklin Frazier, *Black Bourgeoisie* (Glencoe, Ill.: Free Press, 1957), p. 237.

munity. It is of the lower-class Negro that so many stereotypes have developed. These are the blacks who are chronically unemployed, who work at the lowest-paid jobs in industry and domestic service—i.e., who do the back-breaking jobs and are still defined as "lazy"—and who make up a disproportionately high proportion of the welfare rolls in urban areas. The lower-class Negro is most often the recent migrant from the rural South, seeking to improve his status in the city. Among lower-class Negroes disorganized family life is prevalent.[35] It is also to the lower-class blacks that widespread social pathologies are attributed.[36] Finally, it is the lower-class Negro who in many ways is the major target of the War on Poverty. For, historically, these are the individuals who have received fewer social rewards than any other group. They are crowded into the slums of the largest cities and are only noticed when acts of violence (real or imagined) are attributed to them.

Drake and Cayton describe the complexity of the lower class in the black community in Chicago. In addition to those with middle-class aspirations and to the stable "church folk," one finds "the denizens of the underworld—the pimps and prostitutes, the thieves and pickpockets, the dope addicts and the reefer smokers, the professional gamblers, cutthroats, and murderers." [37]

Writing about the residents in America's urban Negro slums, especially New York's Harlem, Kenneth Clark describes the lower class as being "subject peoples, victims of greed, cruelty, insensitivity, guilt, and fear of their masters." [38] Perhaps the most salient characteristics of the lower-class blacks are their powerlessness, hopelessness, and despair. They lack the organization and organizational participation of middle- and upper-class Negroes. Even religious institutions have failed to assist them in coping with their many problems, especially in urban areas. They tend to affiliate themselves with "store-front" Fundamentalist churches which are generally powerless in the larger community. Furthermore, they tend to be rejected by middle- and upper-class Negroes, who feel that identification with the lower class would lower their status.[39]

---

[35] See especially U.S. Department of Labor, Office of Policy Planning and Research, *The Negro Family: The Case for National Action* (Washington, D.C.: Government Printing Office, 1965).

[36] Clark, *op. cit.*, Chap. 5; Frazier, *The Negro in the United States*, pp. 286–87; 303–4.

[37] Drake and Cayton, *op. cit.*, p. 600.

[38] Clark, *op. cit.*, p. 11.

[39] Middle- and upper-class Negroes repeatedly express contempt for lower-class Negroes. Such feelings are frequently expressed in the case histories reported in Abram Kardiner and Lionel Ovesey, *The Mark of Oppression* (New York: World Publishing, 1962), especially Chap. 6; see also Frazier, *Black Bourgeoisie*, pp. 224–29.

Differences in Social
Stratification:
Blacks vs. Whites

Social stratification in the black community differs in some regards from
that found in the white community. Because of the overrepresentation of
Negroes in the lower class, stratification tends to be based to a greater
degree on behavioral patterns and social factors, rather than on income
and occupation, which usually are considered crucial determinants in the
white community. Social stratification in the black community is more
likely to be determined by style of life and family background. Although
a few Negroes who have amassed great wealth or achieved fame in the
larger society might be considered upper class by objective standards,
most blacks who are considered upper class within their own community
would not be so considered if they were white. Schoolteachers are a notable example. Within the black community they are frequently considered
to be upper class; white schoolteachers are rarely so considered. Similarly,
many individuals working as skilled workers, service workers, and even
laborers are considered to be middle class because of their behavior
patterns.

However, behavior patterns, while still salient, are losing force.
Support for this contention is found in a recent view of published literature dealing with prestige criteria among Negroes. This study reveals that
in 16 of the better-known community studies, Negroes traditionally used
different criteria for evaluating one another than did whites.[40] However,
the trend is clearly toward increasing acceptance of the same three main
criteria used in the general community. Thus education is emphasized
more frequently than any other status element, followed by occupation
and income, respectively. Other criteria reported (in order of importance)
are respectability or morality, refinement or "culture," skin color or white
ancestry, family background, and property ownership.[41] Among white
Americans occupation and income have received importance equal to
that of education, and frequently more so.

With increasing urbanization, regional redistribution, educational
achievement, and occupational differentiation, there is a trend toward
the development of socioeconomic status groupings among urban Negroes
that will parallel those among white Americans.

• • •

[40] Norval Glenn, "Negro Prestige Criteria: A Case Study in the Bases of Prestige,"
American Journal of Sociology, Vol. 68 (May 1963), 645–57.
[41] *Ibid.*, p. 647.

As with American communities in general, the black community varies depending on whether it is in the South or outside that region and on whether it is urban or rural. However, certain recurrent patterns exist in black communities throughout the United States. In a study of the Negro community in 11 cities of varying sizes and different regions, Williams reports clearly discernible patterns appearing in each of them.[42] Several of these characteristics are of relevance to the present chapter. The black community tends to be socially isolated from the larger community. Separate social institutions have developed among Negroes to meet needs not served by the larger community. The church continues to play a dominant role in the institutional life of the rural black community but a declining role in the urban community. The black community adheres to a system of social stratification not unlike the larger community. Its members distinguish among themselves on the basis of certain achieved and ascribed criteria.

In addition, the black community in America is like a colonial possession in that it tends to be economically and politically dependent upon the larger community. Its residents provide a source of cheap labor, and, depending on the needs of the larger community, unemployment may be widespread. The residents of the black community are crowded into a geographical area distinguishable from the general community by poor housing conditions and the lack of services provided. Education is controlled from the outside, and the police often assume the posture of occupying forces. In short, all important decisions—political, economic, and educational—affecting the black community are made for its residents by white Americans who have become known as the "white power structure." In periods of disorder (usually in summer) specially trained and equipped police and military forces are rushed in to quell the disturbances with armed force, but little thought is given by public officials to the conditions that produce these disorders.

[42] Robin M. Williams, Jr., *Strangers Next Door* (Englewood Cliffs, N.J.: Prentice-Hall, 1964), pp. 252–54.

SELECTED BIBLIOGRAPHY

Belfrage, Sally, *Freedom Summer*. New York: The Viking Press, Inc., 1965.
Clark, Kenneth, *Dark Ghetto*. New York: Harper & Row, Publishers, 1965.
Davis, Allison, Burleigh Gardner, and Mary Gardner, *Deep South*. Chicago: The University of Chicago Press, 1941.

Dollard, John, *Caste and Class in a Southern Town*. New Haven, Conn.: Yale University Press, 1937.

Drake, St. Clair, and Horace Cayton, *Black Metropolis*. New York: Harcourt, Brace and Co., 1945.

Du Bois, W. E. B., *The Philadelphia Negro*. Philadelphia: University of Pennsylvania Press, 1899.

Frazier, E. Franklin, *Black Bourgeoisie*. Glencoe, Ill.: Free Press, 1957.

——, *The Negro in the United States*. New York: The Macmillan Company, 1957.

——, *Negro Youth at the Crossways*. Washington, D.C.: American Council on Education, 1940.

Johnson, Charles S., *Growing Up in the Black Belt*. Washington, D.C.: American Council on Education, 1941.

Lewis, Hylan, *Blackways of Kent*. Chapel Hill, N.C.: The University of North Carolina Press, 1955.

Osofsky, Gilbert, *Harlem: The Making of a Ghetto*. New York: Harper & Row, Publishers, 1965.

Powdermaker, Hortense, *After Freedom*. New York: The Viking Press, Inc., 1939.

Rohrer, John, and Munro Edmondson, eds., *The Eighth Generation Grows Up*. New York: Harper & Row, Publishers, 1960.

Sutherland, Elizabeth, ed., *Letters From Mississippi*. New York: McGraw-Hill Book Company, 1965.

Taeuber, Karl E., and Alma Taeuber, *Negroes in Cities*. Chicago: Aldine Publishing Co., 1965.

U.S. Department of Labor, Bureau of Labor Statistics, *The Negroes in the United States: Their Economic and Social Situation*. Washington, D.C.: Government Printing Office, 1966.

U.S. Department of Labor, Office of Policy Planning and Research, *The Negro Family: The Case for National Action*. Washington, D.C.: Government Printing Office, 1965.

Warner, Robert, *New Haven Negroes*. New Haven, Conn.: Yale University Press, 1940.

Williams, Robin M., Jr., *Strangers Next Door: Ethnic Relations in American Communities*. Englewood Cliffs, N.J.: Prentice-Hall, Inc., 1964.

Youth in the Ghetto. New York: Harlem Youth Opportunities Unlimited, Inc., 1964.

Compared with most of the other countries in the world at the present time, the United States is essentially a middle-class society. In 1965 the median number of years of school completed for adult Americans (25 years of age and over) was 11.8; in the same year some three-fifths of all workers were employed in high-status white-collar and skilled occupational categories; and in 1964 the median family income was $6,556. Furthermore, the middle class sets standards of behavior which persons of lesser status emulate. Within this middle-class society, however, black Americans as a group are relegated to a lower-class position. They differ significantly from white Americans on all indicators of status. Some black citizens have attained high status in the United States, but they are the exceptions. The vast majority of black Americans occupy the lowest status positions in society. Through the practice of racism, American society has succeeded in relegating a significant segment of its population to a subordinate position.

Education, occupation, and income are three of the most reliable indicators of status in American society. These three variables are usually interrelated, and they reinforce one another. However, they may be usefully distinguished for purposes of analysis.

Socioeconomic Status [1]

EDUCATION

In a highly industrialized nation such as the United States, formal education serves as a key factor in social mobility. Generations of immigrants have been able to improve their status after reaching the United States through the acquisition of formal education. The situation of Negroes has, to some extent, been affected by increasing formal education. Unlike many immigrant groups, however, their advancement has been hampered by the widespread practices of segregation and discrimination which have either denied them access to formal education or relegated them to inferior and inadequate schools.

[1] Data on the Negro population in the United States are sometimes entered as "Negro" and sometimes combined with other "nonwhite" minorities. Since Negroes have made up at least 94 percent of the nonwhite population since the first census, "nonwhite" and "Negro" are frequently used interchangeably.

Quantity of Education

At the time of emancipation a vast majority (90 percent) of the black
people in the United States were illiterate.[2] During slavery it was virtually impossible for the blacks to acquire even the most fundamental
tools of reading and writing. During the 1860's, however, Negroes made
significant strides, to the point where, by 1870, the illiteracy rate had
dropped to 80 percent. In each decade following the Civil War the
illiteracy rate among the blacks declined. Yet the differential between
blacks and whites has persisted (see Table 4–1). For example, in 1940 the

TABLE 4–1

**PERCENT OF ILLITERATES * IN THE UNITED STATES,
BY COLOR, 1870–1959**

Year	Total	Nonwhite	White
1870	20.0	79.9	11.5
1880	17.0	70.0	9.4
1890	13.3	56.8	7.7
1900	10.7	44.5	6.2
1910	7.7	30.5	5.0
1920	6.0	23.0	4.0
1930	4.3	16.4	3.0
1940 **	2.9	11.5	2.0
1947	2.7	11.0	1.8
1952	2.5	10.2	1.8
1959	2.2	7.5	1.6

* Illiterates are defined as persons who
could not both read and write a simple
message either in English or in any other
language.

** estimated

Note: Data for 1870 to 1940 are for population 10 years of age and over; data for
1947, 1952, and 1959 are for population 14
years of age and over.

Source: U.S. Department of Labor, Bureau
of Labor Statistics, *The Negroes in the
United States: Their Economic and Social
Situation,* Bulletin No. 1511, 1966, Table
IV B-1, p. 194.

[2] U.S. Department of Labor, Bureau of Labor Statistics, "A Century of Change:
Negroes in the U.S. Economy, 1860-1960," *Monthly Labor Review* (December 1962),
p. 1361.

illiteracy rate among blacks was comparable to the rate among white Americans in 1870. Although the decline in Negro illiteracy has been a continuous one, the gap between blacks and whites is such that it is unlikely that Negroes will reach the rate among whites in the near future. In 1959 the illiteracy rate among Negroes was 7.5 percent, but among whites it was 1.6 percent.

The extent of literacy among black people is a direct result of their enrollment and length of stay in school. In the decade following the Civil War, when most Negroes lived on farms, few of their children were enrolled in school. Those who were enrolled attended for only short periods. The schools were overcrowded and the buildings dilapidated; the teachers were most often incompetent, rarely possessing as much as a high school education. This situation improved little with the turn of the century. It is reported that only 58 percent of the Negro children between the ages of 6 and 14 were enrolled in school as late as 1912. Significant progress has been made in the 20th century, and the gap between black and white school attendance has continued to narrow. By 1961, 98 percent of all black children and 99 percent of all white children of elementary school age were in school.[3]

The rates of literacy and school attendance have increased substantially in recent decades. Similarly, the median number of years of school completed for blacks has increased, and the gap between blacks and whites in this regard has gradually narrowed through the years. By 1965 the median number of years of school completed for Negroes was 9.0, compared with 12.0 for white Americans (see Table 4–2). Females have a slightly higher median number of years of school completed than males, among both blacks and whites. The three-year gap between Negroes and whites in median number of years of school completed, however, fails to indicate the real difference in educational attainment by these two groups. For example, only 17.7 percent of the black students in the United States in 1965 reported completing high school, whereas nearly one-third (32.1 percent) of the white students completed high school. At the college level the gap widens still further. Negroes constitute 10.8 percent of the population but only 4.6 percent of all college students. Nearly one white American in ten (9.9 percent) had completed four or more years of college, compared with only 4.7 percent of Negroes. On the other extreme, more than half (50.5 percent) of all black people terminated their formal schooling with the completion of elementary school or less, compared with less than one-third (31.2 percent) of white Americans.

[3] *Ibid.*, p. 1361.

TABLE 4–2

NUMBER OF YEARS OF SCHOOL COMPLETED FOR
NEGRO AND WHITE POPULATION, 25 YEARS OF AGE
AND OVER, UNITED STATES, BY SEX, 1965

| | Years of School Completed | | | | | | | |
| | Elementary School | | | High School | | College | | Median |
Race and Sex	Less Than 5 Years	5–7 Years	8 Years	1–3 Years	4 Years	1–3 Years	4 Years or More	School Years Completed
Total: All races	6.8	10.7	15.5	18.0	30.7	8.9	9.4	11.8
Male	7.7	11.1	15.9	17.3	27.1	8.0	12.0	11.7
Female	5.9	10.3	15.1	18.7	34.0	8.8	7.1	12.0
Negro	18.2	19.9	12.4	22.2	17.7	4.7	4.7	9.0
Male	22.4	19.7	11.5	20.6	16.6	4.8	4.9	8.7
Female	14.7	20.1	13.2	23.6	19.2	4.7	4.5	9.2
White	5.5	9.8	15.9	17.6	32.1	9.3	9.9	12.0
Male	6.1	10.3	16.4	17.0	28.1	9.3	12.7	12.0
Female	4.9	9.3	15.4	18.2	35.6	9.3	7.3	12.1

Source: U.S. Bureau of the Census, *Statistical Abstract of the United States,
1966* (87th ed.), 1966, Table 155, p. 113.

Quality of Education

Data on the extent of literacy, the proportion of school-age children
attending school, and the median number of years of school completed
indicate that the quantitative differences in education between black and
white Americans have narrowed in recent years. However, they indicate
little about the differences in the quality of education received by blacks
and whites. At the time of the *Brown* vs. *Board of Education of Topeka*
decision of the Supreme Court in 1954, in which the Court declared
segregation in public education unconstitutional, 68 percent of all Negroes still lived in states which maintained segregated schools. Seventeen
states and the District of Columbia required segregated schools by law,
and four states permitted segregated schools. In many of the remaining
states also, black pupils attended segregated schools. These schools were
inferior to those attended by white pupils in their expenditures per
pupil, capital outlay per pupil for schools, length of the school year,
training of classroom teachers, and number of books in school libraries.

In 1952, for example, Southern states spent an average of $164.83
for the education of one white pupil, compared with $115.08, or 70 per-
cent of that amount, for the education of each black child.[4] The amount

4 Harry S. Ashmore, *The Negro and the Schools* (Chapel Hill, N.C.: The University of North Carolina Press, 1954), p. 153.

of money spent per Negro pupil varied anywhere from 30 percent of what was spent per white pupil in Mississippi to 85 percent in North Carolina. In the same year the capital outlay per pupil for Negro schools in Southern states was $29.58, or 82 percent of the $36.25 per white pupil.[5]

In 1950 the average number of days in the school year for black pupils in the South was 176, compared with 178 for white pupils. The average number of years of college training attained by Negro teachers was 3.3, compared with 3.6 for white teachers. The average number of books in school libraries per Negro pupil enrolled in five Southern states was 1.8, compared with 4.7 per white pupil.[6]

These comparative figures serve to indicate the gap in the quality of public elementary and secondary education received by black and white pupils in the South before the 1954 decision of the Supreme Court. It should also be added that prior to the late 1940's and early 1950's the gap between the quality of Negro education and that received by white pupils was even greater. With increasing pressures for the desegregation of public education, Southern states attempted to forestall this eventuality by increasing the support made available for the education of Negroes. In the large urban centers where a vast majority of Northern Negroes were concentrated, the situation differed little insofar as the quality of education was concerned.

Schools in which black children predominate are more likely to be characterized by inadequate facilities.[7] In 1966, for example, 43 percent of Negro elementary school pupils in the Northeast attended schools which were at least 40 years old, compared with 18 percent of white pupils. In the United States as a whole, there were an average of 32 Negro pupils per room, compared with 29 white pupils. Twenty-seven percent of all Negro elementary school pupils in the United States attended schools without auditoriums, compared with 19 percent of white pupils. Thirty percent of Negro elementary pupils attended schools without full-time librarians, compared with 22 percent of white pupils of the same level. For black students in secondary schools the differential facilities between their schools and those attended by white pupils were as pronounced as on the elementary level. For example, 80 percent of Negro secondary school pupils attended schools equipped with physics laboratories, compared with 94 percent of white secondary pupils.

Since the data on the quality of Negro education in the South pre-

[5] *Ibid.*, p. 156.
[6] *Ibid.*, pp. 157–60.
[7] U.S. Department of Health, Education, and Welfare, Office of Education, *Equality of Educational Opportunity* (Washington, D.C.: Government Printing Office, 1966), pp. 10–13.

date the Supreme Court decision of 1954, it might be suspected that the status of Negro education has changed substantially since that time. However, in the years following the desegregation decision, the changes have been minimal. A vast majority of black pupils continue to attend segregated (and inferior) schools. In the 17 Southern states affected by the decision, only 15.9 percent of the Negro pupils attended schools with white pupils in 1965. The extent of desegregation varies by state. In Alabama, Louisiana, and Mississippi, less than 1 percent of all Negro pupils attended schools with white pupils. On the other extreme, in several states—Delaware, Kentucky, Maryland, Missouri, and West Virginia—and the District of Columbia, more than half of the Negro pupils attended integrated public schools.[8] In the large cities outside the South where Negroes are concentrated, the schools are becoming more segregated with the exodus of white families to the suburbs. According to a report by the U.S. Office of Education, in 1966 more than 65 percent of all black first graders attended schools that were from 90- to 100-percent Negro. Education above the elementary level is less rigidly segregated, but 66 percent of all Negro 12th-grade pupils attended schools that were at least 50-percent Negro.[9]

The greatest impetus to school desegregation in the South occurred ten years after the Supreme Court decision of 1954, as a result of the Civil Rights Act of 1964. At the time of passage of this act only about 1 percent of the Negro pupils enrolled in schools in the 11 states of the original Confederacy were attending integrated schools. Based on this record, one source has projected that it will require 500 years before all Negro pupils will be attending desegregated schools.[10]

At the college level the quality of black education parallels that of the elementary and secondary levels. Most (59 percent) Negroes pursuing higher education attend predominantly Negro colleges and universities in the South and Southwest. In the school year 1963–64 there were 123 predominantly Negro colleges and universities in the United States. These included 17 junior colleges, one autonomous medical school, and one theological center. Less than two-thirds (63 percent) of these institutions were accredited by appropriate regional associations or professional accrediting agencies.[11]

[8] U.S. Bureau of the Census, *Statistical Abstract of the United States, 1966* (Washington, D.C.: Government Printing Office, 1966), p. 123.

[9] U.S. Department of Health, Education, and Welfare, Office of Education, *Equality of Educational Opportunity*, p. 3.

[10] Leonard Broom and Norval Glenn, *Transformation of the Negro American* (New York: Harper & Row, 1965), p. 98.

[11] U.S. Department of Commerce, Business and Defense Services Administration, *A Guide to Negro Marketing Information* (Washington, D.C.: Government Printing Office, 1966), pp. 45–50.

In the predominantly black colleges and universities, faculty members are less well trained than in predominantly white institutions. For example, in 1965 black students attended colleges with lower proportions of faculty members with earned doctorate degrees than white students. Furthermore, Negro students are more likely to attend colleges where faculty members are paid substantially lower salaries than in colleges with predominantly white student populations.[12]

OCCUPATIONAL STATUS

The occupational gap between black and white Americans in the first 100 years since emancipation has remained a wide one. At the end of the Civil War a vast majority of Negroes were employed as either farm laborers or domestic service workers. By 1890, when data on Negro occupational status were first collected, nearly 90 percent of Negro workers were still concentrated in agriculture and domestic service occupations. Sixty percent of white workers were so employed.[13] Since the turn of the 20th century there has been a steady shift among black people away from these occupations, but the shift of white workers has been even greater, with the result that the occupational gap between black and white workers has persisted and in some cases widened. For example, in 1965 only 10.7 percent of white workers were employed as service workers, while 31.7 percent of nonwhite workers were so employed; 4.5 percent of white workers were employed as nonfarm laborers, while 22 percent of nonwhite workers were so employed.[14] Although there has been a shift from farm employment for both white and black workers, a greater proportion of white workers than Negro workers have moved into higher-status occupations. Negro workers continue to be concentrated in the lowest-status positions in industry, government, and service occupations.

The greatest change in the occupational status of black people occurred between 1940 and 1960, when federal, state, and municipal governments enacted laws forbidding the traditional discriminatory employment practices against Negroes. As a result of increasing employment opportunities, significantly greater numbers of blacks were employed in white-collar and skilled occupations. For example, in 1940, 2.6 percent of Negro workers were employed as clerks and sales workers; in 1960, 6.5 percent were so employed. Among Negro women, 1.4 percent

[12] U.S. Department of Health, Education, and Welfare, Office of Education, *Equality of Educational Opportunity*, p. 26.

[13] U.S. Department of Labor, Bureau of Labor Statistics, "A Century of Change . . . ," p. 1360.

[14] U.S. Bureau of the Census, *Statistical Abstract of the United States, 1966*, p. 229.

were employed as clerks and sales workers in 1940, compared with 10.2 percent in 1960. For Negro males there was a comparable shift in skilled workers from 4.4 percent in 1940 to 10.2 percent in 1960. In each of these occupational categories, however, the blacks were vastly underrepresented. In 1960, 14.5 percent of white males were employed as clerks and sales workers, and 41.4 percent of white females were so employed. One-fifth (20.5 percent) of all white male workers were employed as skilled workers (see Table 4–3).

Similar gains for black people from 1940 to 1960 have been reported for professional occupations, but, here again, Negroes are far from being represented in proportion to their numbers in the population. The rate of gain has been such that it is unlikely that the gap between black and white workers will close in the near future. According to one source, at the rate of gain of those two decades it will take 530 years to close the gap between black and white male professional workers; 415 years for Negroes to be proportionately represented as managers, officials, and proprietors; and 270 years to bridge the gap as sales workers.[15]

Black occupational status varies by region and by sex.[16] In 1965, Negroes living outside the South maintained higher occupational status than did those residing in the South. In the South only 6.4 percent of Negro males and 11.9 percent of Negro females were employed as professional, technical, and managerial workers, compared with 10.3 percent of Negro males and 9.8 percent of Negro females living outside the South. Among clerical, sales, and kindred workers, 4.2 percent of Negro males and 7.2 percent of Negro females were so employed in the South, compared with 9.6 percent of Negro males and 18.8 percent of Negro females outside the South. On the other extreme, more than one-fourth (27.3 percent) of Negro males in the South are employed as nonfarm laborers, compared with 15.8 percent outside the South. Similarly, in the South more than two-thirds (68.7 percent) of Negro females are employed in service occupations (including domestic service), compared with 47.6 percent outside the South. Throughout the United States black people are concentrated in the lowest-status occupations, and those in the South are more likely to be so employed than their counterparts elsewhere.[17]

15 Broom and Glenn, *op. cit.*, p. 111.
16 See U.S. Bureau of the Census, "Negro Population: March 1965," *Current Population Reports,* Series P-20, No. 155 (Washington, D.C.: Government Printing Office, 1966), p. 27.
17 Jack P. Gibbs found that occupational differentiation between black and white workers was widespread throughout the United States and that Southern states were not uniformly higher in these practices than non-Southern states. See his "Occupational Differentiation of Negroes and Whites in the United States," *Social Forces,* Vol. 44 (December 1965), 159–65.

TABLE 4-3

EMPLOYED WORKERS, AGE 14 AND OVER,* BY RACE AND SEX, UNITED STATES, 1910–1960

| | Negro | | | | | | | | | | | | White 1960 | |
| | Male | | | | | | Female | | | | | | | |
Occupation	1910	1920	1930	1940	1950	1960**	1910	1920	1930	1940	1950	1960**	Male	Female
Professional, technical, and kindred workers	1.1	1.2	1.5	1.7	2.3	3.9	1.4	2.4	3.3	4.2	5.4	7.5	11.0	13.8
Proprietors, managers, and officials (nonfarm)	1.1	1.0	1.2	1.4	2.1	2.3	0.3	0.5	0.6	0.7	1.1	1.2	11.5	4.0
Clerks and sales workers	1.0	1.5	1.7	2.6	4.3	6.5	0.3	1.0	1.1	1.4	5.4	10.2	14.5	41.4
Skilled, foremen	3.6	4.6	4.8	4.4	7.7	10.2	0.1	0.1	0.1	0.1	0.6	0.7	20.5	1.3
Semiskilled, operatives	4.7	7.0	9.0	11.7	21.0	23.5	5.4	9.0	10.1	13.5	14.6	12.8	19.5	15.7
Unskilled	25.5	30.9	31.7	22.9	23.3	19.4	0.8	2.7	1.7	0.8	1.5	1.0	5.6	0.5
Service, including domestic	6.9	7.1	9.4	13.7	14.4	14.4	39.4	45.5	56.3	63.4	60.7	55.0	5.3	16.5
Farm workers	56.1	46.7	40.7	41.5	23.7	11.5	52.2	38.9	27.0	15.9	9.8	3.6	7.9	1.4
Not reported					1.2	8.4					1.6	8.1	4.3	5.3

* Figures for 1910–1930 are for Negroes 10 years of age and over; for 1940–1960 all figures are for individuals 14 years of age and over.

** All nonwhites

Source: U.S. Department of Labor, Bureau of Labor Statistics, "A Century of Change: Negroes in the U.S. Economy, 1860–1960," *Monthly Labor Review* (December 1962), Tables 5–6, pp. 1363–64.

Black females are more likely to be employed in high-status occupations than black males. In 1960, for example, 7.5 percent of Negro females in the labor force were employed as professional, technical, and kindred workers, compared with only 3.9 percent of Negro males. Again, 10.2 percent of Negro females were employed as clerks and sales workers, compared with 6.5 percent of Negro males. On the other hand, Negro females are vastly overrepresented in some low-status occupations. More than half the Negro females in the labor force were employed as service workers (including domestic service) in 1960, while only 14.4 percent of Negro males were so employed.[18]

A Note on Black People in Government Employment

Black people are overrepresented in the civilian work force of the federal government.[19] In 1964, although they constituted less than 11 percent of the total population and approximately 10 percent of the labor force, Negroes accounted for 13.2 percent of all federal workers. This difference is largely attributed to the government's hiring policies and the concentration of federal jobs in areas with large Negro populations. Within the federal government, Negroes tend to be concentrated in such agencies as the Government Printing Office, the Federal Services Administration, the Veterans Administration, the Department of Labor, and the Department of Health, Education, and Welfare, each of which maintains a labor force that is from 20 percent to 40 percent Negro. In many of the major cities, such as Baltimore, Chicago, Cleveland, Detroit, Los Angeles, New York, Philadelphia, San Francisco, and Washington, D.C., black people account for at least one-fifth of all federal employees.

Although black persons appear to have less difficulty securing employment in the federal government than in private industry, in both instances they occupy a disproportionately large share of the low-paying jobs. In 1965, for example, more than 90 percent of all Negro federal employees earned salaries of less than $6,500 yearly, and a substantial proportion earned less than $4,500.[20] As is generally the case, the proportion of Negroes employed by the federal government, their employment status, and, by extension, their earnings, depend on whether they are employed in the South or elsewhere. Within the South they are under-

---

[18] U.S. Department of Labor, Bureau of Labor Statistics, "A Century of Change . . . ," p. 1364.

[19] See U.S. Department of Labor, Bureau of Labor Statistics, "Employment of Negroes in the Federal Government," *Monthly Labor Review* (October 1965).

[20] U.S. Department of Labor, Bureau of Labor Statistics, *The Negroes in the United States: Their Economic and Social Situation* (Washington, D.C.: Government Printing Office, 1966), p. 44.

represented in federal employment, and, when so employed, they are overrepresented in the lowest-paying jobs.

Unemployment
Among Black People

In addition to being employed in the lowest-status jobs in government and industry, black Americans are much more likely than white Americans to be unemployed. The unemployment rate among Negroes has remained at least twice that of white workers since World War II (see Table 4–4). Furthermore, if the unemployment rates which have persisted for Negroes held for the labor force as a whole, the United States would have been in a state of depression since the end of the war. The rate of unemployment for Negroes has not dropped below 7.5 percent since 1954. During this period white Americans have frequently enjoyed "unparalleled prosperity," depending on the business cycle. As has been noted by one economist, "What is recession for the white (say, an unemployment rate of 6 percent) is prosperity for the nonwhite. He last saw an unemployment rate below 7.5 percent in 1953—a full decade ago." [21] Even in years of peak employment (some economists define "full employment" as an unemployment rate of 4 percent) the unemployment rate for black persons remains high.

Among Negro workers unemployment varies by age and sex. Black males are consistently more likely to be unemployed than black females. The reverse pattern holds for white Americans: females are more likely to be unemployed than males. Among both blacks and whites, younger workers are more likely to be unemployed than older ones. However, all Negro workers—young or old and male or female—maintain rates of unemployment twice those of white workers. Indeed, the unemployment rate among Negroes under 16 years of age which is frequently as high as 20 percent, reached a peak of 28.4 percent in 1963, a year in which the rate for white youths in the same age category was 14 percent and the general white rate was 5.1 percent.

Black Americans are not only twice as likely as whites to be unemployed, but they are also unemployed for longer periods of time. In 1965, for example, nonwhites accounted for 23 percent of workers who were unemployed for 15 weeks or longer and 25.4 percent of workers unemployed 27 weeks or longer, although they represented only 11 percent of the labor force.[22]

[21] Rashi Fein, "An Economic and Social Profile of the Negro American," *The Negro American,* eds. Talcott Parsons and Kenneth Clark (Boston: Houghton Mifflin, 1966), p. 114.

[22] U.S. Department of Labor, Bureau of Labor Statistics, *The Negroes in the United States . . . ,* p. 85.

TABLE 4-4

NONWHITE AND WHITE UNEMPLOYMENT RATES, BY
SEX AND AGE GROUP, UNITED STATES, 1954-1965

Year	Total			Males, 20 Years of Age and Over			Females, 20 Years of Age and Over			Both Sexes, 14 to 16 Years of Age		
	Nonwhite	White	Ratio of Nonwhite to White	Nonwhite	White	Ratio of Nonwhite to White	Nonwhite	White	Ratio of Nonwhite to White	Nonwhite	White	Ratio of Nonwhite to White
1954	8.8	4.5	2.0	9.0	3.9	2.3	7.4	4.4	1.7	13.8	10.3	1.3
1955	8.0	3.6	2.2	7.7	3.0	2.6	6.8	3.4	2.0	14.2	9.2	1.5
1956	7.5	3.3	2.3	6.7	2.7	2.5	6.8	3.3	2.1	15.9	8.8	1.8
1957	8.0	3.9	2.1	7.6	3.2	2.4	6.4	3.8	1.7	17.8	9.9	1.8
1958	12.6	6.1	2.1	12.7	5.5	2.3	9.5	5.6	1.7	25.0	13.0	1.9
1959	10.7	4.9	2.2	10.5	4.1	2.6	8.3	4.7	1.8	23.5	11.9	2.0
1960	10.2	5.0	2.0	9.6	4.2	2.3	8.3	4.6	1.8	22.1	12.4	1.8
1961	12.5	6.0	2.1	11.7	5.1	2.3	10.6	5.7	1.9	25.4	13.8	1.8
1962	11.0	4.9	2.2	10.0	4.0	2.5	9.6	4.7	2.0	23.7	12.0	2.0
1963	10.9	5.1	2.1	9.2	3.9	2.4	9.4	4.8	2.0	28.4	14.0	2.0
1964	9.8	4.6	2.1	7.7	3.4	2.3	9.0	4.6	2.0	26.2	13.3	2.0
1965	8.3	4.1	2.0	6.0	2.9	2.1	7.4	4.0	1.9	25.3	12.2	2.1

Source: U.S. Department of Labor, Bureau of Labor Statistics, *The Negroes in the United States: Their Economic and Social Situation*, Bulletin No. 1511, 1966, Table IIA-2, p. 80.

The disproportionately high rates of Negro unemployment have been explained as a function of the Negroes' unfavorable position in the occupational structure; that is, black people are likely to occupy positions which are becoming obsolete. This explanation is no doubt valid in some cases, but it does not explain the disproportionately high rates of unemployment among Negroes at all occupational levels. In 1962, for example, 11 percent of all nonwhite professional and technical workers with work experience were unemployed, compared with only 6 percent of whites in comparable positions.[23] The Negroes' high rates of unemployment and their tendency to be unemployed for longer periods than white workers are, more than anything else, reflections of the continuing practice of discrimination against them.[24]

Black People in Business

The development of business enterprise among black people has had a long history, beginning with the free Negroes before the Civil War. However, their business ventures have played an insignificant role in the economy of the United States, and they have not been commensurate with the achievements of Negroes in other aspects of American life.[25] Historically, Negro business ventures have generally been small, single proprietorships and have catered to the segregated Negro market. With the decline in segregation in recent years, the black businessman has felt the brunt of changing patterns of race relations. For example, between 1950 and 1960 the total number of Negro businessmen declined by nearly one-fourth, from 42,500 to 32,400. The number of Negro-owned restaurants declined by one-third, and other retail outlets experienced an even greater decline. In addition, there was a decline in the number of black funeral directors and barbers.[26] The gradual decrease in the number of Negro small business enterprises reflects, in addition to decreased segregation, a general economic trend in the larger society. Corporations experience greater rates of return than small independent business organizations.

In 1960, Negroes constituted 2.5 percent of the self-employed businessmen in the United States.[27] The ratio varied greatly by industry. The

[23] Fein, *op. cit.*, p. 116.

[24] Ralph Turner, "Foci of Discrimination in the Employment of Nonwhites," *American Journal of Sociology*, Vol. 58 (November 1952), 247–56.

[25] E. Franklin Frazier, *The Negro in the United States* (New York: Macmillan, 1957), pp. 387–93; Gunnar Myrdal, *An American Dilemma* (New York: Harper, 1944), pp. 307–14.

[26] *The Negro Handbook* (Chicago: Johnson Publishing Co., 1966), pp. 214–15.

[27] Andrew F. Brimmer, "The Negro in the National Economy," *The American Negro Reference Book*, ed. John P. Davis (Englewood Cliffs, N.J.: Prentice-Hall, 1966), pp. 251–336.

largest share (3.4 percent) was concentrated in personal services, and those in banking and finance constituted the smallest share (0.2 percent). Proportionately few Negro businessmen are to be found in manufacturing, construction, communications, wholesale trade, insurance, and real estate; they tend to concentrate in transportation, retail trade, and general services. This differential concentration of black and white businessmen is reflected in their income. In 1960 the median income was $3,368 for nonwhite businessmen and $5,932 for white businessmen.[28]

Black people have achieved a significant measure of success in the life insurance business. These companies developed at about the turn of the 20th century as a result of discrimination. Insurance companies owned and operated by white businessmen either refused to insure Negroes or charged them higher premiums than white persons. In 1963 Negroes owned more than 50 life insurance companies. The 20 largest companies held $311 million in assets in 1962. This figure represented only about 0.23 percent of the $133 billion for insurance companies in the United States.[29] At the present time there is little discrimination against black policyholders by large insurance companies operated by white businessmen, and most of the insurance in force on Negro lives is held by white-owned companies.[30]

In banking and finance black Americans have exerted an insignificant impact on the economy of the United States. In 1963 there were 20 Negro-owned banks in the United States, with assets of $104,174,185, and 40 savings and loan associations, with assets of $318,000,000.[31] These assets represented less than 1 percent of similar financial enterprises in the country as a whole. Negro-owned banks have higher operating expenses and experience lower rates of return on their resources and lower rates of profit; yet the significance of these banks lies in the role they play in the economic development of the black community. They aid in financing the growth and expansion of Negro business by making capital available to these businessmen.[32]

Negroes have made relatively successful strides in the field of publications. The general press has not been responsive to the needs of the black community, so blacks have attempted to meet this need by publishing newspapers and magazines. In 1965 there were 156 such publications in 30 states and the District of Columbia. These publications included

28 *Ibid.,* p. 292.
29 *Ibid.,* p. 309.
30 Broom and Glenn, *op. cit.,* p. 140.
31 *The Negro Handbook,* pp. 218–20.
32 Brimmer, *op. cit.,* pp. 303–6.

daily and weekly newspapers, popular magazines, and professional journals.[33] They ranged in circulation from nearly a million (*Ebony*) to several thousand.

In general, Negro business enterprise has catered to those needs of the black community not met by white businessmen. Few of them compete on the open market with white-owned businesses serving the general public. Yet white businessmen have always successfully competed with Negro businessmen in the black community. Within the black community white businessmen frequently control the business enterprises serving the residents, except for such personal service establishments as barber and beauty shops and funeral parlors. Apartment houses, grocery stores, bars, theaters, and frequently restaurants are likely to be owned by white businessmen who do not live in the community and whose profits are taken from the black community. For example, Drake and Cayton report that, in 1938, Negroes owned 2,600 business establishments in Chicago's black community while white persons owned 2,800. These white businessmen received more than 90 percent of all the money spent by Negroes in these areas.[34]

Negro business enterprises have remained relatively insignificant in the American economy for a variety of reasons. White-owned financial institutions have been reluctant to extend credit to Negroes, considering them poor risks. Black people have therefore been unable to open and expand businesses. In addition, white real estate owners and agents have refused to rent preferred business locations to Negroes. Finally, Negroes lack business experience, knowledge, and tradition. They have been excluded from white-owned businesses where they could get the necessary experience, and few Negro businesses are large enough to provide training for black youth. Because of the lack of business tradition, the tendency has been for black college students to shun the study of business for liberal arts.

With few exceptions, black business accomplishments historically have not been notable, and the future is not promising. The decline of segregation and discrimination lessens the dependence of the Negro customer on Negro businesses. Furthermore, there continues to be a decline in retail trade outlets resulting from competition by large chain stores and supermarkets. Small stores are either purchased by the larger corporations or forced out of business. The economic outlook for the small entrepreneur is not a promising one.

---

33 *The Negro Handbook*, pp. 383–86.
34 St. Clair Drake and Horace R. Cayton, *Black Metropolis* (New York: Harcourt, Brace, 1945), p. 438.

INCOME

The continuing pattern of discrimination against black people in employment, resulting in their being relegated to the lowest-status occupations, coupled with their low and inferior educational status, is reflected in their earnings. Negro family incomes have been and continue to be significantly lower than those for white families. Furthermore, the differential appears to be widening rather than narrowing.[35] Little attention was focused on differential family incomes for blacks and whites prior to World War II, as is reflected in the absence of such data before 1939. Since the war, however, Negro family income has ranged anywhere from 51 percent to 57 percent of white family income (see Table 4–5). As recently as 1963 black families earned only 53 percent of what white

TABLE 4–5

MEDIAN FAMILY INCOME IN THE UNITED STATES,
NONWHITES AND WHITES, 1947–1964

Year	Nonwhite	White	Nonwhite as Percent of White
1947	$1,614	$3,157	57.1
1948	1,768	3,310	53.4
1949	1,650	3,232	51.1
1950	1,869	3,445	54.3
1951	2,032	3,859	52.7
1952	2,338	4,114	56.8
1953	2,461	4,392	56.0
1954	2,410	4,339	55.5
1955	2,549	4,605	55.4
1956	2,628	4,993	52.6
1957	2,764	5,166	53.5
1958	2,711	5,300	51.2
1959	2,917	5,643	51.7
1960	3,233	5,835	55.4
1961	3,191	5,891	53.4
1962	3,330	6,237	53.4
1963	3,465	6,548	52.9
1964	3,839	6,858	56.0

Source: U.S. Department of Labor, Bureau of Labor Statistics, *The Negroes in the United States: Their Economic and Social Situation,* Bulletin No. 1511, 1966, Table IIIA-1, p. 138.

[35] James A. Geshwender, "Social Structure and the Negro Revolt: An Examination of Some Hypotheses," *Social Forces,* Vol. 43 (December 1964), 248–56.

families earned. Although the differential has fluctuated since 1947, the greatest persistent decline in the differential occurred between 1952 and 1955. Since that time the gap has tended to widen.

The earnings of black families vary with the region of the country in which they live. The gap between black and white families has been consistently greater in the South than elsewhere in the United States. For example, in 1964 the median family income for whites in the South was $5,889; for blacks it was $2,898, or 49 percent of the median white family income. In the Northeast black families earned 67 percent of what white families earned. In the North-Central states the ratio was 72 percent, and in the West it was 78 percent.[36]

The differential income between blacks and whites varies by sex, residence patterns (farm or nonfarm), and age. In general the income of black females is closer to that of white females than that of black males to their white male counterparts. In 1959 Negro females earned 61.6 percent of what white females earned, whereas Negro males earned only 47.0 percent of what white males earned. By 1964 the ratio for Negro females was 70.5 percent, and for Negro males it was 56.7 percent. In 1964 black males living in nonfarm regions earned 59.4 percent of what white males earned, while those living on farms earned only 37.1 percent of what white males earned. Negro females in nonfarm regions, on the other hand, earned 73.9 percent of what white females in these regions earned, and those living on farms earned only 46.4 percent of what white females earned.[37] The working Negro wife, therefore, contributes a greater proportion of the family income than does her white counterpart.

In all occupational categories, younger black males have incomes closer to those of white workers than older black males. In 1960 the ratio of nonwhite to white median income outside the South varied from 82 percent in the age category 18 through 24 to 71 percent in the age category 55 through 65. In the South the ratio was significantly lower, but the differential again was narrowest for younger workers (55 percent for those between 18 and 24 and 47 percent for those between 55 and 65).[38] This difference is partially a function of greater similarities in education and experience and partially a function of an increasing trend toward equal pay for equal work.

Black earnings are low, regardless of where blacks are employed. At all occupational levels, Negroes with comparable training and experience can expect to earn somewhat less than white workers. In 1963, for

36 U.S. Department of Labor, Bureau of Labor Statistics, *The Negroes in the United States ...*, p. 139.
37 *Ibid.*, pp. 142–43.
38 *Ibid.*, p. 146.

example, the median annual income for nonwhite workers was $3,217, whereas for white workers it was $5,663. The differential between white and nonwhite workers persists throughout all occupational categories. It is greatest in private industry and least for those employed by federal, state, and local government agencies, where the policy of equal pay for equal work generally prevails. The effects of discrimination in employment are reflected in differential earnings between black and white workers. As Fein reports: "The Negro family whose head had some high school earned less than the white with fewer than eight years of schooling; *the Negro who has attended (but not completed) college earns less than the white with only eight years of elementary school;* the Negro college graduate earns but slightly more than does the white high school graduate." [39]

Although Negroes constituted 10.8 percent of the population of the United States in 1965, they received only 5 percent of the nation's income, or approximately $27 billion.[40]

A Note on Poverty Among Blacks

According to the Social Security Administration, two out of every five (43 percent) nonwhite families live in poverty, as compared with 12 percent of white families. The incidence of poverty is, therefore, three and one-half times as great among nonwhite families as among white families.[41] Poverty varies with residence, age of household head, number of persons in the family, number of dependent children, region of the country, and family type. The differentially high incidence of poverty among nonwhites persists throughout each of these characteristics, but among nonwhites poverty is concentrated in families with two or more children and is especially great among families headed by young adults. Conversely, among white families poverty is most prevalent among the aged and in households with few, if any, children.

Poverty among nonwhites is greater among farm families than among nonfarm families. Three-fifths (60 percent) of all families headed by persons under 24 years of age are poor, and more than half (53 percent) of those headed by persons 65 years of age and over are poor. The

[39] Fein, *op. cit.*, p. 120 (italics in the original).

[40] U.S. Department of Commerce, Business and Defense Services Administration, *A Guide to Negro Marketing Information*, p. 2.

[41] The Social Security Administration defines as poor those farm families of four persons with incomes of less than $1,860 and those nonfarm families of four persons with less than $3,100 income. The index is adjusted to take family size into account. See Mollie Orshansky, "Counting the Poor: Another Look at the Poverty Profile," *Social Security Bulletin* (January 1965), p. 19.

greater the number of persons in the family, the greater the likelihood
that the family lives in poverty. For those families made up of seven or
more persons, 68 percent are poor. Similarly, families with the largest
number of dependent children are poor. Poverty among nonwhites is
greatest in the South and least in the West; also, those in the North-
Central states are slightly more likely to be poor than those in the Northeast. Nonwhite families headed by females are considerably more likely
to be poor (71 percent) than those headed by males (34 percent).[42]

•   •   •

Black Americans are overrepresented in the lowest socioeconomic
status category in society. In the first 100 years after emancipation, Negroes lagged behind white Americans in education, occupational status,
and income. Significant gains have been made in each of these categories,
especially since World War II, but the gap is such that many decades, and
perhaps centuries, will be required before black people can be expected
to occupy a status comparable to that of white Americans.

Education, occupation, and income are interrelated as status variables. Occupation is generally determined by educational background, and
occupation determines income. As long as black people are relegated
to inferior education, the likelihood of their improving their level of
living is minimal. In addition, Negroes face problems which white
Americans are spared. With Negroes, simply improving one's educational status is not necessarily a means to social mobility. Indeed, within
the context of American society race plays the crucial role in all aspects
of life. Once one is identifiable as Negro, he is not simply, say, a male
college graduate, aged 23, who is trained as an engineer, and who is
eligible for a beginning salary of $8,000. His being a Negro takes prece-
dence over whatever other attributes he might possess.

One hundred years after emancipation racism is still the dominant
force in American life insofar as attitudes and behavior toward black
citizens are concerned. Changes in the status of Negroes have occurred
in the last ten years, but the almost total lack of any significant change
in the first 80 years after emancipation has had the effect of compounding
the problem. The black infant born in the 1960's is likely to experience
less difficulty becoming a middle-class American than his ancestor born
in the 1860's or his parent born in the 1930's, but the ease with which
he can achieve this status will not depend solely on his educational

[42] See U.S. Department of Labor, Bureau of Labor Statistics, *The Negroes in the
United States . . . ,* p. 160.

achievement, his occupation, or his income. It will depend to a great extent on the willingness of his fellow white citizens to accord him the rights which they take for granted for themselves, and on the willingness of the government to assume responsibilities toward him in the same way that it makes demands upon him.

SELECTED BIBLIOGRAPHY

Ashmore, Harry S., *The Negro and the Schools.* Chapel Hill, N.C.: The University of North Carolina Press, 1954.

Brimmer, Andrew F., "The Negro in the National Economy," in *The American Negro Reference Book,* ed. John P. Davis. Englewood Cliffs, N.J.: Prentice-Hall, Inc., 1966.

Broom, Leonard, and Norval Glenn, *Transformation of the Negro American.* New York: Harper & Row, Publishers, 1965.

Drake, St. Clair, and Horace Cayton, *Black Metropolis.* New York: Harcourt, Brace and Co., 1945.

Edwards, G. Franklin, *The Negro Professional Class.* New York: Free Press, 1959.

Fein, Rashi, "An Economic and Social Profile of the Negro American," in *The Negro American,* eds. Talcott Parsons and Kenneth Clark. Boston: Houghton Mifflin Company, 1966.

Frazier, E. Franklin, *The Negro in the United States.* New York: The Macmillan Company, 1957.

Kozol, Jonathan, *Death At an Early Age: The Destruction of the Hearts and Minds of Negro Children in the Boston Public Schools.* Boston: Houghton Mifflin Company, 1967.

The Negro Handbook. Chicago: Johnson Publishing Company, 1966.

U.S. Department of Health, Education and Welfare, Office of Education, *Equality of Educational Opportunity.* Washington, D.C.: Government Printing Office, 1966.

U.S. Department of Labor, Bureau of Labor Statistics, *The Negroes in the United States: Their Economic and Social Situation.* Washington, D.C.: Government Printing Office, 1966.

The institutional life of the black community in the United States emerged and developed as a result of the peculiar interaction of black and white Americans through the years. Few aspects of institutional life in Africa survived the transfer of the slaves to North America. With the possible exception of a few aspects of religious life, the distinctive features of Negro life in the United States today stem from the historical, social, and economic forces which these people have encountered since their arrival in North America. Their social institutions are a reflection of their life in a racist society.

In this chapter attention is focused on three social institutions: family life, politics, and religion. Other distinctive social institutions are discussed in appropriate sections of other chapters.

THE FAMILY

The organization and behavioral patterns of the black family in the United States result mainly from economic and social conditions which Negroes have encountered. Few survivals of the original African family system remain. From the breakup of the African family during slavery to the overwhelming urbanization of black people in the 1960's, family life has been in a constant process of change, adapting to economic and social forces emanating from the larger society.

Social

Institutions

Developmental Processes

The family system which developed among black people during slavery was one with few of the characteristics that were normal to the white American family of the time. The very nature of slavery as an economic institution, as well as the attitudes which led to the institutionalization of American Negro slavery, militated against the black family's developing stability. Associations between male and female slaves were frequently engaged in for the sole purpose of satisfying sexual desires. Slaveholders could, and often did, mate their slaves to produce additional property. Male slaves were frequently used as stallions; in such cases, no bonds of affection were likely to develop between them and female slaves. Furthermore, since slaves were the property of slaveholders, any family relationships which might develop could be, and frequently were, dissolved through the sale of one of the parties involved. Any offspring to such a union usually remained with the mother, while the father was permitted to continue his sexual exploits on a new plantation.

Slave mothers frequently were affectionate and devoted to their offspring, but both the separation of the father and the presence of the slaveholder as a promiscuous role model led to the matricentric family, a development which has to some extent persisted to the present time. Children rarely saw their fathers, and their mothers assumed responsibility for whatever parental affection and care they received. When separated from her children, the slave mother often visited them at night. It was the mother, then, who was the dominant and important figure in the black slave family.

Because of the precariousness of their status, economically, socially, and legally, and because of their slave heritage, with its disregard for stable family life, blacks who were free before the Civil War were unable to develop stable family relations.[1] Family disorganization, including sexual promiscuity, was widespread. However, many of the mulatto children born to black women were kept by their mothers and accorded care despite severe hardships. Among the more economically secure free blacks, family relations attained a high degree of stability. Many of them were prosperous mulattoes who patterned their families after the middle- and upper-class white families.

The Civil War and emancipation had a disrupting effect on whatever degree of stability slave families had managed to achieve. Marriage as a formal and legal relationship between males and females was never allowed to become a part of the mores among most slaves. However, during slavery some stable families of husband, wife, and children did develop. With the complete uprooting of the social order in the South, family instability was but one element in the widespread social disorganization found among the ex-slaves. In the exodus from the plantations and in the general aimless wandering which accompanied their freedom, many black mothers left their children behind. Yet many others refused to depart from their children, and reports testify to the sacrifices which many of them made in order to keep their children.[2]

Promiscuous sexual relations and frequent changing of partners became the rule among ex-slaves, especially among those who experienced difficulties adjusting in an era largely characterized by anomie. Religious leaders, state legislatures, military authorities, the Freedmen's Bureau, missionary schools, and the mass media all joined the effort to

---

[1] See E. Franklin Frazier, *The Negro Family in the United States* (Chicago: The University of Chicago Press, 1966), especially Chap. 10.

[2] See, e.g., *ibid.*, Chap. 5.

impose institutional marriage and family norms on the freedmen.[3] These efforts succeeded in some cases, but in others official monogamous marriage and stable family relations required a difficult form of self-discipline. Nevertheless, by the end of the Reconstruction, Negroes had come to accept many of the family patterns of the larger society.

The restoration of white supremacy in the South following the Reconstruction imposed economic and social hardships on the black people. It became virtually impossible for the black man to assume a position of dominance or of equality with the black female. Economic exploitation, unemployment, and social subordination of black males in the larger society served to render them ineffectual as husbands and fathers. The appearance of Jim Crow laws toward the end of the 19th century further served to humiliate the black male. To a great extent these laws were geared toward keeping him "in his place" (i.e., away from the white female). Furthermore, with the widespread urbanization of the blacks since 1900, family life was again disrupted. The social norms which made for family stability in the rural South were without force in the urban slums. Among the lower-income Negroes, social disorganization was manifested in broken families, matricentric families, and illegitimacy. On the other hand, a growing middle class among urban Negroes is characterized by stable family relations and rigid adherence to the norms governing white middle-class families.

The Family in the 1960's:
Demographic Characteristics

As of March 1965, about three-fifths of all Negroes 14 years of age and over in the United States were married.[4] These individuals constituted 4.4 million families, of which 3.2 million were headed by a husband and wife, 1.1 million were headed by a woman, and some 137,000 were headed by a man with no wife present. Thus 72 percent of all black families were composed of both husband and wife, compared with 87 percent for white families. One-fourth of all black families, compared with less than one-tenth (9 percent) of all white families, were headed by females.

Black families were larger than white families. The average size of the Negro family was 4.34 persons, compared with 3.64 persons for

[3] Jessie Bernard, *Marriage and the Family Among Negroes* (Englewood Cliffs, N.J.: Prentice-Hall, 1966), pp. 10–13.

[4] These data are from the U.S. Bureau of the Census, *Current Population Reports*, Series P-20, No. 155, "Negro Population: March 1965" (Washington, D.C.: Government Printing Office, 1966), especially Tables 9–13, pp. 21–26.

white families. There were 2.01 children under 18 years of age per Negro family and 1.38 per white family.

Although black families were larger, they earned significantly less than white families. In 1964 the median income for Negro families was $3,700, or 54 percent of the $6,900 median income for white families. This difference in family income existed despite the fact that black families are much more likely than white families to contain working mothers. In 1965 nearly one-half (47 percent) of the wives in black husband-wife families were gainfully employed, compared with one-third among white husband-wife families.

Regionally, black families in the United States are evenly divided between the Southern and non-Southern states, but within these regions some differences occur. Few (3 percent) Negro families outside the South live on farms, whereas within the South one out of every ten families lives on a farm. The black family is larger in the South than outside that region (mean family size being 4.56 and 4.11, respectively). Southern black families average 2.14 dependent children (under 18 years of age), compared with 1.87 outside the South. Finally, black families in the South include an average of 2.14 related dependent children; outside the South black families contain an average of 1.71 related dependent children.

Black families are less likely than white families to own their own homes. In 1960, for example, less than two-fifths (38.4 percent) of non-whites lived in owner-occupied units, compared with more than three-fifths (61.6 percent) of white Americans.[5]

Because Negro families earn less than white families, they are required to spend more of their smaller earnings for what the U.S. Department of Labor calls the "three basic expenses." Negro and white families spend approximately the same proportion of their incomes for food, but Negroes spend a greater proportion for shelter (including fuel, light, refrigeration, and water) and clothing. These three expenses account for 58 percent of the total black expenditures, compared with 52 percent of white expenditures.[6]

Family Disorganization

The economic and social conditions under which black Americans have

[5] U.S. Bureau of the Census, *Statistical Abstract of the United States, 1966* (Washington, D.C.: Government Printing Office, 1966), p. 752.

[6] U.S. Department of Labor, Bureau of Labor Statistics, *The Negroes in the United States: Their Economic and Social Situation* (Washington D.C.: Government Printing Office, 1966), p. 148.

lived have led to disorganized family life. The legacy of slavery, widespread poverty, and rapid urbanization have militated against the establishment of stable families governed by middle-class norms. The contemporary black family, more than its white counterpart, is plagued by disorganization.

The family structure of lower-class blacks is characterized by instability. There is some evidence that when black people achieve middle-class status, family stability becomes even more important than it is among the white middle class.[7] But a vast majority of black people are found in the lowest socioeconomic status positions in society. Family instability is characterized by the high proportion of marriages dissolved by divorce, desertion, and separation. In 1960 nearly one-fourth (22.9 percent) of all urban Negro women who had ever been married were living apart from their husbands. The figure is 7.9 percent among white women in this same category.[8]

Desertion and separation were the principal means of family dissolution when Negroes were primarily rural dwellers, but increasing urbanization has forced married Negroes to adopt the legal procedure of divorce if they contemplate entering a new marriage relation. Hence the increase in urbanization has been accompanied by an increased divorce rate. According to Frazier, divorce is more prevalent among middle- and upper-class blacks than among the lower class.[9] This fact, he feels, is a reflection of the greater acceptance among these classes of middle-class norms governing family relations.

Separation and desertion have characteristically been utilized by lower-class Negroes to sever marriages. In rural communities in the South such practices were widespread, and these practices have followed the rural migrants to the city. These phenomena are by-products of casual marital relations existing during slavery, economic deprivation, and the loose character of institutional life among Negroes in cities. Marital instability was inherent in the slave system. Since emancipation black men have experienced difficulty providing economic support for their families.[10] And, in cities, family desertion is "one of the inevitable consequences of the impact of urban life on the simple family organization and folk culture which the Negro has evolved in the rural South."[11]

[7] See E. Franklin Frazier, *Black Bourgeoisie* (Glencoe, Ill.: Free Press, 1957), pp. 82–83.

[8] U.S. Bureau of the Census, *Current Population Reports*, p. 23.

[9] Frazier, *The Negro Family in the United States*, pp. 288–91.

[10] See C. Eric Lincoln, "The Absent Father Haunts the Negro Family," *New York Times Magazine*, November 28, 1966, p. 60.

[11] Frazier, *The Negro Family in the United States*, p. 255.

When marriage is dissolved through divorce, desertion, or separation, if children are involved, they generally remain with the mother.
Although the norms of society idealize the small nuclear family of
husband, wife, and children, a significant number of black families are
headed by females. In 1965, for example, one-fourth of all black families
were headed by women, compared with only 9 percent for white families.[12] In addition to dissolved marriages, these families frequently result
from illegitimacy.

The illegitimacy rate among black people is reported to be eight
times the rate among white Americans. Nearly one-fourth of all Negro
births in 1963 were reported to be illegitimate.[13] Illegitimacy among
Negroes has been explained as psychological deviance, inherent sexuality,
or moral decay. Rarely is it seen as a function of historical and contemporary conditions under which black Americans have lived and
continue to live.[14] That is, in addition to the slave heritage, with its
prevention of the emergence of any norm of legitimacy, the social and
economic conditions of black people since emancipation have been
extreme versions of those likely to generate the highest illegitimacy rate
among the population in general.

The effects of family disorganization on the personalities of children have been well documented.[15] Children in broken homes are said
to seek immediate gratification far more than children with fathers
present in the home. This inability to delay gratification has been linked
to immature, neurotic, and criminal behavior. Children from homes
without fathers are reported to experience difficulty in distinguishing
sex roles, a condition which manifests itself in femininity among males,
in delayed marriage or divorce, and in pseudomasculine toughness.
Finally, it has been suggested that families without fathers are more
likely to produce schizophrenics than are families in which the father is
present. Although these relationships between family disorganization
and personality problems in children are not definitive, evidence indicates
that children from broken families are more likely to develop personality problems than those children with both parents present in the
home. A disproportionately high percentage of black children grow up
in broken homes.

[12] U.S. Bureau of the Census, *Current Population Reports*, p. 3.
[13] U.S. Department of Labor, *The Negro Family: The Case for National Action*
(Washington, D.C.: Government Printing Office, 1965), pp. 8–9.
[14] See Andrew Billingsley and Amy T. Billingsley, "Illegitimacy and Patterns of
Negro Family Life," in *The Unwed Mother*, ed. Robert W. Roberts (New York: Harper
& Row, 1966).
[15] Thomas F. Pettigrew, *A Profile of the Negro American* (Princeton, N.J.: Van
Nostrand, 1964), pp. 15–24.

Patterns of Family Life

In many ways black family life in the United States differs from white family life. However, the contention that the deterioration of the Negro family is the main source of problems faced by Negroes in American society clearly overstates the case.[16] Although there is widespread family disorganization frequently manifested in matriarchal family patterns, in a vast majority of black families, as in white families, dominance is shared between the mother and father (egalitarian pattern) or is vested in the father (patriarchal pattern).[17] Where the matriarchal pattern continues to exist, such as among the lower class, it is a result of illegitimacy, the dissolution of institutional life in urban areas, or the father's inability to perform the economic functions traditionally associated with his status. Rural Southern Negroes who moved to urban areas found the church and the family less responsive to their needs in these new environments. As soon as black Americans enter the middle class, family patterns associated with the lower class tend to disappear. The differences between black and white family patterns, then, are largely results of status in the society.

One of the chief societal functions of the family is the socialization of offspring. In the case of black parents this role becomes more difficult, for theirs is not simply a task of instilling skills, knowledge, attitudes, and values; they must also socialize their offspring into the peculiar status of being black in a racist society. Child-rearing practices constitute crucial aspects of the socialization process. In the 1940's Davis and Havighurst conducted a study of racial and class differences in child-rearing practices. They reported that few differences existed when Negro and white families occupied similar social-class positions.[18] Subsequent studies report findings inconsistent with these.[19] One similar study, however, reports that black mothers are less likely to expose

[16] See, e.g., U.S. Department of Labor, *The Negro Family: The Case for National Action*, pp. 29–46.

[17] See Russell Middleton and Snell Putney, "Dominance in Decisions in the Family: Race and Class Differences," *American Journal of Sociology*, Vol. 65 (May 1960), 605–9. In a study of black and white families in the Detroit, Michigan, area and in southeastern Michigan it is reported that, whereas the majority of white families are egalitarian (54 percent), the largest percentage of Negro families are dominated by the wife. The husband was found to be dominant in 19 percent of the Negro families; the wife was dominant in 44 percent; and 38 percent were egalitarian. See Robert A. Blood, Jr., and Donald M. Wolfe, *Husbands and Wives* (Glencoe, Ill.: Free Press, 1960), pp. 34–36.

[18] Allison Davis and Robert J. Havighurst, "Social Class and Color Differences in Child Rearing," *American Sociological Review*, Vol. 11 (December 1946), 698–710.

[19] See, e.g., Martha S. White, "Social Class, Child Rearing Practices, and Child Behavior," *American Sociological Review*, Vol. 22 (December 1957), 704–12.

themselves to child-rearing literature than white mothers, regardless of social-class position, but that black mothers who are so exposed express more favorable attitudes toward child-rearing than do white mothers.[20] Although contradictory findings are reported, there is considerable evidence to indicate that middle-class black parents are more like middle-class white parents in their child-rearing practices than they are like lower-class black parents.

Because of historical and social factors, however, some differences between black and white family patterns are likely to persist. The economic plight of the Negro is not likely to be eradicated in the near future, and the black male will continue to experience difficulties in providing for his family in accordance with the norms of society. The legacy of slavery and the lack of stable family relations fostered by that institution will continue to plague the black family, even if its economic position improves. Frazier sees the high rate of illegitimacy among black Americans as resulting from "naive and ignorant peasant folk who are newcomers to the city." [21] But this phenomenon must be partially explained as a result of slavery and its prohibition of a norm of legitimacy. One researcher attributes more permissive premarital sexual attitudes among Negro high school and college students than among white students to the experience of Negroes during slavery.[22] Illegitimate births are widespread among rural Southern Negroes, as well as among their urban Northern counterparts. Attitudes toward this phenomenon are considerably less harsh and punitive among black than among white Americans. For example, black mothers are more likely to keep their illegitimate offspring than are white mothers.[23] However, Bernard summarizes studies of illegitimacy and presents evidence to support the conclusion that illegitimacy is "not accepted—let alone welcomed," even in low-income black families. For many it is a traumatic experience.[24]

Although some of the patterns of black family life may be accounted for by forces other than their precarious economic situation, when blacks and whites share similar class positions, their family patterns today are remarkably similar.

POLITICS

With rare exceptions, black Americans have played a minor role in the political life of the United States, both in the electoral process and in public office. Historically, black people have been heavily con-

---

[20] Zena S. Blau, "Exposure to Child-Rearing Experts: A Structural Interpretation," *American Journal of Sociology*, Vol. 69 (May 1964), 596–608.

[21] Frazier, *The Negro Family in the United States*, p. 267.

[22] See Ira L. Reiss, "Premarital Sexual Permissiveness Among Negroes and Whites," *American Sociological Review*, Vol. 29 (October 1964), 688–98.

[23] Frazier, *The Negro Family in the United States*, p. 265.

[24] Bernard, *op. cit.*, pp. 50–55.

centrated in the South, and a variety of techniques have been used to keep them from voting. Except during the period of Radical Reconstruction, the South succeeded in virtually disfranchising its many Negroes. In 1898, for example, a Senator from South Carolina boldly declared from the floor of the Senate that his state had virtually eliminated black people from voting. "We have done our best. We have scratched our heads to find out how we could eliminate the last one of them. We stuffed ballot boxes. We shot them. We are not ashamed of it." [25] Because of increasing pressure for greater civil rights, and because of additional civil rights legislation ensuring their voting rights, black people are becoming more active in American political life.

Historical Trends

Black people have been active in varying degrees in the political life of the United States since the beginnings of the Radical Reconstruction. On the national level, three Negroes served in the 41st Congress (1869–71), two in the House of Representatives and one in the Senate.[26] With the exception of the 50th Congress (1887–89), Negroes served in every U.S. Congress from 1869 to 1901. The largest number—seven—served in the 43rd and 44th Congresses. All these Congressmen represented Southern states, and by the turn of the 20th century, Negroes had been effectively disfranchised in that region. The last black man from the South to serve was a Representative from North Carolina whose service ended in 1901.

No Negroes served in the national Congress from the 57th Congress (1901–3) through the 71st Congress (1929–31), but with the widespread migration of black people northward and availability of the franchise to them, the first Negro from the North to serve in Congress was seated in 1931. Since that time one or more Negroes from the North have served in every Congress. With the concentration of black people in large urban centers, as a result of residential segregation, the number of Negroes in Congress has gradually increased to the point where the 90th Congress (1967–69) included seven black Congressmen, six Representatives and one Senator. Each of these Congressmen was from a Northern state, and the Senator (from Massachusetts) was the first Negro elected to that office since 1881.

Although black Americans have frequently constituted a majority in the population of several political subdivisions in the South, since the Reconstruction they have held little, if any, political power. On the state and local levels Negroes held important offices during the Recon-

[25] Cited in Rayford W. Logan, *The Negro in the United States* (Princeton, N.J.: Van Nostrand, 1957), p. 51.

[26] These data are reported in *The Negro Handbook* (Chicago: Johnson Publishing Co., 1966), pp. 271–74.

struction. During this period they were elected or appointed to such public offices as supreme court justice, lieutenant governor, secretary of state, state treasurer, superintendent of public instruction, and virtually every other public office except that of governor. In the state constitutional conventions, Negroes were well represented, especially in South Carolina, Louisiana, Florida, and Virginia. At no time, however, can it be said that they effectively controlled the affairs of any state.

Beginning with the elections for the constitutional conventions in 1867, black people in the South voted in large numbers. At that time the total Negro vote exceeded the vote of white Southerners.[27] Throughout the Radical Reconstruction Negroes actively exercised the franchise. With the restoration of white supremacy in 1877, the gains registered in this period gradually disappeared. The Populist movement in the 1890's witnessed a resurgence of Negro voting, but it was short lived. By the turn of the 20th century, through a series of devices, some legal and some illegal, the South had effectively disfranchised most of its black citizens.[28] At that time so few black people lived outside the South that their voting strength was insignificant.

With the wholesale disfranchisement of black people in the South after 1900, they were hardly represented in public office in that region during the first half of the 20th century. With increased voting guarantees, especially the Voting Rights Act of 1965, Negroes have been elected to public office at various levels—from state senator to local boards of education and, in one case, to county sheriff—since the rise of the civil rights movement.

In the North the concentration of black people in urban areas is a relatively recent development. In the second half of the 20th century, increasingly large numbers of Negroes have held elective and appointive offices at various levels, from state senator to mayor to judges of various levels, including the U.S. Supreme Court. With increasing urbanization among Negroes, New York City provides a clue to their potential role in public life. In 1960, with about a million black people, New York had "17 Negro judges, two supreme court justices, one general sessions judge, four city magistrates, three domestic relations court judges, six municipal court judges, and one city court judge. In addition, in New York City (unlike Chicago) many Negroes hold administrative positions at the cabinet and subcabinet levels." [29] Although New York may be the

27 W. E. B. Du Bois, *Black Reconstruction* (New York: Harcourt, Brace and Co., 1935), p. 371.

28 See, e.g., Gunnar Myrdal, *An American Dilemma* (New York: Harper, 1944), pp. 479–86.

29 James Q. Wilson, *Negro Politics* (Glencoe, Ill.: Free Press, 1960), p. 46.

exception at the present time, there is increasing evidence that black people in large urban areas consider political power a major weapon for improving their status.

With the internal redistribution of black people in the 20th century, Northern cities became the center of black political behavior. Black voters are frequently cultivated by white politicians because in certain "decisive" states black voters hold the balance of power since their voters have determined the outcome of elections.[30] In the South, especially since the passage of the Civil Rights Act of 1964 and the Voting Rights Act of 1965, black people have been registering and voting in increasing numbers. This increased participation in elections was made evident by the election returns in 1964 and 1966, when black people were elected to state legislatures and local offices throughout much of the South, although still not nearly in proportion to their number in the population.

Voting Rights

The right to vote is one of the basic civil rights guaranteed to citizens by the Constitution of the United States. Yet hardly any aspect of the black man's quest for equality has met with greater resistance in the South than the right to vote. Several judicial decrees and legislative acts have not succeeded in fully translating this constitutional guarantee into a reality for millions of black citizens of the United States.[31] With emancipation, two amendments, the Fourteenth and Fifteenth, were written into the Constitution especially to protect the voting rights of the newly freed slaves. These amendments specifically directed states to guarantee voting rights to black citizens.

Three civil rights acts were enacted between 1866 and 1875 as a means of assuring equality of treatment (including the right to vote) to America's Negroes. These acts—the Civil Rights Act of 1866, the Civil Rights Act of 1870, and the Civil Rights Act of 1875—together with constitutional guarantees, served to permit black people in the South to exercise the right to vote with relative ease during the Reconstruction. After the Reconstruction, however, several states adopted so-called grandfather clauses, which restricted registration and voting to persons who had voted prior to emancipation. This practice was finally declared unconstitutional by the Supreme Court in 1915.[32] With this defeat

---

[30] See D. W. Brogan, *Politics in America* (New York: Harper, 1954), p. 116ff. See also Oscar Glantz, "The Negro Voter in Northern Industrial Cities," *The Western Political Quarterly*, Vol 13 (December 1960), 999–1010.

[31] For a review of these acts and rulings see Charles Aiken, *The Negro Votes* (San Francisco: Chandler Publishing Co., 1962).

[32] *Ibid.*, pp. 21–35.

Southerners adopted the "white primary," in which the Democratic Party prohibited Negroes from participating in primary elections in nine states. When the white primary was outlawed, many Southern states resorted to the gerrymander as a means of disfranchising Negroes. In a long series of cases the Supreme Court eventually curbed this practice also.

In addition to the above techniques, the poll tax, property, educational, and "character" requirements were used to keep black citizens from voting. Perhaps the most effective means of disfranchising Negroes, however, were those of intimidation and violence.[33]

Because of the difficulties encountered by black people attempting to vote in the South, special legislation was again enacted in the 1950's and 1960's. The Civil Rights Act of 1957 attempted to guarantee that any Negro so desiring could vote. The federal government, through the Justice Department, was empowered to institute law suits to ensure Negroes the right to vote. The Civil Rights Act of 1960 empowered the Attorney General ultimately to certify Negroes as qualified voters in areas where they had been kept from voting through discrimination. And the Civil Rights Act of 1964 included voting rights guarantees. One important aspect of this act is the provision that a sixth-grade education is a presumption of literacy for voting purposes.

In spite of the Constitution, the 19th-century civil rights acts, the judicial rulings of the Supreme Court, and the 20th-century civil rights acts, black Americans have continued to experience difficulties in voting throughout the Deep South. After the Civil Rights Act of 1964, civil rights organizations were urged to discontinue direct action protests and to concentrate on voter registration among black people. It was felt that the most effective means of achieving their goals was through registering Negroes to vote. When large-scale attempts were made to register black people in the South, voting registrars again utilized a variety of techniques to keep them from voting. Acts of violence (so characteristic in the South) met voter registration workers and black people attempting to vote. Civil rights workers and the leaders of civil rights organizations urged the enactment of new legislation to guarantee Southern Negroes the right to vote. As a result of these pressures, the Voting Rights Act of 1965 was enacted by Congress and signed into law on August 6. This act contains many provisions designed to assure black people that devices previously employed to disfranchise them would no longer serve this purpose. For example, literacy as a qualification for

[33] See Paul Lewinson, *Race, Class, and Party* (New York: Oxford, 1932); Myrdal, *op. cit.*, pp. 485–86.

voting was suspended, and voter registration may be supervised by federal officials in political subdivisions where a pattern of discrimination is discerned.

Although intimidation and threats will no doubt continue to deter many eligible black voters, a long series of legislative acts and judicial rulings, over a period of more than 100 years, has finally established, in principle, the right of black people to vote.

Political Organization and Behavior

The second half of the 20th century has seen the growth of greater cohesiveness in the black community than has existed since emancipation as a direct result of increasing identification among black people and the demand for greater civil rights. The black community nowhere represents a completely unified force, however. Clearly some communities are better organized than others. The Atlanta, Georgia, black subcommunity, for example, is described by Hunter as a community with a high degree of social organization.[34] The black leadership of Atlanta followed the pattern of leadership in the larger community. However, the black community exerted less influence on policy decisions in the larger community than other associational groupings, such as organized labor or the Jewish subcommunity. Other subcommunities were represented on policy-making committees in the larger community, but the black subcommunity was not represented: "... the [Negro] subcommunity ... stands alone in its isolation from the sources of power as no other unit within the metropolitan area. Its channels of communication in most of its power relations with the larger community are partially blocked, if not totally closed." [35] Because of the large number of Negroes, and because of the relatively high proportion of middle-class Negroes, there was a high degree of civic participation among Atlanta's Negroes. Even there, however, they were powerless to influence basic community decisions.

As a political force, black people lack the organization necessary for effective action. In many urban areas the black community has enough numerical strength to organize effective civic action, but its members have relied on the courts and direct action demonstrations to gain political ends. Several factors account for this lack of conventional

---

34 Floyd Hunter, *Community Power Structure* (Chapel Hill, N.C.: The University of North Carolina Press, 1953), Chap. 5.
35 *Ibid.*, p. 184.

political behavior among black people.[36] They are overrepresented in the lower class, and lower-class people are less likely to participate in political activities. In addition to the general tendency of lower-class people to shun political activity, social disorganization is widespread among lower-class Negroes. Their lives are such that the personal problems of employment and maintenance are so pervasive as to rule out politics. In addition, lower-class Negroes lack a sense of identification with their communities.

Within the black community there is a tendency for middle-class Negroes to avoid associations with the lower class.[37] Since the middle class characteristically assumes positions of political leadership in the community, the antipathy which middle-class Negroes maintain toward the lower class renders cooperation difficult. Furthermore, the middle class and the lower class represent divergent values. Most middle-class blacks occupy this status as a result of social mobility, and they are eager to forget their lower-class heritage.

Few individuals in the black community possess the requisite wealth for large-scale political undertakings. The middle class is usually made up of professionals, and few black businesses are of such magnitude as to provide their owners with the wealth required for political leadership. Even civic and civil rights organizations within the black community are usually lacking in membership and funds. Rarely are they maintained by the residents of the community.

The structure of the black community, then, is such that widespread conventional political activity has been lacking. Black leaders have tended to rely on the courts and demonstrations to achieve political ends. There is some evidence, however, of a trend toward conventional political behavior on the part of Negroes.[38] There is increasing recognition that the problems confronting Negroes—in employment, in education, and in housing—are of such magnitude that it is unlikely that they can be solved simply by achieving full constitutional rights.

In recent years black citizens have registered to vote in increasing numbers in the South, and they have elected Negroes to political offices throughout the United States. For example, the Justice Department

[36] See Edward Banfield and James Q. Wilson, *City Politics* (Cambridge, Mass.: Harvard, 1963), Chap. 20.

[37] Frazier, *Black Bourgeoisie*, pp. 224–29.

[38] See James Q. Wilson, "The Negro in Politics," in *The Negro American*, eds. Talcott Parsons and Kenneth Clark (Boston: Houghton Mifflin, 1966); for a recent study of the changing role of Negroes in Southern political life, see Donald R. Matthews and James W. Prothro, *Negroes and the New Southern Politics* (New York: Harcourt, Brace & World, 1966).

reported that 47.8 percent of the eligible Negroes in the Deep South registered for the 1966 elections. This figure represented an increase of 28.6 percent over the preceding year.[39] When they vote, Negroes usually exert a "liberalizing" influence on an election. It is often said that the black voter votes "race" first. The character of American society being what it is, a vote on an issue beneficial to Negroes or for a politician who campaigns on behalf of Negroes is likely to exert a liberalizing influence, especially in the South. The likelihood is that Negroes will continue to vote for issues and politicians who serve their interests and against those who do not.[40]

Changes are occurring in the nature of black leadership.[41] Traditionally, the black leader was acceptable to the larger (i.e., white) community. These leaders were usually moderate and were often ministers. However, Negroes are now demanding that their leaders be responsible to the black community. The more militant they are, especially on race issues, the greater their likelihood of receiving community support.

Public Officials

When the 90th Congress convened in January 1967, its membership included seven Negroes, six Representatives and one Senator. These seven Congressmen represented the largest number of black Americans in Congress since the Reconstruction. Furthermore, the Senator was the first Negro elected to the Senate from a non-Southern state. Several other Negroes held elective or appointive offices on the national level. There were a total of 12 judges serving on the U.S. Court of Appeals, the Customs Court, U.S. District Courts, and the U.S. Supreme Court. Seven Negroes were serving as ambassadors, and there were 19 Foreign Service officers and 38 Foreign Service reserve officers.[42]

In 1965 approximately 1,800 black Americans held elective or appointive offices in state, county, and municipal agencies throughout the United States.[43] These positions varied from membership on a local antipoverty committee to mayor of a medium-sized city (Springfield, Ohio). By 1967 Negroes had been elected to the office of mayor in Cleveland,

[39] *The New York Times,* November 12, 1966, p. 16, col. 2.

[40] See Russell Middleton, "The Civil Rights Issue and Presidential Voting Among Southern Negroes and Whites," *Social Forces,* Vol. 40 (March 1962), 209–15; Henry Lee Moon, "The Negro Vote in the Presidential Election of 1956," *Journal of Negro Education,* Vol. 26 (Summer 1957), 219–30.

[41] James Q. Wilson, *Negro Politics,* especially Chap. 12.

[42] These data are reported in *The Negro Handbook,* pp. 271–79.

[43] *Ibid.,* pp. 429–70.

Ohio; Gary, Indiana; and Flint, Michigan. In addition, a Negro was appointed mayor of Washington, D.C. Throughout the North many black people held important elective and appointive positions. In the South the positions were the less influential ones, often ceremonial in nature. The elections of 1964, however, signaled a turning point in politics for Negroes. Armed with protective legislation, they voted in record numbers and elected 280 Negroes to public office.[44] These included 90 members of state legislatures and 184 persons in state and local offices, such as justices of the peace and members of county boards of revenue and boards of education. In many of the Southern states Negroes were elected to state legislatures for the first time in the 20th century.

In 1966 the Voter Education Project of the Southern Regional Council reported that 20 black citizens were elected to Southern legislatures.[45] This number was a gain of nine. Georgia led all other Southern states combined with a total of 11 black legislators. Many other Negroes were elected to local and county offices throughout the South.

The Department of Justice, which supervised voter registration and observed the 1966 elections in counties in Alabama, Georgia, Louisiana, and Mississippi, reported that, because of the heavy black voter turnout in the rural South, at least ten Negroes were elected to public office in rural areas in the Deep South for the first time since Reconstruction.[46] In one rural Deep South county—Macon County, Alabama—blacks were elected to important political offices, including those of sheriff, tax collector, and member of the board of education. Macon County is the first in the South to elect a Negro to the position of sheriff since Reconstruction. The county has a population of 27,000, 84 percent of whom are black, the highest ratio of blacks to whites of any county in the United States. In addition to these three public officials, Negroes occupy two of the five posts on the city council, two of the four elective posts of the county commission, a majority of the county's jury list, a majority of the police force in the major city, and a majority of the county's Democratic executive committee. Macon County, and its principal city, Tuskegee, have perhaps the most integrated local governments in the United States today.[47]

In general, however, black Americans hold disproportionately few elective and appointive offices. The pattern varies with the region of the country, and, although they tend to hold more influential positions

[44] *The New York Times,* December 23, 1964.
[45] *Ibid.,* November 27, 1966, p. 74, col. 1.
[46] *Ibid.,* November 12, 1966, p. 16, col. 2.
[47] Gene Roberts, "A Kind of Black Power in Macon County, Ala.," *New York Times Magazine,* February 27, 1967, p. 32.

outside the South, political activity among black people in these regions is a relatively recent phenomenon. There is some evidence that with the concentration of Negroes in large urban centers outside the South, increasing numbers of elective and appointive offices will be held by them.[48] Within the South increased voter registration, resulting from increased voting guarantees, is likely to change the political climate of that region.

All evidence indicates that black people are an emerging political force in American society. They are likely to vote in increasing numbers and to elect more and more Negroes to political office. Such political activity is important in the black man's quest for equality. However, many of the problems faced by black people are not amenable to political solutions. Therefore conventional political behavior is likely to prove ineffective in dealing with many of the problems encountered by black people. They have been virtually ignored as citizens for so long that any solutions to the many problems they face in American society are likely to require radical social action on many fronts.[49]

RELIGION

Religion has traditionally played an important role in the life of black Americans. The character of their religion is a reflection of their precarious status in the larger society. Denied the opportunity to participate as equals in the religious life and other institutions of the larger society, black people organized their own religious denominations as a means of coping with the social isolation which they encountered. Although their religious institutions contain the same basic elements as white Protestantism, it is especially in their religion that some elements of their African heritage are to be found.[50]

Developmental History

The first black people to settle permanently in what is now the United States were systematically stripped of their traditional culture, including their religious practices. In contrast to those who settled in the Caribbean and South America, the slaves in North America did not establish their traditional cults in the New World. Slaveholders succeeded in forcing slaves to abandon the outward manifestations of their "heathen" re-

48 See Charles Silberman, *Crisis in Black and White* (New York: Random House, 1964), Chap. 7.

49 For a discussion of the limitations of political action, see James Q. Wilson, "The Changing Political Position of the Negro," in *Assuring Freedom to the Free,* ed. Arnold Rose (Detroit, Mich.: Wayne State University Press, 1964), pp. 163–84.

50 See Melville Herskovits, *The Myth of the Negro Past* (New York: Harper and Brothers, 1941), especially Chap. 7: "The Contemporary Scene: Africanisms in Religious Life."

ligions. Few of the slaves had been converted to Christianity before their arrival in North America, and throughout much of the slavery era many slaveholders opposed religious instruction for slaves. Negro slaves had been baptized since their first importation, but ". . . it was not until the opening of the 18th century that a systematic attempt was made on the part of the Church of England to Christianize Negroes in America." [51] These efforts were carried out by the Society for the Propagation of the Gospel in Foreign Parts, which was chartered in England in 1701. Soon afterward white Baptist and Methodist ministers and missionaries began proselytizing among the slaves. The slaves responded considerably more enthusiastically to these efforts than they had to those from ministers and missionaries of the Church of England. Frazier sees the uneducated and emotional appeals of the Baptists and Methodists as fulfilling a special need of the slaves.[52]

On many plantations slaves were allowed to worship in churches with white persons, often seated in the gallery but sometimes in a separate section on the main floor. In such cases the services were invariably conducted by white ministers, but there were occasionally black ministers among the slaves. Black ministers were viewed by slaveholders with distrust, especially after the rebellion of Nat Turner, who was himself a minister. But black ministers were tolerated as long as they confined themselves to sermons in which they instilled in the slaves acceptance of their status. As Myrdal has written, "Undoubtedly the great bulk of the Southern Negro preachers advocated complete acceptance of slave status." [53] By emancipation a significant proportion of the slaves had been converted to Christianity, and their religious practices provided them with some outlet for the frustrations resulting from their status. Furthermore, religion gave them a basis of social cohesion for the first time since their arrival in the New World.

The religious life of the free Negroes during the slavery era differed from that of the slaves. At first black people in the North and South attended services along with white worshipers. And in both regions Negro ministers served mixed Negro-white congregations as well as all-Negro congregations. Several black ministers achieved widespread distinction as orators and preached to predominantly white congregations. The separate black church was established in the 1770's because of increasing tension resulting from Negroes' attendance at predomi-

[51] E. Franklin Frazier, *The Negro Church in America* (New York: Schocken Books, 1964), p. 6.
[52] *Ibid.,* p. 8.
[53] Myrdal, *op. cit.,* p. 860.

nantly white churches.[54] By the turn of the 19th century free blacks had established both Methodist and Protestant Episcopal churches. Baptist churches, independent of white churches, were also organized during this time. In the North the churches of the free blacks served to assist their counterparts who were enslaved in the South in two ways. They were frequently centers of Abolitionist activity, and they aided runaway slaves by serving as stations in the Underground Railroad.

During the Reconstruction the black church provided a source of social organization and social control in a time of social disruption for the newly freed slaves. There were initial conflicts between the freedmen and those blacks who had been free before the Civil War, but these were short lived. Perhaps the most important role of the black church in this period was played in political life.[55] Since the Negro in the South enjoyed civil rights on a wide scale, many of the politicians of this period were recruited from among religious leaders. They served in state legislatures, in the Freedmen's Bureau, and in many federal appointive positions. Two of the 20 Negroes elected to the federal House of Representatives between 1869 and 1901 were ministers, as was one of the two Senators.

The restoration of white supremacy to the South served to strip these leaders of their political power in the larger community, and many of them became leaders in education and other community institutions serving black people. The black church as a separate institution was the primary source of social life among black people. The ministry was the main source of leadership, and it was through the ministry that the black community maintained contact with the larger community. As Myrdal has written:

> In practically all rural areas, and in many urban ones, the preacher stood out as the acknowledged local leader of the Negroes. His function became to transmit the whites' wishes to the Negroes and to beg the whites for favors for his people. He became—in our terminology—the typical accommodating Negro leader. To this degree the Negro church perpetuated the traditions of slavery.[56]

The frustrations inherent in the lives of black Americans were such that some form of outlet was essential. The character of black religion being what it was, that is, concerned with other-worldly matters, meant that

[54] Benjamin E. Mays and Joseph W. Nicholson, *The Negro's Church* (New York: Institute of Social and Religious Research, 1933), pp. 29–33.
[55] Frazier, *The Negro Church in America*, pp. 42–44.
[56] Myrdal, *op. cit.*, p. 861.

it posed no serious threat to established patterns of white supremacy. Therefore religious activity among Negroes was not only tolerated but encouraged. The minister could be trusted, and the church served to contain the black masses.

In the North, where white supremacy was less well institutionalized, the black church remained somewhat more independent. Unlike their Southern counterparts, Northern black ministers were more responsive to the needs of their followers than to the white community. Therefore they were more likely to become involved in the politics of the larger community, and they frequently became leaders in opposition to segregation and discrimination against Negroes. Furthermore, within the black community they engaged in social service work. On the whole, however, the black church in the North was not a militant force for social change.

With the widespread urbanization of black people beginning in the second decade of the 20th century, the focus of black life shifted from the rural South to the cities in the South and elsewhere. This radical change, like that brought about by emancipation, had a disrupting effect on the lives of black people. The uprooted masses flocked to cities, and again the church provided a basis for social organization. But within the urban environment the black church, like religious institutions in the larger society, addressed itself to problems facing its members and de-emphasized its other-worldly outlook. At the same time the established urban black church gradually became less emotional in its services. Because of the widespread social disorganization accompanying the urbanization of Negroes, many of them continued to feel the need for outlets from the frustrations they faced. Therefore they sought refuge in "store-front" churches and in the many cults which developed. The black church continued to be the primary source of social cohesion, but it did not play an important role in the endeavors of black people to achieve greater civil rights during the first half of the 20th century.

With the greater emphasis on civil rights at midcentury, the black church became one of the prime agencies advocating social change in the realm of race relations. Black ministers became leaders in the civil rights movement, and the movement has to a large extent continued to have a religious base. Since religion had always been the only well-organized institution within the black community, such a development was inevitable.

Religious Affiliation

The black man's lack of participation in the organized religious life of American society in general reflects his lack of acceptance by the larger society. In some respects the Christian church is one of America's most

segregated institutions. The major churches are undergoing some transformation, however, and black people are gradually being accepted into
membership in predominantly white churches.

It is impossible to specify the exact membership of any of the
major religious denominations at any point in time because the census
does not collect this information at its regular enumerations. Therefore
it is necessary to rely on data provided by the religious organizations.
Most black Christians are concentrated in six predominantly black denominations. Of these, the National Baptist Convention, U.S.A., claiming 5.5 million members in 1953, was the largest. Its membership, as large
as the other five combined, was distributed among 26,000 member
churches with a total of 27,000 ministers.[57] The National Baptist Convention of America, the second largest predominantly black denomination, reported 2,668,000 members in 1956. In this group there were 11,398
churches and 7,598 ministers. The Progressive National Baptist Convention, Incorporated, the third of the major Baptist denominations,
reported 505,000 members, 411 churches, and 450 ministers in 1965.
These three Baptist denominations combined, with 8.6 million members,
represent more than half of the black church members in the United
States, including the members of predominantly white denominations.

Following Baptists, Methodists rank second among the predominantly Negro denominations. The African Methodist Episcopal Church,
with 1,166,000 members, 5,878 churches, and 7,079 ministers in 1951,
was the largest of the Methodist denominations. The African Methodist
Episcopal Zion Church, with 770,000 members, 4,083 churches, and
2,480 ministers in 1959, ranked second. The Christian Methodist Episcopal Church, with 444,500 members, 2,523 churches, and 1,914 ministers,
ranked third in size.

In addition to the black denominations, several of the predominantly white religious groups and denominations had sizable black
memberships. Of these, the Roman Catholic Church reported the largest
black membership. In 1963 the Roman Catholic Church reported a
black membership of 722,609 out of a total membership of more than
45 million. The Methodist Church reported 373,327 black members out
of a total membership of more than 10 million in 1964. In 1963 the
American Baptist Convention reported 200,000 black members out of a
total of 1.5 million. The Seventh-Day Adventists reported 167,892 black
members out of a total of 370,880 members in 1964, giving it the highest
proportion of black members of any predominantly white religious
group in the United States. Other denominations, such as the Christian

[57] These data and those which follow are reported in *The Negro Handbook*,
pp. 307–8.

Churches (Disciples of Christ), the Protestant Episcopal Church, the Congregational Christian Churches, the United Church of Christ, and the United Presbyterian Church in the United States of America, include Negroes as members, but except for the Congregational Christian Churches, with approximately one-third Negroes in its membership, the proportion of Negro members is small.

Black people tend to worship with other blacks. A vast majority of them are members of black denominations of the Christian church, and even when they hold membership in a predominantly white religious group or denomination, the likelihood is that they worship in segregated black churches.

Beginning with the rapid migration of black people to cities during the second decade of the 20th century, many of them became members of less well-organized "store-front" churches, many of which are affiliated with the more institutional denominations. Others affiliated themselves with the many religious cults, such as the Holiness churches, or with non-Christian religions. More recently urban black people have flocked to the Nation of Islam, popularly known as the Black Muslim sect. It is impossible to estimate accurately the membership of these religious groups, but they thrive in black residential sections of large cities throughout the United States.

Structure and Patterns

Since black religion in America, like other aspects of black life, is highly segregated, it might be expected to differ in some regards from religion in the larger society. The black church runs the gamut from the separationist sects and cults in large urban centers, which appeal to the lower classes and where emotionalism is an important part of the services, to the upper-class Protestant churches represented by the Congregationalist, Episcopal, and Presbyterian denominations, which are totally devoid of emotionalism in their services. Regardless of the type of service, black people are more likely to be affiliated with some form of church than are white Americans. Myrdal reports that in the 1930's, 44 percent of the black population were members of churches, compared with 42 percent of the white population.[58] This figure probably represented an underenumeration among Negroes, because they are more likely than whites to attend services at store-front churches and to be members of small religious cults and sects whose membership is rarely reported in church statistics.

The black community is noted for the number of churches it includes. Drake and Cayton enumerated some 500 churches in Chicago

[58] Myrdal, *op. cit.*, p. 864.

that served some 200,000 members. These churches represented more than 30 denominations. Seventy-five percent of these churches were store-front churches or "house churches" with an average membership of fewer than 25 persons.[59] A study of central Harlem in the 1960's enumerated 418 church buildings. Of this number only 122 were housed in conventional church buildings; 232 were located either in store fronts or in residential buildings; and the remainder were located in large meeting halls, private homes, or social agencies.[60]

Among conventional black Protestants, religious services follow a pattern similar to that of white Protestant churches. In general, few innovations have been made in the services. The choir sings alone or is joined by the congregation in the singing of hymns; music is supplied by an organ (a piano in smaller churches); prayer is recited by the minister; the sermon (the center of the service) is delivered by the minister; and the collection, an essential part of the service, frequently consumes a significant proportion of the time allocated to the service.[61] In some Baptist and Methodist churches the services frequently assume a more emotional tone than in other Protestant denominations. There are frequent responses to the sermon on the part of the congregation. These responses take the form of "yes" or "Amen." Such practices are characteristic of churches which cater to the lower classes, because middle-class Baptists and Methodists avoid outward displays of emotionalism. As Baptist and Methodist churches have altered the content of their services, some of their members have sought refuge in store-front churches and Holiness sects: ". . . the popular Protestant denominations (Methodist and Baptist) do not generally meet the emotional, psychological, and economic needs of traditionalists and/or submerged socioeconomic groups; consequently there has been a striking attraction of some groups who are not adjusted to religious and social change to faiths which emphasize emotion and sometimes economic provision."[62]

The Protestant denominations serving middle- and upper-class blacks do not differ in their religious services from similar white denominations. A small minority of Negroes are members of such predominantly white denominations as the Congregational, Episcopal, and Presbyterian churches. Such black membership is drawn from the middle and upper classes. Similarly, what Frazier calls "a small intellectual

[59] St. Clair Drake and Horace Cayton, *Black Metropolis* (New York: Harcourt, Brace, 1945), pp. 412–16.

[60] *Youth in the Ghetto* (New York: Harlem Youth Opportunities Unlimited, 1964), p. 111.

[61] Myrdal, *op. cit.,* pp. 866–67.

[62] Ruby F. Johnston, *The Development of Negro Religion* (New York: Philosophical Library, 1954), pp. 129–30.

fringe among middle-class Negroes" has affiliated with the Unitarian Church. He sees these affiliations on the part of Negroes as attempts to enhance their professional and social status and to lose their racial identity.[63]

The Roman Catholic Church in America is predominately a white church. However, it has never been so segregated in its services as Protestant churches are.[64] In many areas of the South the Roman Catholic Church is the only church which black people have traditionally attended along with white worshipers. Because of its rigid hierarchical structure, the Catholic Church has the advantage over Protestant churches in that integration can be imposed from the top of the organization. Catholic schools and other facilities in the South were among the first to desegregate their facilities, although not without strong resistance from Catholic laymen. Because of its racial attitudes regarding religious services, the Catholic Church has tripled its black membership in less than three decades.[65]

The typical black church attempts to serve its members as well as God. The 11 o'clock Sunday morning service is usually the main event of the day, although many of the churches conduct Sunday evening services as well. Sunday school is maintained for the children, and there is usually a variety of other services, such as special rallies, women's day, children's day, and other services conducted during the week. There are numerous men's and women's organizations associated with the church. The church building may be used for a variety of functions, including meetings for community organizations, social events, concerts, and mass meetings. In many ways the black church building serves as a community center for social and civic activities.

The foregoing description is characteristic of the urban black Protestant church, the predominant black church. Rural churches in the South and the many urban sects differ in some regards. The rural church remains more conservative and other-worldly than its urban counterpart. It is more emotional in its services, and the members participate more freely. Frazier describes a typical rural service as follows:

> After the congregation has assembled, someone—usually a deacon or a prominent member—"raises a hymn," that is, begins singing. The noise dies down, and, as the singer's voice grows in volume, the congregation joins in the singing. The singing is followed by a prayer by a deacon, which

[63] Frazier, *The Negro Church in America*, pp. 76–81.

[64] See Joseph H. Fichter, "American Religion and the Negro," in Parsons and Clark, *op. cit.*, pp. 401–22.

[65] *The Negro Handbook*, p. 307.

is approved by "Amens" on the part of the congregation. Then follow more spontaneous singing and prayer. After this comes the sermon, which is characterized by much dramatization on the part of the minister. Members of the audience express their approvals by "Amens," groans, and such expressions as "Preach it," and "Yes, Lord." As the minister reaches the climax, "shouting" or a form of ecstatic dancing begins. The contagion often spreads until most of the congregation is "shouting." As the "shouting" dies down, someone—very likely the minister, who has not lost control of the services—"raises a hymn." Afterward the minister turns to such practical matters as collection and announcements concerning future services.[66]

Rural black churches in the South are usually small, wood structures. They are unpretentious and are frequently dilapidated. Ministers lack formal religious training, and in the 1930's a vast majority of them had completed no more formal education than grammar school.[67] Their sermons are usually other-worldly in their content, having no relevance to the day-to-day lives of their worshipers. Nevertheless, the rural church is perhaps the outstanding social institution among rural Negroes. It serves as a means of escape from the harsh lives they lead. Furthermore, it is the medium through which the community maintains its social cohesion.

With increasing urbanization and the changing character of Baptist and Methodist services, many rural black migrants have flocked to store-front churches, which do not differ significantly in their services from the rural church. Still other black people have flocked to the many new cults which have developed.[68] Some of these cults seek to "purify" Christianity by requiring their members to reject "sinful" activities, such as drinking alcoholic beverages, dancing, playing cards, and swearing. Perhaps the best known of the Holiness sects are the Father Divine Peace Mission Movement and the Unified House of Prayer for All People, founded by Bishop Charles Emanuel Grace. Other cults have rejected Christianity and are linked to the non-Christian religions of the world. These churches include the Church of God (or Black Jews), the Moorish Science Temple of America, and, more recently, the Nation of Islam. These cults represent a radical departure from Christianity, and services are frequently conducted in languages other than English, such as Hebrew and Arabic.

The Church and Civil Rights

The Montgomery Bus Boycott, originating in 1955, signaled the beginning, in modern times, of mass direct action on the part of black people

[66] E. Franklin Frazier, *The Negro in the United States* (New York: Macmillan, 1957), p. 351.

[67] Mays and Nicholson, *op. cit.*, pp. 238–41.

[68] Frazier, *The Negro Church in America*, pp. 55–57.

to improve their status in the United States.[69] The bus boycott was organized and led by the late Martin Luther King, Jr., a Baptist minister who had become the acknowledged leader of the movement for greater civil rights for America's Negroes. It is unlikely that the success of this act of mass protest could have been achieved without the involvement of the black church. Since the Civil War the black church has been the most cohesive social institution in the black community. Therefore it was inevitable that the church would play a dominant role in any emerging movement for greater civil rights. Historically, the black church played an insignificant role in matters pertaining to civil rights, concentrating rather on other-worldly matters in adherence to the norm of the larger society—that the church should not involve itself in politics. Radical social action is not alien to black religion, however. Three of the most famous of the slave insurrections were led by black ministers, Gabriel Prosser, Nat Turner, and Denmark Vesey. But the discrepancy between Christian teachings and American social practices served to thrust the black church into the forefront of the black rebellion against segregation and discrimination.

Since the Montgomery Bus Boycott, the civil rights movement has changed strategy on occasion, but it has remained an essentially religious movement. Moreover, it has belatedly involved white religious leaders and laymen as well as Negroes. Initially the civil rights movement was strongly tied to such Christian precepts as love of one's adversary and nonviolent resistance. Response on the part of many white Americans, especially in the South, has led many black people to question the wisdom of these techniques. Although, until his assassination in April 1968, Martin Luther King remained the undisputed leader of the black protest movement, his strategy had been questioned.[70] For example, during the summer of 1964, in Mississippi alone, white Christians bombed or burned 34 Negro churches. These churches had long been sanctuaries in which blacks could be immune to outside intrusion. These and hundreds of similar acts of violence, including the murder of ministers, have led black people to question the notion that nonviolence and love disarm one's adversary.

Civil rights protest meetings, voter registration drives, mass action demonstrations, and "freedom schools" continue to be held in churches, and black ministers continue to play a dominant role in civil rights activities. The role of the black church in the protest movement has

[69] Martin Luther King, *Stride Toward Freedom* (New York: Harper and Brothers, 1958).

[70] See Kenneth Clark, "The Civil Rights Movement: Momentum and Organization," in Parsons and Clark, *op. cit.*, pp. 595–625.

accounted for much of the movement's early success in breaking down barriers of segregation in the South. The protest movement had its origins in religion.[71] Negro ministers continue to occupy leadership positions in civil rights activities. Furthermore, because of its religious orientation, thousands of white religious leaders and laymen have been impelled to align themselves with the black protest movement.[72] Hundreds of white clergymen have been arrested in civil rights demonstrations, and during the civil rights march from Selma to Montgomery, Alabama, in March 1965, leaders of each of the major religious organizations were either present or represented as a means of demonstrating their support. In recent years the leaders of each of the national organizations representing the three major religious groups in the United States—Protestants, Catholics, and Jews—have appealed to their followers to discontinue practices of segregation and discrimination in religious worship, education, employment, and housing and to adopt attitudes of love and brotherhood toward Negroes.

Both the role of the black church in civil rights protest activities and the religiousness of black people have been noted. The question of the link between these two elements might be raised. That is, does religion serve as a deterrent or motivation for civil rights activities? In a recent nationwide survey of black people an attempt was made to answer this question.[73] In general it was found that greater religious involvement was accompanied by diminished militancy in civil rights. Furthermore, Negroes who were members of predominantly black denominations, such as Baptists and Methodists, were less militant about civil rights than those who were members of predominantly white denominations, such as Episcopalians, members of the United Church of Christ, Presbyterians, and Catholics. The members of the various religious sects and cults were the least militant. The author concludes: "Until such time as religion loosens its hold over these people or comes to embody to a greater extent the belief that man as well as God can bring about secular change, and focuses more on the here and now, religious involvement may be seen as an important factor working against the radicalization of the Negro public." [74] Nevertheless, the church has been the focal point of organizing for protest, and a small minority of militant ministers have been powerful catalysts without which the movement might never have achieved the success it has.

[71] See Carleton L. Lee, "Religious Roots of the Negro Protest," in Rose, *op. cit.*, pp. 45–71.

[72] Fichter, *op. cit.*, pp. 401–22.

[73] Gary T. Marx, "Religion: Opiate or Inspiration of Civil Rights Militancy Among Negroes," *American Sociological Review*, Vol. 32 (February 1967), 64–72.

[74] *Ibid.*, p. 72. Used by permission of The American Sociological Association.

•   •   •

Three of the primary social institutions in the black community are the family, politics, and religion. Each of these institutions generally parallels its counterpart in the larger society, but each has its distinct elements. The differences result from a long history of oppression, and there is some evidence that urbanization and improvements in standard of living are serving to minimize the differences. This fact is especially true of family patterns and religious practices. The likelihood is, however, that because of the racist nature of American society, and because of increasing black consciousness, the distinctive aspects of these institutions will persist.

Politics is perhaps the institution in which the greatest changes have taken place in recent years. Armed with the vote, black people are turning to politics as a means of forcing the society to address itself to the needs of their communities.

SELECTED BIBLIOGRAPHY

Aiken, Charles, *The Negro Votes*. San Francisco: Chandler Publishing Co., 1962.

Banfield, Edward, and James Q. Wilson, *City Politics*. Cambridge, Mass.: Harvard University Press, 1963.

Bernard, Jessie, *Marriage and the Family Among Negroes*. Englewood Cliffs, N.J.: Prentice-Hall, Inc., 1966.

Blood, Robert A., Jr., and Donald M. Wolfe, *Husbands and Wives*. Glencoe, Ill.: Free Press, 1960.

Brogan, D. W., *Politics in America*. New York: Harper and Brothers, 1954.

Du Bois, W. E. B., *Black Reconstruction*. New York: Harcourt, Brace and Co., 1935.

Frazier, E. Franklin, *Black Bourgeoisie*. Glencoe, Ill.: Free Press, 1957.

———, *The Negro Church in America*. New York: Schocken Books, Inc., 1964.

———, *The Negro Family in the United States*. Chicago: The University of Chicago Press, 1966.

Hunter, Floyd, *Community Power Structure*. Chapel Hill, N.C.: The University of North Carolina Press, 1953.

Johnston, Ruby F., *The Development of Negro Religion*. New York: Philosophical Library, Inc., 1954.

King, Martin Luther, Jr., *Stride Toward Freedom*. New York: Harper and Brothers, 1958.

Lewinson, Paul, *Race, Class, and Party*. New York: Oxford University Press, Inc., 1932.

Matthews, Donald R., and James W. Prothro, *Negroes in the New Southern Politics*. New York: Harcourt, Brace & World, Inc., 1966.

Mays, Benjamin E., and Joseph W. Nicholson, *The Negro's Church*. New York: Institute of Social and Religious Research, 1933.

Myrdal, Gunnar, *An American Dilemma: The Negro Problem and Modern Democracy*. New York: Harper and Brothers, 1944.

The Negro Handbook. Chicago: Johnson Publishing Company, 1966.

Pettigrew, Thomas F., *A Profile of the Negro American*. Princeton, N.J.: D. Van Nostrand Co., Inc., 1964.

Silberman, Charles, *Crisis in Black and White*. New York: Random House, Inc., 1964.

U.S. Department of Labor, Office of Policy Planning and Research, *The Negro Family: The Case for National Action*. Washington, D.C.: Government Printing Office, 1965.

Wilson, James Q., "The Changing Political Position of the Negro," in *Assuring Freedom to the Free*, ed. Arnold Rose. Detroit: Wayne State University Press, 1964.

———, *Negro Politics: The Search for Leadership*. Glencoe, Ill.: Free Press, 1960.

Youth in the Ghetto. New York: Harlem Youth Opportunities Unlimited, Inc., 1964.

"I can conceive of no Negro native to this country who has not, by the age of puberty, been irreparably scarred by the conditions of his life. . . . The wonder is not that so many are ruined but that so many survive." [1] This statement by James Baldwin capsules the role of environmental factors in producing in black Americans deviations from the professed norms of the larger society. Black people are forced to live under harsh conditions in the United States; yet high standards of civic responsibility are expected of them.

No discussion of social deviance among black Americans can ignore the role of racism in American life. Individuals, social agencies, and social institutions responsible for the enforcement of social norms in American society operate within a long-established framework which precludes equality of treatment for black citizens. In no case is this situation more pronounced than in the relationship between the police and the black community. Policemen, like citizens in general, operate with a set of assumptions about black people which predisposes them to differential treatment.[2] In this regard policemen do not differ significantly from other public officials in the United States. Therefore such circumstances must enter into any discussion of the extent and causes of social deviance among black people in the United States.

Social Deviance

In this chapter attention is focused on three areas in which behavior is reported to exceed the "tolerance limit of the community." [3] Crime and delinquency, mental illness, and drug addiction have been selected because of the availability of research findings in these areas and because other areas (e.g., family disorganization) are discussed elsewhere.

CRIME AND DELINQUENCY

Statistics on crime and delinquency in the United States are notoriously inaccurate. In addition to differences among various administrative agencies in compiling statistics on criminal and delinquent behavior,

[1] James Baldwin, *Notes of a Native Son* (Boston: Beacon Press, 1957), p. 71.
[2] See, for example, Aaron V. Cicourel, *The Social Organization of Juvenile Justice* (New York: Wiley, 1968); Jerome H. Skolnick, *Justice Without Trial: Law Enforcement in Democratic Society* (New York: Wiley, 1966).
[3] See Marshall B. Clinard, *Sociology of Deviant Behavior* (New York: Holt, 1963), pp. 22–31.

special problems arise in connection with black people.[4] The position occupied by black people in a racist society means that they are more likely than whites to be arrested, indicted, and convicted. Furthermore, black people are less likely than white persons to receive probation, parole, suspended sentence, pardon, or commutation of the death sentence.[5] In short, black people are discriminated against in the administration of justice, just as they are in virtually every aspect of American life. The relative proportion of crimes recorded for black people, therefore, must be questioned.

For a variety of reasons, official statistics on Negro criminality are exaggerated.[6] Many acts that are considered crimes among black persons are not so considered when they are committed by white persons. In several political subdivisions laws relating to such practices as segregation and vagrancy are especially designed for black people. Black men have been arrested and convicted for such acts as "looking at a white woman" and refusing to comply with the racial etiquette of the South. Black people are frequently blamed and falsely convicted for crimes which have actually been committed by white persons.

Black people are especially vulnerable to misuse of power by the police. Police sometimes arrest Negroes on the slightest suspicion and obtain "confessions" through the excessive use of force. Similarly, Negroes are often arrested in police raids as a means of earning fees. Once arrested, Negroes face a series of acts of discrimination in the courts, on the part of juries, judges, and prosecutors. Anti-Negro prejudice on the part of court officials frequently results in Negroes' being convicted for crimes which they have not committed. One of the most clear-cut cases of discriminatory behavior is the disproportionately high percentage of black people executed under capital punishment. For example, between 1930 and 1963, 54 percent of the 3,833 persons executed in the United States were black.[7]

Because they are poor and frequently unable to pay fines, convicted Negroes are less likely than convicted white persons to escape prison sentences. On their arrival at prison, Negroes again encounter a series of acts of discrimination. Prison officials share the same anti-Negro

[4] See, for example, Ronald H. Beattie, "Problems of Criminal Statistics in the United States," *The Journal of Criminal Law, Criminology and Police Science*, Vol. 46 (July–August 1955), 178–86.
[5] See Donald Cressy, "Crime," *Contemporary Social Problems*, eds. Robert K. Merton and Robert A. Nisbet (New York: Harcourt, Brace, 1966), pp. 151–53; Guy B. Johnson, "The Negro and Crime," *The Annals of the American Academy of Political and Social Science*, Vol. 271 (September 1941), 93–104; Gunnar Myrdal, *An American Dilemma* (New York: Harper, 1944), pp. 966–79.
[6] This discussion relies heavily on Johnson, *op. cit.*, pp. 95–103.
[7] *The Negro Handbook* (Chicago: Johnson Publishing Co., 1966), p. 111.

prejudice that pervades the larger society. Black prisoners are frequently required to perform the most difficult work tasks. They are less likely to be pardoned because they cannot usually exert the political pressure necessary for such acts. Similarly, they are discriminated against in the use of parole as a method of release and rehabilitation.

Despite the many shortcomings in collecting crime statistics and in the administration of justice for black people, official reports usually form the basis for estimating the extent of criminal behavior in the United States. These statistics report that the crime rate for black people exceeds that for whites in all categories. The proportionate number of arrests is greater, as is the rate of commitments to state and federal prisons.

Crime

Official crime statistics in the United States have been reported yearly since 1930 by the Federal Bureau of Investigation (FBI) of the Department of Justice. These data are based on the number of arrests reported by police departments throughout the United States. In 1965 reports were received from law enforcement agencies having jurisdiction over 92 percent of the population. Reports are made in accordance with a handbook supplied to local law enforcement officials by the FBI. This handbook outlines the procedures for scoring and classifying crimes. Thus the annual report of the FBI is the most comprehensive index of arrests available.

According to the 1965 report, Negroes, comprising 10.8 percent of the population, accounted for 28.4 percent of the arrests for criminal acts (see Table 6–1). The proportion of arrests varied by offenses charged. Nearly three-fourths (73.2 percent) of all persons arrested for gambling were Negroes, compared with only 14.2 percent of the persons arrested for embezzlement. In all categories of offenses, however, the rate of arrests for black people was higher than that for white persons. Assuming that the arrests reported by the FBI represent a reasonably reliable indicator of conventional crimes committed in the United States, arrests for specific offenses in which Negroes significantly exceed their proportion in the total population may provide some clues to an explanation of differential rates of criminality among black and white persons.

Inspection of the table reveals little about the crimes for which black people are arrested other than the general observation that they were vastly overrepresented in the total arrests when compared with their numbers in the population. However, a few patterns emerge. (1) The rate of arrests for those crimes which are defined as "serious" (the

TABLE 6–1

TOTAL ARRESTS AND NEGRO ARRESTS, UNITED STATES,
1965

Offense Charged	Total	Negro	Percent Negro
All Arrests	4,743,123	1,347,994	28.4
1. Criminal homicide			
(a) murder and nonnegligent manslaughter	6,509	3,704	56.9
(b) manslaughter by negligence	2,457	541	22.0
2. Forcible rape	9,328	4,665	50.0
3. Robbery	39,854	22,546	56.6
4. Aggravated assault	70,285	36,558	52.0
5. Burglary (breaking and entering)	181,429	59,673	32.9
6. Larceny (theft)	364,072	109,792	30.2
7. Auto theft	93,108	26,372	28.3
8. Other assaults	193,475	73,284	37.9
9. Arson	5,516	1,127	20.4
10. Forgery and counterfeiting	27,477	5,440	19.8
11. Fraud	49,537	8,252	16.6
12. Embezzlement	6,781	966	14.2
13. Stolen property (buying, receiving, or possessing)	15,869	5,463	34.4
14. Vandalism	82,798	16,074	19.4
15. Weapons: carrying, possessing, etc.	49,731	26,226	52.7
16. Prostitution and commercialized vice	30,635	17,598	57.4
17. Sex offenses (except forcible rape and prostitution)	53,422	13,759	25.7
18. Narcotic drug laws	31,294	12,069	38.6
19. Gambling	86,627	64,135	73.2
20. Offenses against family and children	59,958	19,699	32.9
21. Driving under the influence of alcohol	231,899	38,966	16.8
22. Liquor laws	167,815	31,929	19.0
23. Drunkenness	1,516,548	354,158	23.4
24. Disorderly conduct	503,849	179,506	35.6
25. Vagrancy	115,305	28,161	24.4
26. All other offenses (except traffic)	511,121	135,946	26.6
27. Suspicion	76,183	21,721	28.8
28. Curfew and loitering violations	71,138	14,521	20.4
29. Runaways	88,103	15,142	17.2

Source: Compiled from Federal Bureau of Investigation, *Uniform Crime Reports—1965*, Table 25, p. 117.

first seven in the table) was greater than for "minor" crimes. For example, black people accounted for at least one-half of the arrests for murder and nonnegligent manslaughter, forcible rape, robbery, and aggravated assault. (2) The arrest rate for black people was lowest for crimes which are directly related to socioeconomic status. These crimes, which include forgery and counterfeiting, fraud, and embezzlement, generally involve the use and misappropriation of money and defrauding. They usually involve larger financial transactions than Negroes are capable of engaging in *and* positions in the social structure of business which are usually denied black people. (3) The arrest rate for black people was especially high for the illegal possession of weapons (52.7 percent of total), prostitution and commercialized vice (57.4 percent of total), and gambling (73.2 percent of total). The latter two crimes are clearly related to the precarious economic position which black people occupy, whereas the possession of weapons is no doubt a function of the frustrations which result from this depressed state.

The arrest rate for black people may be compared with the rate of court commitments involving felony prisoners and with the characteristics of prisoners in state prisons. In 1960 black people accounted for 35 percent of all court commitments for felony prisoners and 38.7 percent of all prisoners confined in state prisons.[8] There is a sizable discrepancy between the arrest rate of black people (30 percent of the total in 1960), the rate of court commitments, and the proportion of prisoners in state prisons. This discrepancy between arrests and commitments represents, among other things, discrimination on the part of court personnel, the inability of black people to pay cash fines in lieu of prison sentences, and the lack of access to bail and efficient legal counsel. The discrepancy between the rate of commitment and the state prison census no doubt reflects discrimination against black people insofar as pardon and parole are concerned.

Despite the shortcomings enumerated above, it is likely that black people commit a disproportionately high percentage of crimes in the United States.[9] Numerous reasons for this phenomenon may be advanced. (1) In the United States black people occupy a separate and subordinate economic and social position which leads to frustration. Their frustrations are usually displaced in acts of aggression against fellow Negroes, thus leading to a high proportion of intraracial criminal acts. (2) As Myrdal has demonstrated, the caste system under which black people live operates in such a way as to prevent them from identifying with the society and the law. The very legal system itself is manipulated

[8] U.S. Department of Justice, Federal Bureau of Prisons, *National Prisoner Statistics* (Washington, D.C.: Federal Bureau of Prisons, 1960), pp. 40, 57.

[9] See, for example, J. T. Blue, "The Relationship of Juvenile Delinquency, Race, and Economic Status," *Journal of Negro Education,* Vol. 17 (Fall 1948), 469–77; Earl R. Moses, "Differentials in Crime Rates Between Negroes and Whites Based on Comparisons of Four Socio-Economically Equated Areas," *American Sociological Review,* Vol. 12 (August 1947), 411–20.

to discriminate against black peope.[10] (3) Black persons, far more than white persons, are forced to live in deteriorated sections of cities. These areas are characterized by widespread social disorganization and organization in terms of criminal values, as well as poverty, poor housing, restrictions on settlement, and limited outlets for recreation and employment. "Out of these and similar conditions arise elements conducive to greater criminality, as well as other forms of pathology, among the Negro population." [11] (4) The high crime rate among black people is partially a function of their reaction to having their means to success blocked by discriminatory behavior. "Crime may thus be utilized as a means of escape, ego enhancement, expression of aggression, or upward mobility." [12] Black people have internalized the cultural goals of the larger society, but the socially acceptable means for achieving these goals are unavailable to them. (5) Black people are overrepresented in the lower class, and recorded crime tends to be concentrated in this class.[13] "White-collar crime," the middle- and upper-class specialty, is far less likely to be recorded as such.[14] Lower-class people, both black and white, live in a society in which they are surrounded by affluence, yet they must live in poverty. The association between economics and recorded crime is a pronounced one.

Juvenile Delinquency

It is impossible to estimate the amount of juvenile crime committed in the United States for the same reasons that statistics on crime in general are unreliable indicators of criminal behavior.[15] Age, rather than offense, is the defining characteristic of juvenile delinquents, and the age at which an offender is defined as a juvenile varies from state to state. Usually, however, juveniles are defined as persons under the age of 18. As with adults, black youths are far more likely to be arrested for criminal acts than white youths. In 1965, for example, the FBI re-

10 Myrdal, op. cit., pp. 975–76.

11 Moses, op. cit., p. 420; See also Albert K. Cohen, Delinquent Boys (Glencoe, Ill.: Free Press, 1955); and W. B. Miller, "Lower Class Culture as a Generating Milieu of Gang Delinquency," Journal of Social Issues, Vol. 14 (1958), 5–19.

12 Thomas F. Pettigrew, A Profile of the Negro American (Princeton, N.J.: Van Nostrand, 1964), p. 156.

13 Albert J. Reiss, Jr., and Albert L. Rhodes, "The Distribution of Juvenile Delinquency in the Social Structure," American Sociological Review, Vol. 26 (October 1961), 720–32; Calvin F. Schmid, "Urban Crime Areas: Part I," American Sociological Review, Vol. 25 (August 1960), 527–42; Calvin F. Schmid, "Urban Crime Areas: Part II," American Sociological Review, Vol. 25 (October 1960), 655–78.

14 E. H. Sutherland, White Collar Crime (New York: The Dryden Press, 1949).

15 See Albert K. Cohen and James F. Short, "Juvenile Delinquency," in Merton and Nisbet (eds.), op. cit., pp. 90–91.

ported that Negroes accounted for 23 percent of all arrests of persons under 18 years of age.[16] Other investigations corroborate these findings.[17] The same factors operating to inflate the Negro crime rate in general must be considered in any discussion of juvenile delinquency among Negroes. Black youths encounter the same types of discrimination as do black adults. Studies report that black youths accused of criminal acts are more likely to be institutionalized than white youths and that they are likely to be committed younger, for less serious offenses, and with fewer court appearances.[18]

Even when allowances are made for discrimination against black youths and for inaccuracies in reporting, rates of juvenile delinquency among Negroes are reported to be especially high compared to white youths in large urban centers. For example, between 1951 and 1962 the rate for central Harlem was reported to be at least twice as high as the rate for New York City as a whole.[19] Data on delinquency from predominantly Negro sections of several other cities—St. Louis, Missouri; Boston, Massachusetts; Minneapolis, Minnesota; Cleveland, Ohio; and Syracuse, New York—indicate that the rates in these sections vary anywhere from twice to four times the rates for the cities as a whole.[20] It is reported that in 1960, almost one-third (31 percent) of the juvenile delinquents in the Lexington, Kentucky, Standard Metropolitan Statistical Area were Negroes, although nonwhites comprised only 15 percent of the population from ages 5 to 19.[21] The likelihood, then, is that Negro (and other minority) youths commit a disproportionately high percentage of acts of juvenile crime in the United States.

In addition to factors contributing to the high crime rate among black people in general (as enumerated above), black youths in the

[16] Federal Bureau of Investigation, *Uniform Crime Reports—1965* (Washington, D.C.: Government Printing Office, 1966), p. 118.

[17] Joseph H. Douglass, "The Extent and Characteristics of Juvenile Delinquency Among Negroes in the United States," *Journal of Negro Education,* Vol. 28 (Summer 1959), 214–29.

[18] Sidney Axelrod, "Negro and White Male Institutionalized Delinquents," *American Journal of Sociology,* Vol. 57 (May 1952), 569–74; Mary H. Diggs, "Some Problems and Needs of Negro Children as Revealed by Comparative Delinquency and Crime Statistics," *Journal of Negro Education,* Vol. 19 (1950), 290–97; Irving Piliavin and Scott Briar, "Police Encounters with Juveniles," *American Journal of Sociology,* Vol. 60 (September 1964), 206–14.

[19] *Youth in the Ghetto* (New York: Harlem Youth Opportunities Unlimited, 1964), p. 138.

[20] Kenneth Clark, *Dark Ghetto* (New York: Harper & Row, 1965), pp. 86–87.

[21] James K. Ball, Alan Ross, and Alice Simpson, "Incidence and Estimated Prevalence of Recorded Delinquency in a Metropolitan Area," *American Sociological Review,* Vol. 29 (February 1964), 90–93.

United States are distinguishable from youths in the dominant society in ways which are likely to contribute to nonconforming behavior. Even when compared with black adults, black youths are especially vulnerable to arrest. For example, in one city where two-thirds of the police interviewed openly admitted anti-Negro prejudice, a policeman was asked why he had apprehended a Negro youth. He replied that he "looked suspicious," which he explained by saying, "He was a Negro wearing dark glasses at midnight." [22] The appearance of black youths frequently corresponds to the policeman's perception of the confirmed delinquent.

The family in which the black youth lives serves to contribute to nonconforming behavior as defined by the dominant middle-class society. The black family, with its lower-class status, is more likely than the white family to be characterized by disorganization.[23] The family is frequently incomplete, often lacking the father. The incidence of juvenile delinquency among children from broken homes is greater than among children who come from homes where both parents are present. In such families the mother is frequently required to work outside the home, and the child lacks parental supervision or guidance. Interpersonal relations between parents and children in lower-class families are frequently characterized by indifference, hostility, fear, and the absence of sympathy and kindness. These elements are reported to be associated with delinquency in youth.[24]

Within the black community the youths frequently see aggressive behavior as a means of obtaining and maintaining status.[25] Having been rejected, as well as subjected to constant threats, by the larger society and by middle-class Negroes, these youths resort to aggressive behavior. "Deviant conduct, therefore, might be approached as a nonconforming means of survival in a segregated, presumably hostile society." [26] Techniques are thereby developed for dealing with the emotional frustrations which black youths encounter.

Finally, acts of deviance on the part of black youths are much more likely to come to the attention of official agencies than are those of white youths.[27] Deviant acts on the part of white youths are more likely to be

[22] Piliavin and Briar, *op. cit.*, p. 212.

[23] Ruth S. Cavan, "Negro Family Disorganization and Juvenile Delinquency," *Journal of Negro Education*, Vol. 28 (Summer 1959), 230–39.

[24] See Sheldon Glueck and Eleanor Glueck, *Unraveling Juvenile Delinquency* (Cambridge, Mass.: Harvard, 1950).

[25] Kenneth Clark, "Color, Class, Personality and Juvenile Delinquency," *Journal of Negro Education*, Vol. 28 (Summer 1959), 240–51.

[26] Mozell Hill, "The Metropolis and Juvenile Delinquency Among Negroes," *Journal of Negro Education*, Vol. 28 (Summer 1959), 278.

[27] Douglass, *op. cit.*, p. 215.

handled by private social agencies, whereas for black youths they are handled by legal authorities.

MENTAL ILLNESS

Statistics on the incidence of mental illness among black people are both insufficient and contradictory. Since black people are separated from the larger society by a caste barrier which relegates them to a precarious existence, the assumption is frequently made that they are more likely to be scarred by their existence than are white Americans. This theory holds that for black people the U.S. social environment is one of oppression and that this situation adversely affects their mental health. Numerous social pressures to which Negroes, more than white Americans, are exposed leave their impact on their personalities. Such circumstances, it is assumed, contribute to differentially high rates of mental illness among black people.

Mental illness is usually divided into two types, psychoses and psychoneuroses. Psychoses are more easily diagnosed and are therefore more often studied. However, studies show conflicting findings. For a period of some three decades one researcher had studied the incidence of mental illness among black persons, compared with white persons, in New York State. The statistics for New York State are reasonably complete for patients hospitalized for psychoses because they are collected by a central agency from both public and private hospitals. Malzberg reports that, in 1930 and 1931, the rate of first admissions of Negroes to mental hospitals or mental wards in other hospitals was 150.6 per 100,000 population, compared with 87.7 whites per 100,000 population, or a ratio of 1.7 to 1.[28] By 1939 both black and white rates had increased, but the Negro rate of increase is reported to have been greater—48 percent, compared with a 14-percent increase among whites.[29] He reports that, between 1948 and 1951, Negroes continued to have significantly higher rates of hospitalization for psychoses than whites.[30] Moreover, in 1960 and 1961, Negroes constituted only 8.4 percent of the population of New York State but accounted for 13.8 percent of the admissions to mental hospitals.[31] Although the differential between blacks and whites

[28] Benjamin Malzberg, *Statistical Data for the Study of Mental Disease Among Negroes in New York State, 1939–1941* (Albany, N.Y.: State Department of Mental Hygiene, 1955), p. 1.

[29] *Ibid.,* p. 9.

[30] Benjamin Malzberg, *The Mental Health of the Negro* (Albany, N.Y.: Research Foundation for Mental Hygiene, 1962).

[31] Benjamin Malzberg, *New Data on Mental Disease Among Negroes in New York State, 1960–1961* (Albany, N.Y.: Research Foundation for Mental Hygiene, 1965).

had diminished, blacks were still overrepresented in first admissions to mental hospitals in New York State.

The data from New York State show a persistent excess of psychoses among Negroes. Findings from other states frequently differ, however.[32] It is reported that in Pennsylvania from 1943 to 1947 the incidence of mental illness was higher for blacks than for whites. In South Carolina the numbers of Negroes in state mental hospitals in 1948 were proportionate to their numbers in the population. A comparable finding is reported for Mississippi from 1945 to 1947. Data from Louisiana report that the incidence of mental illness among whites was greater than among Negroes in 1941. A study in Illinois reports no greater incidence of psychoses among blacks than among whites in 1948.[33] A study of the Cincinnati, Ohio, General Hospital revealed that the proportion of Negro admissions to the psychiatric wards was not significantly higher than the ratio of Negroes in the population of that city.[34]

A recent, impressively comprehensive study in Baltimore, Maryland, reports that Negroes do not have higher rates of psychoses than do whites.[35] Data reported in this study are based on sample surveys and on public and private institutional rates. In state hospitals nonwhite rates were higher, but in private hospitals and Veterans Administration hospitals rates were higher among whites. And, among the noninstitutional population the white rate of psychosis was more than 10 times as great as the black rate. The overall rate from all sources in Baltimore was 9.46 per 1,000 whites, compared with 7.04 per 1,000 Negroes. Finally, a widely publicized study reported that in Virginia the rates of black mentally ill patients have always been higher than those for whites and that in recent years there has been a significant increase in the Negro rate.[36]

The findings from these diverse studies are so contradictory as to make generalizations hazardous. Nevertheless, the assumption that black people suffer disproportionately high rates of the most serious forms

[32] Data for Pennsylvania, South Carolina, and Louisiana are reported in Ernest Y. Williams and Claude P. Carmichael, "The Incidence of Mental Disease in the Negro," *Journal of Negro Education*, Vol. 18 (Summer 1949), 276–82.

[33] Helen V. McLean, "The Emotional Health of Negroes," *Journal of Negro Education*, Vol. 18 (Summer 1949), 283–90.

[34] A. B. Sclare, "Cultural Determinants in the Neurotic Negro," *British Journal of Medical Psychology*, Vol. 26 (1953), 279–88.

[35] Benjamin Pasamanick, "Some Misconceptions Concerning Differences in Racial Prevalence of Mental Disease," *American Journal of Orthopsychiatry*, Vol. 93 (January 1963), 72–86; Benjamin Pasamanick, "A Survey of Mental Disease in the Urban Population," *American Journal of Psychiatry*, Vol. 119 (October 1962), 299–305.

[36] David C. Wilson and Edna M. Lantz, "Culture Change and Negro State Hospital Admissions," *American Journal of Psychiatry*, Vol. 114 (July 1957), 25–32.

of mental illness persists.[37] Furthermore, two recent studies report an inverse correlation between social class and the incidence of psychoses.[38] Since Negroes are overrepresented among the poor, it might be expected that psychoses would be more prevalent among them. On the other hand, it is generally reported that white Americans, more than Negroes, are likely to suffer from psychoneuroses, the milder form of mental illness. Pasamanick reports that in Baltimore the rate of psychoneuroses among whites was more than twice as great as among blacks. The rate among whites was reported to be 62 per 1,000 population, compared with 28 per 1,000 among Negroes.[39] Williams and Carmichael report that the incidence of psychoneuroses among black people in state hospitals is much lower than among whites. In New York State it is reported that the rate of psychoneuroses among whites was three times as great as among Negroes from 1949 to 1951.[40] Both Hollingshead and Redlich, and Srole, et al., report a direct correlation between social class and the prevalence of psychoneuroses. Again, since black people are underrepresented among the middle class, it might be expected that the incidence of psychoneuroses among them would be lower than among white Americans. Although the data on psychoneuroses are less complete, they are also less contradictory than data on psychoses.

Psychoses are usually considered to be of two types, organic and functional. Studies reporting the differential incidence of mental illness among blacks and whites report that blacks are more likely to suffer from such organic psychoses as general paresis and alcoholic psychoses and from such functional psychoses as dementia praecox (schizophrenia); whites are more likely to suffer from manic depressive (functional) psychoses.[41] Pettigrew, after a review of studies of mental illness among Negroes, concluded: "Particular psychoses contribute disproportionately to the greater Negro rates. Schizophrenia, the bizarre condition of social withdrawal and personality disorganization, is especially frequent among Negro first admissions." [42] Therefore it is reported that the incidence of mental illness among black people is greater for both organic and functional psychoses.

37 Cf. Thomas F. Pettigrew, op. cit., p. 75.
38 See August B. Hollingshead and Frederick C. Redlich, Social Class and Mental Illness (New York: Wiley, 1958); Leo Srole et al., Mental Health in the Metropolis: The Midtown Manhattan Study (New York: McGraw-Hill, 1962).
39 Pasamanick, op. cit., p. 83.
40 Malzberg, New Data on Mental Disease . . . , pp. 58–59.
41 Malzberg, Statistical Data for the Study of Mental Disease . . . , pp. 4–6; Malzberg, New Data on Mental Disease . . . , pp. 51–59; Benjamin Malzberg, "Mental Disease Among Native and Foreign Born Negroes in New York State," Journal of Negro Education, Vol. 25 (Spring 1956), 175–81; Wilson and Lantz, op. cit., p. 32.
42 Pettigrew, op. cit., p. 75.

Pasamanick reports that in Baltimore nonwhites have higher rates of mental deficiency than do whites. He reports that between 1952 and 1955 the rate was 21.3 per 1,000 Negro population, compared with 13.2 per 1,000 white population. He attributes this difference to environmental (rather than hereditary) factors, such as lack of motivation and less stimulation among poor people.

Conflicting data on the differential incidence of mental illness among blacks and whites usually result from incompleteness and from difficulties in diagnosing mental illness. As one writer has concluded, ". . . inadequate appreciation of the sociological dimensions in the differential racial environments may lead the researcher or clinician to overlook variations in the development of the personality with consequent difficulties in assessing etiological factors, accurate diagnosis, or therapeutic proceedings." [43] Nevertheless, differentially high rates, when reported, are usually explained in terms of social factors. For example, the Malzberg studies explain the differential in New York State as a function of migration, which results in a more precarious standard of living. Furthermore, statistics are more often reported for public than private institutions. Because black people are overrepresented in the lower class, they are forced to seek treatment in public institutions, whereas white Americans seek care in private institutions or through noninstitutional arrangements. Black people are often denied treatment in private hospitals and clinics. Williams and Carmichael reported in 1949 that "No private institution in the United States at the present time will accept the Negro as a mental patient, and the number of whites treated in these institutions is difficult to evaluate. . . ." [44]

Data from Southern states which generally show that black people are proportionately represented in mental hospitals no doubt reflect a tendency to hospitalize only the most severe cases of mental illness among black people. This tendency may result in underenumeration. On the other hand, the overrepresentation of black people in some studies may reflect faulty diagnoses. Clinical studies on mental illness among black people which frequently report extreme paranoia may actually describe an accurate perception of the hostile environment in which they are forced to live. As Kardiner and Ovesey have written, "Such anxieties mean one thing in the white and another in the Negro. In the white they mean paranoid tendencies; but not in the Negro. For the latter, to see hostility in the environment is a normal perception." [45] Or, as Schermer-

[43] R. A. Schermerhorn, "Psychiatric Disorders Among Negroes: A Sociological Note," *American Journal of Psychiatry*, Vol. 112 (May 1956), 882.

[44] Williams and Carmichael, *op. cit.*, pp. 281–82.

[45] Abram Kardiner and Lionel Ovesey, *The Mark of Oppression* (New York: World, 1962), p. 343.

horn has written, ". . . mistakes in diagnosis could result from uncritical use of case history materials in a Negro patient, if given the same weight that they were given for a white patient. For example, the irregular school attendance or job history of a Negro patient may be less a sign of neurotic instability than of economic deprivation and the consequent ability to do nothing but odd jobs." [46]

The harshness of the environment in which black people are forced to live may contribute to their being reported as overrepresented among Americans suffering from functional psychoses. Studies indicate that the culture in which one lives plays an important role in the incidence of psychoses and that the incidence varies from culture to culture.[47] The effect of American culture on the personalities of black people has been summarized by Kardiner and Ovesey: Cultural factors ". . . force the Negro to live within the confines of a caste system which not only interferes seriously with all varieties of social mobility through class lines, but, simultaneously, tends to stifle effective protest by the threat of hostile retaliation by the majority of whites. Such oppression cannot but leave a permanent impact on the Negro's personality." [48] That living in a state of oppression in the United States has contributed to a disproportionately high incidence of mental illness among black people is usually assumed, but empirical data, where they exist, are so contradictory as to preclude firm generalizations.

DRUG ADDICTION

Data on the extent of drug addiction in the United States are extremely crude because the use of narcotics for nonmedical purposes is generally prohibited by federal, state, and municipal laws. Nonmedical users and dispensers of narcotics must exercise secrecy in these activities, and addicts usually become known only when they are arrested or when they seek treatment. Therefore, published statistics probably represent a small fraction of the narcotics addicts in the United States.

There are several types of addicting drugs commonly used in the United States. They may be classified in two broad types, stimulants and depressants.[49] The stimulants include cocaine, benzedrine, and mescaline. The depressants, which induce sleep and lessen nervous tension,

[46] Schermerhorn, op. cit., pp. 881–82.
[47] See Joseph W. Eaton and Robert J. Weil, Culture and Mental Disorders (New York: Free Press, 1955).
[48] Kardiner and Ovesey, op. cit., p. 11. For a review of cultural factors in mental illness in one Negro community see Seymour Parker and Robert J. Kleiner, Mental Illness in the Urban Negro Community (New York: Free Press, 1966).
[49] Facts About Narcotics Addiction (New York: Department of Health, n.d.).

include morphine and all its derivatives (e.g., heroin, dilaudid, and co-deine), synthetic analgesics (e.g., methadone and demerol), and the hypnotics and sedatives (e.g., bromides and the barbiturates). Although habitual marijuana use is considered a form of drug addiction by law-makers and narcotics control personnel, it is not considered by medical practitioners to be a form of drug addiction because it does not entail physiological dependence.

Recent statistics show that among drug addicts heroin (a depres-sant) is used by a vast majority.[50] An earlier study of 1,036 patients in a federal hospital for narcotic addicts reported that morphine was pre-ferred by the patients and that it was the first used and the last used by a majority of them. This drug was followed in expressed preference and usage by heroin.[51] The typical addict is likely to take heroin, morphine, or a similar drug intravenously. In recent years such practices as glue sniffing, gasoline addiction, and the use of hallucinogenic drugs (LSD–25, psilocybin, and mescaline) have reportedly increased, especially among younger Americans.

The Federal Bureau of Narcotics was created in 1930 to implement laws governing the use and sale of narcotics and to supervise the produc-tion and importation of these drugs. One of its primary functions is the apprehension of violators of an elaborate network of narcotics control laws. According to the Federal Bureau of Narcotics, which compiles sta-tistics on drug addiction from state police reports, there were approxi-mately 60,000 drug addicts in the United States in 1965. This figure is obviously a gross underenumeration, as one study estimated that there were 90,000 addicts in New York City alone.[52] Estimates of the number of narcotic addicts in New York vary widely. The Federal Bureau of Narcotics estimates the number at 35,000, the New York State Narcotic Addiction Control Commission estimates the number at 60,000, and the New York City Narcotics Coordinator estimates the number at 100,000.[53]

It is invariably reported that black people are overrepresented among drug addicts in the United States. The Federal Bureau of Nar-cotics reports that in 1965 more than one-half (51.6 percent) of all nar-cotics addicts in the United States were Negroes.[54] Similarly, the New

[50] Bureau of Narcotics, *Annual Report on Narcotic Addiction in the United States* (Washington, D.C.: Treasury Department, 1966), Table I.

[51] Michael J. Pescor, "A Statistical Analysis of the Clinical Records of Hospital-ized Drug Addicts," *Public Health Reports,* Supplement 143 (1938), Appendix, p. 24.

[52] *Report of Study of Drug Addiction Among Teenagers* (New York: Mayor's Committee on Drug Addiction, 1951).

[53] *The New York Times,* March 27, 1967, p. 26, col. 8. For a comprehensive report of narcotic drug use in the United States, see the series in *The New York Times,* January 8–12, 1968.

[54] Bureau of Narcotics, *Annual Report . . . .*

York City Health Department reports that 47.8 percent of all newly reported habitual users of narcotic drugs in 1964 were Negroes.[55] It is generally believed that from 40 to 60 percent of all addicts in the United States live in New York, and in central Harlem the rate is reported to be approximately seven times as high as that in New York City as a whole.[56]

Although data on drug addiction are inadequate, all available evidence indicates that black people are disproportionately represented among reported narcotic addicts. (It must be remembered, however, that the likelihood is that reported addicts represent a small proportion of those addicted to the use of narcotics.) A vast majority of known narcotic addicts use depressant drugs, such as heroin and morphine, which serve as a means of escape from the precarious existence which black people in the United States lead. Clausen describes their effects: "Their depressant actions include relief of pain, muscular relaxation, drowsiness or lethargy, and (before extreme tolerance has been developed) euphoria, a sense of well-being and contentment." [57] Similarly, other economically deprived groups, such as Puerto Ricans and Mexican Americans, are overrepresented among reported narcotic addicts. In 1965 Puerto Ricans accounted for 13.1 percent of all narcotic addicts reported by the Federal Bureau of Narcotics; Mexican Americans accounted for 5.6 percent.[58]

Drug addiction in the United States is an urban phenomenon. More than one-half (51.6 percent) of the addicts reported by the Federal Bureau of Narcotics live in New York, primarily in New York City. One-fourth live in California and Illinois, mainly in Los Angeles and Chicago. The remaining one-fourth live in other large cities, such as Detroit, Philadelphia, Washington, D.C., Baltimore, and Newark. Each of these cities contains large proportions of deprived Negroes. Drug addiction is most prevalent in urban areas because of the lack of institutional (family, religious) controls, the accessibility of supply, greater anonymity (decreasing the likelihood of detection), and the presence of social norms favorable to such behavior.

Drug addiction is most acute among young males. Approximately 82 percent of all reported addicts were male, and almost half (46.5 percent) of them were between the ages of 21 and 30. Fifty percent were over 30 years of age, and nearly 38 percent were between 31 and 40. Of addicts under 21 years of age, black youths were vastly overrepresented,

[55] *Narcotics Register Project, Report Number 1* (New York: Department of Health, 1966), Table 4.

[56] *Youth in the Ghetto*, pp. 144–45.

[57] John A. Clausen, "Drug Addiction," in Merton and Nisbet (eds.), *op. cit.*, p. 197.

[58] Federal Bureau of Narcotics, *Annual Report* . . . .

but the proportion is significantly lower than among the older addicts. Negroes constituted only one-fourth of the addicts under 21 years of age, and Puerto Ricans constituted another one-fifth. These figures indicate that within the category with the highest rates of unemployment, young adult black and Puerto Rican males, the rate of drug addiction is highest. Furthermore, the high rate of drug addiction among adolescents no doubt reflects the increasing use of drugs among middle-class white youth.

Drug addiction is most prevalent in those sections of metropolitan centers that are most often inhabited by members of ethnic minorities. Certain social characteristics prevail throughout these areas.[59] These areas have high rates of crime, prostitution, and illegitimacy. Family disorganization is widespread, and the areas are densely populated. Living quarters tend to be deteriorated, and families frequently live in cramped quarters, often with several people sharing a single bedroom. Mothers frequently work outside the home, and fathers experience difficulties providing support for the family. Children rely heavily on peer groups for support, which often results in gangs and other youth groups within which social pressures force experimentation with narcotics.

According to one researcher, a distinctive subculture of drug addicts exists.[60] Within this subculture the young drug addict displays a highly developed sense of taste in clothes, speaks with a distinctive vocabulary, thrives on the exploitation of women, and, in general, maintains a superior attitude accompanied by a disdain for work and the conventional daily routine. He is frequently able to live without working, and his main purpose in life is to experience the "kick," an unconventional experience which serves to distinguish him from those he defines as "squares." The ultimate "kick" is the use of heroin because of the extreme proscription on its use in conventional middle-class society.

The habitual use of narcotics is expensive. The New York City Health Department estimates that addicts require $75 a day for drugs. Because of the precarious economic existence of most reported addicts, such a sum of money is far beyond their means. Therefore it is said that they resort to other criminal acts to maintain their "habit." There is some evidence of a correlation between narcotics usage and crime; however, addicts are not prone to crimes of violence. Rather, their criminal behavior is likely to involve some type of theft. For example, "According

---

[59] See Clausen, *op. cit.*, pp. 210–12; Isidor Chein, "Narcotics Use Among Juveniles," in *Narcotic Addiction*, eds. John A. O'Donnell and John C. Ball (New York: Harper & Row, 1966), pp. 123–41.
[60] See Harold Finestone, "Cats, Kicks, and Color," *Social Problems*, Vol. 18 (July 1957), 3–13.

to 1951 Chicago data, arrests for nonviolent property offenses are proportionately higher among addicts, whereas arrests of addicts for violent offenses against the person, such as rape and aggravated assault, are only a fraction of the proportion among the population at large." [61] Addicts are most likely to be convicted of larceny and robbery.

Recent reports by the Federal Bureau of Narcotics show a decline in the number of narcotic addicts among black people. At the same time an increase in narcotic addicts is reported among whites. In the decade from 1956 to 1966 the proportion of Negro addicts is reported to have declined from 57.8 percent of the total to 40.2 percent.[62] Several explanations for this decline have been advanced: increasing racial pride, brought about by the civil rights movement; increased education on the effects of drug addiction; and increased observations by Negroes of the harmful effects of narcotics on relatives and friends.

The evidence indicates that black people are overrepresented among drug addicts in the United States. Despite the shortcomings of the data, they are persuasive. The daily experiences of black people, in many regards, are traumatic. They face indignities which most white persons are spared. The use of narcotizing drugs represents one means of escaping from a harsh environment.

●   ●   ●

Data on crime and delinquency, mental illness, and drug addiction among black Americans are inadequate and, in some cases, contradictory. However, it is frequently reported that black people contribute disproportionately high rates to each of these social problems in the United States. Because of discrimination in the administration of justice, the reported differentially high crime and delinquency rates among black people must be questioned. It is virtually impossible for black Americans to secure impartial treatment at any step in the judicial process. It is possible that black people commit proportionately more conventional crimes than white Americans, but economic and social factors are responsible. The racist nature of American society frequently forces them to resort to nonconforming behavior as a means of surviving the daily hazards to which they are subjected.

The inadequacy of statistics on mental illness renders the making of firm generalizations impossible. Furthermore, subcultural differences

61 Clinard, *op. cit.*, p. 312.
62 *The New York Times*, March 6, 1967, p. 1, col. 4.

between black Americans and mental heath personnel call the validity of such diagnoses into question. As a form of social deviance the extent of drug addiction as reported in official sources is questionable. The likelihood is, however, that the precarious existence which black people lead gives rise to disproportionately high rates of drug addiction.

When black people deviate disproportionately from the norms of society, such behavior must be explained as resulting from the social environment. These phenomena (crime and delinquency, mental illness, and drug addiction) are referred to as "social problems" because they are products of the society in which they are found. For black citizens American society is one which has, through the years, made it difficult for them to conform to standards of behavior which the society sets for all citizens.

SELECTED BIBLIOGRAPHY

Baldwin, James, *Notes of a Native Son*. Boston: Beacon Press, Inc., 1957.

Cicourel, Aaron V., *The Social Organization of Juvenile Justice*. New York: John Wiley & Sons, Inc., 1968.

Clark, Kenneth, *Dark Ghetto*. New York: Harper & Row, Publishers, 1965.

Clinard, Marshall B., *Sociology of Deviant Behavior*. New York: Holt, Rinehart & Winston, Inc., 1963.

Cohen, Albert K., *Delinquent Boys*. Glencoe, Ill.: Free Press, 1955.

Cressy, Donald, "Crime," in *Contemporary Social Problems*, eds. Robert K. Merton and Robert A. Nisbet. New York: Harcourt, Brace & World, Inc., 1966.

Crossack, Martin M., *Mental Health and Segregation*. New York: Springer Publishing Co., Inc., 1965.

Federal Bureau of Investigation, *Uniform Crime Reports—1965*. Washington, D.C.: Government Printing Office, 1966.

Glueck, Sheldon, and Eleanor Glueck, *Unraveling Juvenile Delinquency*. Cambridge, Mass.: Harvard University Press, 1950.

Hollingshead, August B., and Frederick C. Redlich, *Social Class and Mental Illness*. New York: John Wiley & Sons, Inc., 1958.

Jahoda, Marie, *Race Relations and Mental Health*. New York: Columbia University Press, 1960.

Kardiner, Abram, and Lionel Ovesey, *The Mark of Oppression*. New York: World Publishing Co., 1962.

Malzberg, Benjamin, *The Mental Health of the Negro*. Albany, N.Y.: Research Foundation for Mental Hygiene, 1962.

———, *Statistical Data For the Study of Mental Disease Among Negroes in New York State*. Albany, N.Y.: State Department of Mental Hygiene, 1955.

Parker, Seymour, and Robert Kleiner, *Mental Illness in the Urban Negro Community*. New York: Free Press, 1966.

Pettigrew, Thomas F., *A Profile of the Negro American*. Princeton, N.J.: D. Van
    Nostrand Co., Inc., 1964.
Skolnick, Jerome H., *Justice Without Trial: Law Enforcement in Democratic
    Society*. New York: John Wiley & Sons, Inc., 1966.
Srole, Leo, *et al.*, *Mental Health in the Metropolis: The Midtown Manhattan
    Study*. New York: McGraw-Hill Book Company, 1962.
Sutherland, E. H., *White Collar Crime*. New York: The Dryden Press, 1949.
U.S. Department of Justice, Federal Bureau of Prisons, *National Prisoner Statis-
    tics*. Washington, D.C.: Federal Bureau of Prisons, 1960.
Youth in the Ghetto. New York: Harlem Youth Opportunities Unlimited, Inc.,
    1964.

The black people who settled in North America brought with them representative elements of the elaborate cultures they left behind in Africa. Some of these African culture patterns have persisted, but the nature of slavery in North America was such that it precluded both the retention and the borrowing by whites of any appreciable amount of these cultural elements. The influence of the African culture on contemporary American life is perhaps most pronounced in music, religion, the dance, and language.[1] Individual black people have made notable contributions to all aspects of American life, and they have excelled in certain realms (e.g., sports and entertainment) in which they have not been perceived of as threats to the larger society; but the general pattern has been that the dominant society has rejected virtually all aspects of African cultures.

The nature of the contact between the slaves and the slaveholders was such that the blending of cultures which customarily occurs did not take place. The slaves were considered "uncivilized," and every aspect of their culture was considered inferior to that brought by the many Europeans who settled in North America. Furthermore, attempts were made systematically to strip these people of their native culture, while denying them the chance to participate in and

Contributions to American Life

thereby adopt the culture of the larger society. It therefore became necessary for the slaves to survive somehow in a world that was both strange and hostile. In the process of surviving, they developed a way of life which was geared toward making a difficult life livable.

The difficulties which black people continue to encounter in the United States have been enumerated previously. That they have managed to survive in the face of these difficulties is noteworthy. Moreover, they continue to make notable contributions to a society which has persistently denied them equal membership in it. In the realm of art, literature, and music, it has frequently been necessary for young Negroes to journey to Europe as "cultural exiles" to find an atmosphere that is conducive to creative expression. The nature of American society is such that it is impossible for a Negro to be simply a painter, a writer, or a musician. He is first and foremost a Negro, and whatever else he may be must be secondary to this fact. In a way, then, black Americans

[1] See Melville J. Herskovits, *The Myth of the Negro Past* (New York: Harper and Brothers, 1941).

have been isolated from the mainstream of the nation's cultural life. This isolation has had its impact on their creativity. Yet many of the contributions made by black people represent some of the most lasting contributions made by Americans to world culture.

In the present chapter attention is turned to the contributions of black people to American music, literature, the dance, and social values. The selection is somewhat arbitrary, and the omission of numerous other areas in no way implies the absence of contributions in these areas. In recreation, especially competitive sports, and in popular entertainment, black people have frequently contributed far in excess of their proportion in the population. Black people were publishing newspapers as early as 1827. They played significant roles in all the many wars in which the United States has been engaged. Scientists and inventors have been active since the middle of the 18th century, when a 22-year-old Negro constructed the first clock in America. The first blood bank was established by a black man, and the first heart operation was performed by a black surgeon. While most of their fellow Negroes were enslaved, many were excelling in higher education, the first attending college in 1774. The poetess Phillis Wheatley gained an international reputation for her verse as early as 1773. In 1821 a group of free Negroes established a theater known as the African Grove in New York's Greenwich Village, where they performed plays by Shakespeare.

A significant proportion of the entire wealth of what is now the United States came from the labor of black people. The magnitude of the economic contribution of black people is frequently overlooked. At the end of the slave era, some 4 million slaves, out of a total population of slightly more than 31 million, were enumerated. They constituted a free labor force of considerable magnitude. Slavery had been in existence for nearly two and one-half centuries, during which time all slaves, including children and the elderly, were required to work, often 16 to 18 hours daily. They received no compensation for their labor, and the cost of their maintenance was minimal. In addition to the various agricultural and domestic jobs, slaves on farms and in cities worked at a variety of other occupations.[2] They worked as engineers, carpenters, blacksmiths, brick makers, stonemasons, mechanics, shoemakers, weavers, lumber jacks, and in many other skilled occupations. Both the construction industry and the iron industry were dependent on slave labor. Almost every railroad in the antebellum South was constructed by slaves, and the iron industry also depended upon their labor. Slaveholders who did not have enough work for their slaves adopted the practice of hiring

[2] See Kenneth M. Stampp, *The Peculiar Institution* (New York: Knopf, 1956), pp. 34–85.

them out to others as a means of income. Virtually all of the wealth of the antebellum South was derived from the unpaid labor of the slaves. For nearly 100 years after slavery was abolished, the Negro labor force, especially in the South, was systematically exploited and controlled. The contribution of black Americans, then, has been an immense one.

Indeed, it is difficult to imagine what contemporary America would be like without the contributions of black people through the years. At the same time one can imagine how much greater the contributions of black people would have been if they had been responded to simply as people.

MUSIC

In many ways the music which developed from the experiences of black people in the United States stands as America's greatest artistic contribution to world culture. Its influence has been widespread within certain segments of the population in the United States and even more so abroad. Music developed by black people, especially jazz, has achieved the status of a universal language. Europeans study it seriously, and black American musicians abroad are frequently in greater demand than other artists. Margaret Just Butcher identifies three strains in the music of the Negro.[3] The first she identifies as Negro folk music, that "produced without formal musical training or intention by the greatest and most fundamental of all musical forces—emotional creation." This music includes the original work songs. The second strain she identifies as "light, mock-sentimental, full of pagan humor and sharp irony." This music— the blues—is the predecessor of much of contemporary American popular music and in its pure form is rare today. The third strain, a direct outgrowth of the second, is more highly stylized and formal. It is represented by the various forms of jazz.

The first African settlers in North America brought their native music with them.[4] These songs had accompanied their work in the fields in Africa, and in the United States this music served to make their difficult lives on Southern plantations somewhat less painful. Soon after their arrival, however, "work songs," as LeRoi Jones [5] calls them, or "sorrow songs," as Du Bois [6] calls them, developed. These songs be-

[3] Margaret Just Butcher, *The Negro in American Culture* (New York: Knopf, 1964), pp. 42–43.

[4] Marshall Stearns, *The Story of Jazz* (New York: Oxford University Press, 1956), especially Part I.

[5] LeRoi Jones, "Blues, Jazz, and the Negro," in *The American Negro Reference Book*, ed. John P. Davis (Englewood Cliffs, N.J.: Prentice-Hall, 1966), pp. 759–65.

[6] W. E. B. Du Bois, *The Souls of Black Folk* (Chicago: A. C. McLurg and Company, 1903), Chap. 14.

came distinctively American in character because of the different circumstances of the lives of black people. They were working in the fields of the slaveholders, rather than in their own fields, and references to African religion were suppressed by the slaveholders.[7] These songs represent the beginning of Negro music in the United States, and, like the music which evolved from them, they are a reflection of the social situation within which these uprooted people found themselves. This early Negro music has been persistently neglected and misunderstood by Americans. It has nevertheless persisted as the spiritual heritage of black Americans. As Du Bois writes, "They are the music of an unhappy people, of the children of disappointment; they tell of death and suffering and unvoiced longing toward a truer world, of misty wanderings and hidden ways."[8] These songs of an unhappy people contained an element of hope that ultimately justice would triumph, either in the present world or in the world beyond death.

Negro spirituals emerged from the earlier work songs somewhat before the advent of blues. These songs sprung up wherever black slaves happened to be—in the fields, in the kitchens, in the slave cabins, or in the forests. They served to bring some relief from the hardships facing these peasant people. The present-day spirituals, or what LeRoi Jones calls "Afro-Christian music,"[9] developed after black people were forced to abandon their native religions and after Christianity made its inroads among them. The spirituals are not wholly otherworldly. They "tell of hard trials, great tribulations; or wanderings in some lonesome valley, or down some unknown road, a long ways from home, with brother, sister, father, mother gone."[10] To a great degree these songs expressed the desire on the part of the black people to escape the hardships of their lives and to experience life in the Promised Land. These people saw no hope for improved living conditions. It was through their music that they were able to envision ultimate happiness.

The religious music of black people, most often represented by the spirituals, was essentially a new creation. Although it drew to some extent on the African religious music and the earlier work songs, it represented an amalgamation of diverse strains. Like most of the Negro music, it was a product of the circumstances under which these people lived, and the songs have persisted until the present time, no doubt because of their relevance to the continuing struggles of black Americans.

[7] LeRoi Jones, *Blues People* (New York: Morrow, 1963), pp. 19ff.

[8] Du Bois, *op. cit.*, p. 353.

[9] Jones, *Blues People*, Chap. 4.

[10] Sterling A. Brown, Arthur P. Davis, and Ulysses Lee (eds.), *The Negro Caravan* (New York: The Dryden Press, 1941), p. 419.

With emancipation, Negro music adapted to the circumstances of the freedmen. It differed from the earlier work songs in that it was sung for pleasure, and it differed from the religious music in that it was purely secular. The blues deals primarily with love. It represents the first purely secular Negro music sung for entertainment. In addition, blues saw the introduction of musical instruments. In this way blues served as a form of entertainment. Audiences could sit and listen to a blues singer re-create significant aspects of their lives. Unlike Negro spirituals, which were usually sung in groups, blues is generally sung by one person. LeRoi Jones distinguishes two types of early post-emancipation music among black people—primitive blues and classic blues.[11] Both were peculiarly Negro and grew out of the experiences of the time. Primitive blues was closer to the earlier work songs in both form and content, and musical instruments were not widely used. Although widespread social disorganization accompanied the emancipation of the slaves, they gained a degree of freedom of movement. They were able to move from city to city. Furthermore, they were not forced to work the conventional 16- or 18-hour day. Consequently there was time for rest and relaxation and for music.

Classic blues developed in the first decade of the 20th century, largely through the influence of traveling minstrel and vaudeville shows. It became a vehicle for entertaining the public, for it was less a recounting of personal experiences than primitive blues. That is, it was universal in its message. According to Sterling Brown, the universal appeal of the blues lies in its "elemental honesty, depth of insight, and strong original phrasing." Blues songs "belong with the best of folk poetry." [12] Whereas primitive blues singers were usually accompanied by one or two instruments—a guitar or a banjo—the classic blues singers tended to be accompanied by larger groups of instrumental musicians. The blues continues to appeal to large audiences. "The form is simple, but well adapted to express the laments of folk Negroes over hard luck, 'careless' or unrequited love, broken family life, or general dissatisfaction with a cold and trouble-filled world." [13] The blues contains an honesty and a frankness which are most often absent from popular American music. The lyrics are the most important folk poetry produced in the United States.

[11] Jones, *Blues People,* Chaps. 6 and 7.
[12] Sterling A. Brown, "The Blues," *Phylon* (Fourth Quarter 1952), p. 292.
[13] Brown, Davis, and Lee, *op. cit.,* pp. 426–27. One of the more perceptive studies of the blues is Charles Keil, *Urban Blues* (Chicago: The University of Chicago Press, 1966).

Classic blues served as a forerunner to jazz. The various stages of evolution through which jazz has gone, from boogie woogie to bebop, to progressive jazz, to the free jazz of the 1960's, represent an evolution of instrumental music derived from the blues. ". . . it is a new music of a certain distinct rhythmic and melodic character, one that constantly involves improvisation of a minor sort in creating music extemporaneously, on the spot." [14] Jazz is clearly the most cosmopolitan of Negro music, and it stands as one of the most significant artistic contributions in the history of the United States. Jazz has become popular, in part, because, as Stearns has written: "In a society of increasingly mass-produced, assembly-line entertainment, when every individual is treated like an empty pitcher to be filled from above, jazz retains something of the handicrafts of yesteryear. The print of the human spirit warms it." [15]

In recent years controversy has centered around whether white musicians are capable of playing jazz as well as Negroes.[16] Several black musicians and writers maintain that, since jazz comes from within the black people, white musicians are incapable of playing it and white critics are incapable of understanding it.[17] Jazz, according to this view, grew out of the various experiences which black people have encountered, and since white Americans have been spared these experiences, they are incapable of "feeling" jazz as a black person does. To use Nat Hentoff's phrase, "they have not paid the emotional 'dues'" which Negroes have been assessed from birth. Given the peculiar history of the black man in the United States, to label such an assertion as "reverse racism," as is frequently the case, is perhaps to render too hasty a judgment.

In addition to sacred and secular folk and popular music, black Americans have made their impact on music in other realms. For example, many talented composers, black and white, have used Negro thematic material in their compositions.[18] Among the more notable white composers are Anton Dvořak and Igor Stravinsky. And on the concert stage such gifted artists as Marian Anderson, Dorothy Maynor, Roland Hayes, Paul Robeson, Todd Duncan, Mattiwilda Dobbs, Carol Brice, Leontyne Price, William Warfield, Adele Addison, Lawrence

[14] Barry Ulanov, *A History of Jazz* (New York: The Viking Press, Inc., 1957), p. 7.

[15] Stearns, *op. cit.*, p. 306.

[16] See Nat Hentoff, *The Jazz Life* (New York: Dial Press, 1961), p. 251; George E. Simpson and J. Milton Yinger, *Racial and Cultural Minorities* (3rd ed.) (New York: Harper & Row, 1965), pp. 466–68.

[17] Sterling Brown, on the other hand, feels that "In the jazz world, white bands play instrumental music with real feeling." See his "The Blues," p. 291.

[18] See Zelma George, "Negro Music in American Life," in Davis (ed.), *op. cit.*, pp. 747–49.

Withers, Duke Ellington, and Dean Dixon have demonstrated that, given the chance, black people could achieve the highest realms of artistic performance as musicians.[19]

It is in the realm of popular music, however, that Negro music has made its greatest impact. As one authority has written, "From the days of minstrelsy to the latest Broadway hit, the Negro community has been the chief source of styles, form, and much of the content and spirit which have characterized each of the different periods of popular music. In the diffusion of this music through the world there has been a revolution in musical tastes." [20]

LITERATURE

Since their importation to what is now the United States, black people have demonstrated an ability for writing poetry and prose which is especially notable considering the difficulties they have encountered in publishing their writings. The literature of black people, like their music, grew out of their experience in a hostile society. Black writers have been criticized for (1) the small volume of their work, and (2) their emphasis on social protest, which, it is sometimes assumed, indicates a lack of mastery of craftsmanship.[21] Perhaps the most severe criticism was made by Blyden Jackson. He wrote, "An old complaint of mine is that Negroes habitually do not even begin to write enough so that they can learn to write well." [22] The dearth of published works by black people is a clear reflection of the difficulty they face in getting their works published, and the concentration of their creative efforts on the ever-present problems they face as black people in a society which deprecates blackness says nothing about the artistic quality of their products. Social protest is a valid theme for artistic expression, as many writers, Negroes included, have demonstrated. As Ralph Ellison has written:

> I recognize no dichotomy between art and protest. Dostoevski's *Notes from Underground* is, among other things, a protest against the limitations

[19] See Richard Bardolph, *The Negro Vanguard* (New York: Vintage Books, 1961), pp. 385–99.

[20] George, *op. cit.*, p. 756; see also Bardolph, *op. cit.*, pp. 400–411.

[21] See a review of Herbert Hill (ed.), *Anger and Beyond: The Negro Writer in the United States,* by Jervis Anderson, in *Commentary*, Vol. 43 (March 1967), 100–104; Bardolph, *op. cit.*, pp. 382–83; Butcher, *op. cit.*, pp. 183ff; Blyden Jackson, "The Continuing Strain: Resume of Negro Literature in 1955," *Phylon* (First Quarter 1956), pp. 35–41.

[22] Jackson, *op. cit.*, p. 35; see also Nick Aaron Ford, *The Contemporary Negro Novel* (Boston: Meador, 1936), p. 102.

of 19th-century rationalism; *Don Quixote, Man's Fate, Oedipus Rex, The Trial*—all these embody protest, even against the limitation of human life itself. If social protest is antithetical to art, what shall we make of Goya, Dickens, and Twain? [23]

The body of literature created by black people including poetry, prose, and plays, stands as a major contribution to American letters. Some of the contemporary writers have demonstrated an extraordinary talent unexcelled in the English language today. Occasionally a writer excels in several media. LeRoi Jones is such an artist. He has been acclaimed for his poetry, plays, novels, short stories, and social history.

The early writings of black Americans centered around antislavery themes. Thus it was a literature of protest. The sacred and secular music of Negro slaves was indeed poetry. In a more formal vein, poetry was written by slaves and free Negroes in the 18th century. According to Arna Bontemps, a semiliterate slave girl named Lucy Terry, in Massachusetts, commemorated an Indian raid on the town of Deerfield in 1746 with a poem which she called "Bars Fight." [24] A decade later Phillis Wheatley gained an international reputation as a poetess with the publication in England of her book of verse, *Poems on Various Subjects: Religious and Moral.* She was said to be the best known of living American poets at the time. Moreover, a slave preacher named Jupiter Hammond published a volume of poetry as early as 1760.

Later, in New Orleans, the first anthology of Negro poetry was published in 1845.[25] This anthology was written by an educated group of Negroes who had studied in France, and it differed in both form and content from the poetry of the slaves and other free Negroes of the time. Two other black poets, George Moses Horton of Chapel Hill, North Carolina, and Frances Ellen Harper, published several volumes of poetry. It is estimated that, altogether, some 30 volumes of poetry were published by black people between Phillis Wheatley's collection and the first volume published by Paul Laurence Dunbar in 1893.[26] Dunbar was perhaps the most famous of all black poets. The son of a slave mother, he had never experienced plantation life and had never lived in the Deep South, but he wrote his poetry in folk dialect. Because he wrote in an amusing vein, often ignoring the hardships of slavery, he

[23] Ralph Ellison, *Shadow and Act* (New York: Random House, Inc., copyright 1966), pp. 170–71. For a strong defense of the protest theme in Negro literature see Herbert Hill (ed.), *Anger and Beyond: The Negro Writer in the United States* (New York: Harper & Row, 1966), p. xiv.
[24] Arna Bontemps, "The Negro Contribution to American Letters," in Davis (ed.), *op. cit.,* p. 850.
[25] *Ibid.,* pp. 852–53.
[26] *Ibid.,* p. 856.

has been called "a part of the apologist tradition." [27] In his lifetime Dunbar published seven volumes of poetry.

Following the death of Dunbar in 1906, several black Americans continued to write poetry, but it was not until the 1920's that Negro poetry appeared on a large scale. Several black poets—James Weldon Johnson, Angelina Grimke, Ann Spencer, Georgia Douglas Johnson, Claude McKay, Jean Toomer, Langston Hughes, and Countee Cullen— became active in publishing verse during what has been called the Negro Renaissance. Of the earlier Negro Renaissance poets, Jean Toomer and Claude McKay were the best known, but they were soon to be overshadowed by Countee Cullen and Langston Hughes. Both Cullen and Hughes achieved international reputations for their verse, the former winning many awards for his poetry and the latter living to see his poetry translated into many languages. The Negro Renaissance in Harlem ended in the 1930's, but several black poets, including Langston Hughes, Frank Horne, and Sterling Brown, continued to publish poetry throughout that decade.

Since that period black poets have continued to publish. They include Margaret Walker, whose "For My People" won the Yale University Younger Poets Award, and Gwendolyn Brooks, the first Negro to win the Pulitzer Prize for poetry. The line of black poets since Phillis Wheatley has been unbroken. Today such gifted poets as Melvin B. Tolson, Robert Hayden, Gloria Oden, Russel Atkins, Conrad Kent Rivers, and LeRoi Jones continue to publish poetry.[28]

Negro poetry evolved from the social protest against slavery, and it has kept pace throughout the years with the struggles of black people in the United States.[29] During World War I it protested against the economic conditions black Americans encountered, and during the New Deal it reflected the egalitarian ethos of the time, which indicated the greater self-assurance of its authors. During World War II black poets concerned themselves with the problem of war, and, as Butcher has written, "Younger Negro poets writing today include a group of highly cultivated and thoroughly sophisticated intellectuals who, like their white peers, reveal an increasing preoccupation with style and technique." [30]

The first prose writings of black Americans, like their poetry, was literature of protest. They were slave narratives and protests against slavery by free Negroes. Both the slaves and their nonslave brothers cried out for freedom. The first slave narrative to be published, *A Narrative*

[27] Butcher, *op. cit.,* p. 121.
[28] Bontemps, *op. cit.,* pp. 862–63.
[29] Butcher, *op. cit.,* Chap. 6.
[30] *Ibid.,* p. 140.

of the Uncommon Sufferings and Surprising Deliverance of Briton Hammond, A Negro Man, appeared in 1760.[31] Since that time a steady stream of slave narratives, often in autobiographical form, has appeared in the United States. In addition, several ex-slaves wrote fictionalized accounts of the lives of the slaves. Perhaps the most important body of Negro literature to appear at this time was that written by fugitive slaves. Their accounts of what it had meant to be enslaved served as important ammunition for the antislavery movement, especially in the 1840's, a period of widespread Abolitionist activity. *The Narrative of the Life of Frederick Douglass, an American Slave, Written by Himself,* which first appeared in 1845, was perhaps the most important of the slave narratives, and it has been reprinted in numerous editions, the most recent published by Harvard University Press in 1960.[32]

Besides the narratives of ex-slaves, a sizable group of free Negroes published accounts of their travels, histories of the Negro in the United States, novels, plays, magazines, and newspapers.[33] The first play written by a Negro was published in 1858, and the first newspaper, *Freedom's Journal,* appeared as early as 1827. In 1847 Frederick Douglass published *The North Star,* a newspaper which enjoyed wide circulation. The first novel by a Negro, William Wells Brown, a fugitive slave, was published in England in 1853; it was later published in Boston. Brown enjoyed a distinguished literary career which continued until 1880. According to Bontemps, Brown was the first black person in the United States to earn a living from his writings.[34] The publication of slave narratives did not cease with emancipation. They continued to appear as late as the turn of the 20th century, when Booker T. Washington published his *Up from Slavery.*

Paul Laurence Dunbar, in addition to his popularity as a poet, published several works of fiction in the early 1900's. His novels gained wide popularity, and his short stories appeared in the leading literary magazines of the day. Like Dunbar, Charles Waddell Chestnutt published several collections of short stories and novels at the turn of the century. At the same time the works of William Edward Burghardt Du Bois began to appear both in literary magazines and in book form. Du Bois was the first black person to earn the Ph.D. degree from Harvard, where his doctoral dissertation, *The Suppression of the African Slave Trade,* became the first book published in the Harvard Historical

[31] Bontemps, *op. cit.,* p. 863.

[32] This edition was edited by Benjamin Quarles.

[33] John Hope Franklin, *From Slavery to Freedom* (New York: Knopf, 1948), pp. 230–31.

[34] Bontemps, *op. cit.,* p. 870.

Studies.[35] His was one of the most productive literary and educational careers in American history, spanning a period of more than 65 years. Du Bois published more books and articles than any other black person. Several of his books, such as *The Souls of Black Folk,* which was first published in 1903, continue to be reissued in the 1960's because of their relevance to present-day conditions. Du Bois' contribution to American literature includes novels, histories, biographies, autobiographies, scholarly articles, and short stories.

James Weldon Johnson was also among the Negroes writing in the period preceding the Negro Renaissance in Harlem. Du Bois and Johnson were followed by a series of black novelists who lived in Harlem in the 1920's. This period was one of unexcelled productivity for black writers. Such prose writers as Jesse Fauset, Walter White, Claude McKay, Eric Walrond, Wallace Thurmond, Rudolph Fisher, and Langston Hughes were among the towering literary figures of the Negro Renaissance. They were followed, during the Depression, by an even more impressively talented group of writers, which included Zora Neal Hurston, Mercedes Gilbert, George Wylie Henderson, George W. Lee, Waters Edward Turpin, William Attaway, and Dorothy West and, later, by Ralph Ellison, Willard Motley, Richard Wright, and Frank Yerby.

One critical review of the novels written by Negroes in the decade from 1940 to 1950 found that their works achieved high levels of competence and literary ability. "American literature in the hands of Negro practitioners is impressive indeed during the '40's." [36] According to this account they became less preoccupied with racial themes and concerned themselves with the more general problems of American society.[37]

Many of the writers of this and the next decade achieved fame, but the two most highly praised for their literary achievement were clearly Richard Wright and Ralph Ellison. Wright is considered one of the most impressive black American literary talents, and his works have been translated into some 50 foreign-language editions.[38] In the later stages of his career, Wright moved to Paris, from where he traveled widely throughout Europe, Africa, and Asia. On a world scale, Wright was regarded as one of the most important literary figures of his day.

[35] Benjamin Quarles, *The Negro in the Making of America* (New York: Collier Books, 1964), p. 172.

[36] See Carl Milton Hughes, *The Negro Novelist* (New York: Citadel, 1953), p. 250.

[37] This view was shared by Alain Locke. See his "The High Price of Integration. A Review of the Literature of the Negro for 1951," *Phylon* (First Quarter 1952), pp. 7–18. See also Herbert Hill (ed.), *Soon One Morning: New Writing by American Negroes, 1940–1962* (New York: Knopf, 1963), pp. 3, 17.

[38] Bontemps, *op. cit.,* pp. 875–76.

Ralph Ellison's first novel, *Invisible Man,* was greeted with widespread critical acclaim, was awarded several literary prizes, and is still considered one of the outstanding literary achievements of this century. Among its many prizes was the National Book Award, won the year when Ernest Hemingway was a competitor.[39] One literary critic rendered this judgment: "By far the best novel yet written by an American Negro, *Invisible Man* is quite possibly the best American novel since World War II." [40]

Whereas Ellison and Wright concentrated, often indirectly, on the position of the Negro in America, Motley and Yerby refrained from dealing with Negro life. They became the first black writers to deal with so-called popular themes. The works of these writers—Ellison, Wright, Motley, and Yerby—were the predecessors of those of a talented group of young writers that includes Ann Petry, Roi Ottley, William Demby, Owen Dodson, Alden Bland, William Gardner Smith, Lloyd Brown, and Willard Savoy. Saunders Redding appeared at the same time as novelist, essayist, and critic.

Easily the most acclaimed of young black writers is James Baldwin, whose novels, essays, plays, and short stories have established him as one of the most important literary figures writing in English today. Baldwin is best known for his essays, which have been acclaimed as among the best writing in the English language. A less well-known, but talented, group of black writers of the present time, including Alston Anderson, Frank London Brown, Rosa Guy, the late Lorraine Hansberry, LeRoi Jones, William Melvin Kelly, John Oliver Killens, Paule Marshall, Julian Mayfield, Herbert Simmons, and John A. Williams, has continued the tradition of quality prose writing which has had a long, although often unacknowledged, history dating back to slavery.

In this last group are to be found some of the most talented and creative of young Americans. In a survey of novels written by Negroes between 1890 and 1952, Bone catalogs 103. In a five-point rating scale (major, superior, good, mediocre, and poor), he rates three novels as major, four as superior, and eight as good. The remaining 88 were classified as either mediocre or poor.[41] The three major novelists, in his judgment, were Ralph Ellison, Jean Toomer, and Richard Wright. This judgment was rendered, of course, before many of the younger black writers had published their works. Although the conditions under which black people have been forced to live in the United States have served as

[39] Bardolph, *op. cit.,* p. 380.
[40] Robert A. Bone, *The Negro Novel in America* (New Haven, Conn.: Yale, 1958), p. 212.
[41] *Ibid.,* pp. 227–32.

subject matter for much of their literary output, and although the present period has all the earmarks of another "renaissance," it is possible that, if black people had been responded to as other Americans, rather than as Negroes, their contribution might have been even greater.

THE DANCE

Virtually all the popular dance forms in the United States, from the Cakewalk down to the Boogaloo, originated among America's black people. In the realm of more formal dance on the concert stage, black people have excelled despite serious handicaps. Yet it is in the realm of popular dance that they have made their most widely accepted contributions.

The earliest African slaves to reach North America excelled in the mastery of rhythm. The dance had always been an important part of African tribal life; hence the slaves brought with them an appreciation for dancing. As Margaret Just Butcher has written, "Dancing, for the Negro, has always been a spontaneous and normal mode of expression, rather than an artificial and formalized one." She continues, "Although Negro dancing is seemingly a matter of foot movements, the rhythm always begins from within as a body vibration, and throughout the whole body vibrates sympathetically. The Negro dancer's capacity to elaborate upon a basic rhythm by changing, doubling, and skipping beats bewilders those less expert in rhythmic patterns and designs." [42] The Negro dancer, then, because of his cultural background, is less inhibited in his movements than is his white counterpart. This freedom of movement accounts, in part, for the widespread imitation of Negro dancing by white youths who are eager for release from the tensions they feel in contemporary America.

Ritualistic dancing played an important role in the life of black people in Africa. Hence the slaves brought with them their native dances. These forms were modified in the New World, but in the dance, as in music, aspects of their traditional African cultures managed to survive the impact of slavery throughout the Western Hemisphere. Even in North America, where African cultures suffered their greatest destruction, it is still possible to find traces of ritualistic or religious dancing in religious services and in secular dances. African dance patterns have been incorporated into Christian ideology and into secular dance. Furthermore, African dance patterns have merged with purely secular European dances.[43] Hand clapping and foot tapping, as well as ritual-

[42] Butcher, *op. cit.,* pp. 44–45.
[43] See Katherine Dunham, "The Negro Dance," in Brown, Davis, and Lee (eds.), *op. cit.,* pp. 991–1000.

istic leaps during religious services, are examples of these cultural survivals. In Africa tribal drums accompanied the dance, and it has been suggested that foot tapping serves as a substitute for drums.[44] In recent years, however, traditional African drums have become more prevalent in the United States, especially in black neighborhoods in large cities.

The Cakewalk was the first major popular dance of Negro origin to gain widespread acceptance in the United States. It grew out of the long tradition of folk dancing among Negroes. Other Negro dance steps have gained widespread popularity in the United States and have spread throughout the world. These dances include the Charleston, the Lindy Hop, and the Jitterbug, among the earlier forms.[45] In more recent years such dances as the Twist, the Monkey, the Frug, and the Boogaloo are even more reminiscent of the earlier Negro folk dances.

Dunham sees the Big Apple as being directly derived from the category of plantation dances known as the Juba, a popular West Indian dance. The pattern is not exclusively African, but it is typical of African tribal dances, and in the United States it has merged with English square dances. She sees popular dances in the United States as differing from their counterparts in the West Indies because of the different sociological processes occurring in the two areas. "The entire process here has been accelerated and condensed, not only by the uniquely rapid industrialization of America but also by the position of Negro culture in American society." [46] Because of these differences, African tribal dances survived the transition into folk dances to a greater extent in the West Indies and elsewhere in the Western Hemisphere than in the United States. The earlier American Negro plantation circle dances and hand-clapping dances, which were prevalent in Louisiana and in the islands off South Carolina, were roughly equivalent to the present-day folk dances of the West Indies. According to Dunham, these dances became transformed into popular American dances through the emergence of the minstrel tradition, which preceded the urbanization of Negro folk dance patterns. It is through the minstrel that Negro folk dance patterns spread throughout the larger society and ultimately throughout the world.

In the 1920's several shows, *Shuffle Along, Put and Take, Liza* and *Running Wild,* all introducing popular dances of Negro origin, especially the Charleston, served rapidly to popularize Negro dance steps throughout the world.[47] Since that time the impact has accelerated, and at no

[44] Butcher, *op. cit.,* p. 47.

[45] See Langston Hughes, "The Negro in American Entertainment," in Davis (ed.), *op. cit.,* p. 831.

[46] Dunham, *op. cit.,* p. 998.

[47] Hughes, *op. cit.,* p. 841.

point in history has the impact been more pronounced than at the present time.

On the American stage, African culture has served as a source for both ballet and dance opera. Beginning with the 1930's a series of dance concerts was performed on stages throughout the United States. The Federal Theater Project, which was organized during the Depression of the 1930's, included an African dance unit, and several Negro colleges have presented African ballet and folk dances. In the realm of modern dance such choreographers as Martha Graham, Anga Enters, and Tamaris have reflected African- and Afro-American-inspired dances in their repertories. Carmen de Lavallade, Geoffrey Holder, and Jean-Leon Destine are among the major interpreters of the dance in the United States. In addition, both Katherine Dunham and Pearl Primus have established concert dance troupes which concentrate exclusively on Negro dance derived from Africa and the Americas. Dunham and Primus have established international reputations as dancers, choreographers, and scholars of the dance. Janet Collins became a major dancer with the Metropolitan Opera in New York City.

Black people have, therefore, distinguished themselves in all areas of the dance, but their influence has been most widespread in the popular dance forms. In the opinion of one writer, "The American dance, both on the stage and in the nightclub, is largely of Negro origin." [48]

VALUES

Perhaps the single most important contribution (past, present, and future) of black people to American culture is to be found in the realm of social values. Their long history of suffering and the ability somehow to survive with a degree of humanity are achievements of some note. Furthermore, the ability somehow to transcend the example set by the oppressor, and to respond with charity and patience to acts of cruelty fostered by adherence to the ideology of white supremacy, requires an inner strength which, through its example, might lead to the gradual transformation of the United States into a more humane society. John Killens sees the black man as the hope for America. He writes: "Just as most Negroes still believe that the ultimate solution for us is in America, I am firmly convinced that the ultimate salvation of America is the Negro." He sees the black man as playing the dominant role in the transformation of American society because of qualities which have persisted despite severe handicaps: "To live castrated in a great white

[48] Edwin R. Embree, *Brown Americans* (New York: The Viking Press, Inc., 1946), p. 192.

harem and yet somehow maintain this black manhood and humanity—
this is the essence of the new man created out of the Negro invention." [49]

Throughout their long history in America, black people have
eagerly sought to become full-participating members of a society which
has constantly rebuffed them. Being forced to stand outside the society,
they have been able to appraise it with a degree of objectivity which is
difficult for full participants. Negroes, because of their peripheral position in the society, have been able to see that many of the cultural values
of the larger society—equality, justice, democracy, and freedom—lose
meaning in the face of widespread poverty, oppression, and racism. They
know that these high-sounding concepts apply to whites but not to them.
As Killens has written, "To the average white man, a courthouse, even
in Mississippi, is a place where Justice is dispensed. To me, the black
man, it is a place where justice is dispensed-with." [50] The result has been
attempts to reconstruct the organization of American society, and, where
these attempts have failed, an alienation from the dominant values of
the larger society has resulted. Several events attest to this development,
which has accelerated in the last decade.

Black students at Columbia University have organized a Students'
Afro-American Society and have elected to isolate themselves from their
white fellow students because they consider themselves a part of a cultural
tradition that is fundamentally different from white middle-class society,
which gives them a special identity as Negroes. Writing about the
alienation of black students from their white fellow students and from
the values of white middle-class society, one student had this to say:

> The classes of black students that follow us will also realize that member-
> ship in the campus society merely grants one access to the same plethora
> of social ills which presently decay white society. The subsequent classes
> of black students will not only reject the mediocre goals this institution
> says they ought to aspire to; they will resolutely refuse the man's benevo-
> lent offer of a '32nd Vice-Niggership' at General Motors.[51]

Some 200 black students from 14 New England colleges and
universities met at Harvard University on May 13, 1967, and demonstrated against the "racist war in Vietnam." In a statement outlining

---

[49] John O. Killens, "We Refuse to Look at Ourselves Through the Eyes of White
America," in Francis L. Broderick and August Meier (eds.), *Negro Protest Thought in
the Twentieth Century* (Indianapolis, Ind.: Bobbs-Merrill, 1965), p. 356. Copyright ©
by John Oliver Killens. Reprinted by permission of Ashley Famous Agency, Inc. Originally published in *The New York Times.*

[50] *Ibid.*, p. 354.

[51] Marvin S. Kelly, "Pride in Blackness," *The Supplement of the Columbia
Daily Spectator*, April 26, 1967, p. S-2.

the purpose of the demonstration, the students declared: "We believe that America is the black man's battlefield, and that the black man must not join the atrocities of this war." [52]

One of the 300 black students at the University of Alabama commented on why black students remain there in view of the constant rebuffs and insults from white students. "We're not trying to be carbon copies of the white man," she said. "We just want to be accepted for what we are—individuals who are trying to get an education." [53]

Writing about the mood of the young black militants, the past chairman of the Student Nonviolent Coordinating Committee defines their aspirations: "The society we seek to build among black people, then, is not a capitalist one. It is a society in which the spirit of community and humanistic love prevail." [54]

James Baldwin has written:

> I cannot accept the proposition that the 400-year travail of the American Negro should result merely in his attainment of the present level of American civilization. I am far from convinced that being released from the African witch doctor was worthwhile if I am now—in order to support the moral contradictions and the spiritual aridity of my life—expected to become dependent on the American psychiatrist. It is a bargain which I refuse. The only thing that white people have that black people need, or should want, is power—and no one holds power forever. White people cannot, in the generality, be taken as models of how to live.[55]

A civil rights worker from Mississippi, addressing a meeting in Washington, D.C., began her speech by saying, "Children, I don't want to be like white folks. I want to be better than white folks."

The mood expressed in these passages is one of rejection of the notion of "integration" as an end to the society as it is presently organized; that is, black Americans question the value to be derived from integration into a society which has denied a large segment of its population its humanity because of the most superficial of human characteristics—skin color. As James Baldwin phrases the question, "Do I really *want* to be integrated into a burning house?" While it is unlikely that a majority of black Americans subscribe to this point of view, the feeling is widespread among the younger militants, and it is gaining support among other segments of the black community.

Because black people have never subscribed to the myths that

[52] *The New York Times,* May 14, 1967, p. 3, col, 3.
[53] Gertrude Samuels, "There are 300 Negroes at the University of Alabama," *The New York Times Magazine,* May 14, 1967, p. 80.
[54] Stokely Carmichael, "What We Want," *The New York Review of Books,* September 22, 1966, p. 8.
[55] James Baldwin, *The Fire Next Time* (New York: Dial, 1963), p. 110.

most white Americans value, they have responded to oppression not with vindictiveness but with compassion. They have retained a degree of open-mindedness about white Americans which has never been reciprocated. In interpersonal relations they have been responded to with irrationality by white Americans, yet they have maintained a notable degree of rationality in their relations with white Americans. Public opinion polls and sample surveys attest to the relatively low degree of prejudice on the part of Negroes toward white Americans.[56] Considering the experience of black people in America, it would not be surprising if they were filled with hatred for white Americans, but the magnitude of their very experience appears to have taught them a lesson about the futility of hate. They continue to send their young children to school through mobs of screaming and jeering white adults with the hope that they will not be forced to repeat the humiliating experiences which they have encountered. And, unlike the mobs of screaming and jeering white Americans, they do not teach their children to hate those distinguished from themselves by superficial differences. Black Americans have always been more accepting of racial and cultural differences than white Americans. Mass irrationality in regard to physical differences has never been widespread within the black community.

During the spring of 1965 the late Martin Luther King, Jr., of the Southern Christian Leadership Conference, issued a nationwide call for supporters of greater civil rights for Negroes to join in a march from Selma to Montgomery, Alabama. Thousands of white sympathizers from throughout the United States and abroad responded to this call. The march was delayed for several days, but, upon reaching Selma, the poor, local black people served as hosts for these activists. The simple hospitality of the hosts was one of the aspects of the experience most talked about by the white visitors. The contrast between the friendliness of the local blacks and the hostility of the local whites was striking. Many of the whites who had journeyed from the North had never visited a Negro home, and they were surprised at the congenial welcome they received. Similar acts of kindness and acceptance had been accorded the many white civil rights volunteers who journeyed to Mississippi and lived among that state's poor Negroes during the Mississippi Summer Project

[56] See William Brink and Louis Harris, *The Negro Revolution in America* (New York: Simon and Schuster, 1964), especially Chaps. 5 and 10; Gary T. Marx, *Protest and Prejudice* (New York: Harper & Row, 1967); Donald L. Noel, "Correlates of Anti-White Prejudice in Four American Cities" (unpublished Ph.D. thesis, Cornell University, 1961); Donald L. Noel and Alphonso Pinkney, "Correlates of Prejudice: Some Racial Differences and Similarities," *American Journal of Sociology,* Vol. 59 (May 1964), 609–22; Robin M. Williams, Jr., *Strangers Next Door* (Englewood Cliffs, N.J.: Prentice-Hall, 1964), pp. 276–82.

in 1964. Although it might be argued that the white civil rights workers were welcomed, as any people would have been, because they came to help the Negroes, it is unlikely that middle-class Negroes under similar circumstances would have received comparable treatment from poor white Southerners. No matter how much the black people had suffered, they retained a degree of basic humanity which rigid adherence to white supremacy had denied their fellow white citizens.

Black people today are taking the lead in the recasting of American values. For centuries they have been the recipients of few of the rewards of society, especially its material rewards. Consequently they have learned that many of the material creations of society, to which the dominant majority has ready access, have not led to the enhancement of the dignity of man and of his ability to live with himself and others, but, rather, they have created a situation in which varieties of forms of destruction abound. Lerone Bennett sees the recasting of American values as being at the core of the black rebellion. He writes:

> Integration and transformation: these two themes are at the heart of the rebellion which holds enormous possibilities for all Americans. For if the rebellion fulfills itself, it will stimulate our creativity, which only comes from diversity; it will relieve the drab sameness of our middle-class minds and our middle-class neighborhoods; it will give us an America more concerned about the claims of human personality and less concerned about color and machines.[57]

Historically, Americans have been intolerant of cultural differences, both domestically and in international relations. Internally the cultures of the colored minorities, American Indians, Negroes, and Spanish-speaking Americans, have been either suppressed or ignored. It was assumed that these cultures were inferior, and representatives of these cultures either withdrew from the larger society or attempted to assimilate the culture of the dominant white population. Among Negroes this action frequently took the form of self-hate, leading to total rejection of any aspect of the African culture which managed to survive and the adoption of white patterns, including standards of beauty. Skin whiteners and hair straighteners have historically been among the most widely selling cosmetics in black communities. There is some evidence, however, that black people are beginning to manifest increasing pride in the characteristic which they are powerless to change—their blackness. They are abandoning skin whiteners and hair straighteners.[58] They are reject-

---

[57] See Lerone Bennett, *The Negro Mood* (New York: Ballantine Books, Inc., 1965), p. 82.
[58] See "The Natural Look," *Ebony*, June 1966.

ing what they consider the superficial racist values of the larger society.

The demand on the part of black people for acceptance on their own terms (i.e., social and cultural pluralism), which has resulted from the refusal of white Americans to consider seriously the assimilation of Negroes into American life, has had the effect of challenging the societal notion of Americanization through assimilation. Black Americans are not demanding that cultural differences be changed. Rather, the notion of the existence of a distinct black subculture is gaining recognition as a valid sociological process resulting from the meeting of individuals with different life experiences.

This notion has also had its impact on America's conduct of foreign relations. As one writer has put it, "The Negro has learned to detect the realities behind democratic generalizations. He has learned that, just as solemn mouthings frequently conceal differentials in domestic affairs, so they disguise nationalistic bias in foreign relations." [59] Because of his special plight in the United States, the Negro is sensitive to the struggles of fellow oppressed peoples throughout the world. This sensitivity was expressed in the policy statement issued by the Student Nonviolent Coordinating Committee opposing the war in Vietnam: "We believe the U.S. government has been deceptive in claims of concern for the freedom of the Vietnamese people, just as the government has been deceptive in claiming concern for the freedom of the colored people in such other countries as the Dominican Republic, the Congo, South Africa, Rhodesia, and in the United States itself." [60]

In a speech proclaiming his opposition to the war in Vietnam, the late Martin Luther King, Jr., had this to say:

> We are taking the young black men who have been crippled by our society and sending them 8,000 miles away to guarantee liberties in Southeast Asia which they had not found in Southwest Georgia and East Harlem. So we have been repeatedly faced with the cruel irony of watching Negro and white boys on TV screens as they kill and die together for a nation that has been unable to seat them together in the same schools. So we watch them in brutal solidarity burning the huts of a poor village, but we realize that they could never live on the same block in Detroit.[61]

King continues, "I am convinced that if we are to get on the right side of the world revolution, we as a nation must undergo a radical revolution of values. When machines and computers, profit and property rights are

[59] Butcher, op. cit., p. 292.
[60] The New York Times, January 7, 1966, p. 2, col. 8.
[61] Martin Luther King, Jr., "Declaration of Independence from the War in Vietnam," Ramparts, May 1967, p. 33. Reprinted by permission of Joan Daves. Copyright © 1967 by Martin Luther King, Jr.

considered more important than people, the giant triplets of racism, materialism, and militarism are incapable of being conquered." [62]

The opposition by many black Americans (in both positions of leadership and rank and file) to the war in Vietnam serves to highlight their continuing role in pressing for the development of a more humane society at home and a more humanitarian foreign policy. Although centuries of oppression have had the effect of making for callousness among some Negroes, they have, at the same time, made the Negroes more keenly aware of human suffering. As one writer has commented, black people possess "an expressive quality, a strength that comes from suffering, a feel for life that hasn't been leached out of us by a fat, complacent, meaningless existence; a basic health in the midst of sickness around us, and . . . once we are given the opportunity for this to come to flower, we will be a formidable people." [63] It is unlikely that the moral example being set by black people more than three and one-half centuries after their arrival in North America will fail to make its impact on the society at large, both in its domestic relations and in the conduct of foreign affairs.

•   •   •

In music, literature, the dance, and in the realm of social values, the contributions of black people to American society have resulted from their unique experience in the society. In the United States most black people have always been, and continue to be, isolated from white Americans. For these people life has been difficult, and it became necessary somehow to survive in the face of extraordinary disadvantages. Hence a way of life developed which is, in many respects, distinct from that of the larger society. At the same time Western culture made its impact on black people. Because of this unique, dual set of circumstances, distinctive contributions to society were inevitable, and in recent years increasingly large numbers of Americans are recognizing and acknowledging the magnitude of these cultural contributions.

In the realm of social values, black Americans are in the vanguard of social change. Their impact on society has been, and continues to be, profound. At the recent Conference of New Politics in Chicago, this sentiment was summed up by a black delegate who, addressing a largely white audience, declared: "If you're not going to support us, you go your

[62] *Ibid.,* p. 37.
[63] Quoted from Paule Marshall in *Ebony,* August 1966, p. 149.

merry way, and we're going to liberate you whether you want to be liberated or not." [64]

[64] From a speech by James Foreman of the Student Nonviolent Coordinating Committee, as reported in *The New York Times,* September 4, 1967, p. 15, col. 2.

SELECTED BIBLIOGRAPHY

Baldwin, James, *The Fire Next Time.* New York: The Dial Press, Inc., 1963.

Bardolph, Richard, *The Negro Vanguard.* New York: Vintage Books, 1961.

Bennett, Lerone, *The Negro Mood.* New York: Ballantine Books, Inc., 1965.

Bone, Robert A., *The Negro Novel in America.* New Haven, Conn.: Yale University Press, 1958.

Bontemps, Arna, ed., *American Negro Poetry.* New York: Hill & Wang, Inc., 1963.

Broderick, Francis L., and August Meier, eds., *Negro Protest Thought in the Twentieth Century.* Indianapolis, Ind.: Bobbs-Merrill Company, Inc., 1965.

Brown, Sterling, Arthur P. Davis, and Ulysses Lee, eds., *The Negro Caravan.* New York: The Dryden Press, 1941.

Butcher, Margaret Just, *The Negro in American Culture.* New York: Alfred A. Knopf, Inc., 1964.

Carmichael, Stokely, "What We Want," *The New York Review of Books,* September 22, 1966.

Du Bois, W. E. B., *The Souls of Black Folk.* Chicago: A. C. McLurg and Company, 1903.

Ellison, Ralph, *Shadow and Act.* New York: Random House, Inc., 1966.

Embree, Edwin R., *Brown Americans.* New York: The Viking Press, Inc., 1946.

Ford, Nick Aaron, *The Contemporary Negro Novel.* Boston: Meador Publishing Co., 1936.

Hentoff, Nat, *The Jazz Life.* New York: The Dial Press, Inc., 1961.

Herskovits, Melville J., *The Myth of the Negro Past.* New York: Harper and Brothers, 1941.

Hill, Herbert, ed., *Anger and Beyond: The Negro Writer in the United States.* New York: Harper & Row, Publishers, 1966.

———, *Soon One Morning: New Writing By American Negroes, 1940–1962.* New York: Alfred A. Knopf, Inc., 1963.

Hughes, Carl Milton, *The Negro Novelist.* New York: Citadel Press, 1953.

Jones, LeRoi, *Black Music.* New York: William Morrow & Co., Inc., 1968.

———, *Blues People: The Negro Experience in White America and the Music That Developed from It.* New York: William Morrow & Co., Inc., 1963.

Keil, Charles, *Urban Blues.* Chicago: The University of Chicago Press, 1966.

Marx, Gary T., *Protest and Prejudice.* New York: Harper & Row, Publishers, 1967.

Quarles, Benjamin, *The Negro in the Making of America*. New York: Collier Books, 1964.

Simpson, George E., and J. Milton Yinger, *Racial and Cultural Minorities*. New York: Harper & Row, Publishers, 1965.

Stearns, Marshall, *The Story of Jazz*. New York: Oxford University Press, Inc., 1956.

Ulanov, Barry, *A History of Jazz*. New York: The Viking Press, Inc., 1957.

The extent to which black Americans are assimilated into the larger society is the subject of considerable debate. They were among the earliest arrivals to North America, but they were quickly stripped of their native African cultures. Their tribal organization, religion, family life, and language were systematically destroyed. It thus became necessary for them to adopt the patterns of life of the white Europeans with whom they were forced to live. The adoption of Western culture became a difficult task, for they were permitted to assimilate into the society only to the extent that their services could be utilized by their white rulers. In general, they were forced to live a dual existence: their lives had to be structured in terms of the demands made on them by the larger society and in terms of the necessity to survive in a generally hostile environment. When formal slavery ended more than a century ago, it was replaced by a caste system which prevented substantial alteration of the dual environment within which black people lived. A rigid system of segregation and discrimination replaced the institution of slavery, and this system continues to preclude assimilation into the larger society.

Assimilation into American Society

Being in the society but not a part of it has fostered a conflict among black Americans: Some strive to identify with white middle-class values, and others reject all aspects of white culture. The former attitude sometimes leads to negative identification (self-hatred), while the latter frequently manifests itself in black nationalism. The majority of Negroes would no doubt welcome the chance to become assimilated into the larger society. To the extent that there are forces among Negroes resisting such an eventuality, these forces are a result of widespread rejection by white Americans.

There have been few systematic attempts to examine the extent to which black people are assimilated into the larger society, partly because the assimilation process has only recently been systematically analyzed. Milton Gordon sees the process of assimilation as one involving several steps or subprocesses.[1] Each step represents a "type" or "stage" in the assimilation process. He identifies seven variables by which one may gauge the degree to which members of a particular group are assimilated into the host society which surrounds them. The stages and the subprocesses follow.[2]

[1] Milton M. Gordon, *Assimilation in American Life* (New York: Oxford University Press, 1964), Chap. 3.
[2] *Ibid.*, p. 71.

Type or Stage of Assimilation	Subprocess or Condition
Cultural or behavioral assimilation	Change of cultural patterns to those of host society
Structural assimilation	Large-scale entrance into cliques, clubs, and institutions of host society, on primary-group level
Marital assimilation	Large-scale intermarriage
Identificational assimilation	Development of a sense of peoplehood based exclusively on host society
Attitude receptional assimilation	Absence of prejudice
Behavior receptional assimilation	Absence of discrimination
Civic assimilation	Absence of value or power conflict

It is possible systematically to apply these variables to the status of black people in the United States at the present time in an attempt to determine the extent to which these people have assimilated into American society.

CULTURAL ASSIMILATION

To what extent have black Americans adopted the cultural patterns of the larger society in which they find themselves? The systematic stripping of the slaves of their African cultures has been detailed previously.[3] Debate persists, however, on the extent and nature of the survival of African cultures among black people in the United States. In the more than three and one-half centuries that black people have inhabited what is now the United States, they have adopted the culture of the larger society to the extent that it is difficult to detect any significant vestiges of their original cultures. In North America small numbers of slaves were scattered over a large area on numerous plantations and farms. Even when a sizable number of slaves were held by the same owner, they were likely to have been from a variety of cultures in Africa. Under such circumstances the retention of aspects of their original cultures was difficult. In addition, it was forbidden for them to speak their native languages, and their family patterns were systematically destroyed. Although it is still possible to detect survivals in religious life,[4] Christianity made significant inroads among the slaves, and their

[3] Chap. One. See also E. Franklin Frazier, *The Negro in the United States* (New York: Macmillan, 1957), Chap. 1.

[4] See Melville J. Herskovits, *The Myth of the Negro Past* (New York: Harper, 1941); Frazier, *op. cit.*, pp. 14–19.

religious practices developed along the lines of those of white Christians. Indeed, ". . . the religion of the slaves was, in essence, strikingly similar to that of the poor, illiterate white men of the antebellum South." [5] In other aspects of culture as well, few survivals of African civilizations remain.

There have been frequent attempts by some individual Negroes and organizations to re-emphasize aspects of traditional African cultures, but among the majority of Negroes these attempts have been unsuccessful. Historically the most successful of these movements was the Universal Negro Improvement Association, led by Marcus Garvey.[6] The most recent is the Nation of Islam (popularly known as the Black Muslims), led by Elijah Muhammad.[7] In urban areas throughout the United States Black Nationalist groups continue to search for aspects of their past that were destroyed by the institution of slavery.

According to Gordon, the extent to which black people have adopted the cultural patterns of the host society varies by class. He sees the middle- and upper-class Negroes as being totally acculturated, while ". . . lower-class Negro life . . . is still at a considerable distance from the American cultural norm." [8] A vast majority of black Americans are poor (lower class), and in some respects their cultural patterns deviate from those of the larger society. To a large extent, however, these differences are a function of class rather than race. Gordon's analysis posits "middle-class white Protestant Americans as constituting the 'core society.'" Clearly many lower-class Negroes deviate from the norms of this group, as do lower-class white Protestant Americans. In the sense that lower-class Negroes adhere to lower-class American culture patterns, they may be said to be acculturated. Poor Negroes in the rural South are not significantly different from their poor white counterparts in, for example, food habits or religious practices. They eat the less expensive foods and tend to be more emotional in their religious practices, but the same phenomena are true of poor rural white Southerners. Negroes in non-Southern urban areas may differ in these regards from poor whites in the same areas, but the differences are a function of their Southern, not their African, heritage.

[5] Kenneth M. Stampp, *The Peculiar Institution* (New York: Knopf, 1956), p. 377.
[6] See Edmund D. Cronon, *Black Moses* (Madison, Wis.: The University of Wisconsin Press, 1964).
[7] See E. U. Essien-Udom, *Black Nationalism* (Chicago: The University of Chicago Press, 1962); C. Eric Lincoln, *The Black Muslims in America* (Boston: Beacon Press, 1961).
[8] Gordon, *op. cit.*, p. 76.

Middle- and upper-class Negroes are hardly distinguishable from white Americans of comparable social class level in cultural patterns. There is even some evidence that they frequently overconform to middle-class standards of behavior in religious observances, in dress, in sexual behavior, and in child-rearing practices.[9] In virtually all aspects of life, then, Negroes have adopted the cultural patterns of the host society. When differences occur, they are more likely to be functions of their being victims of oppression than of their systematic retention of elements of the cultures which they left in Africa. Such differences are of American, not African, origin. The acculturation process is virtually complete for black Americans. Culturally, they are clearly products of life in the United States.

STRUCTURAL ASSIMILATION

Black Americans usually maintain their own separate institutions within the black community. (See Chap. Three.) Historically this situation has not been a result of voluntary isolation; rather, a caste system of segregation and discrimination against them has tended to preclude their large-scale entrance into cliques, social clubs, and other social organizations and activities along with white Americans on a primary-group level. However, with increasing racial pride among black people today, voluntary racial separation is not uncommon. In the "rank order of discriminations" against Negroes by white Southerners, as enumerated by Gunnar Myrdal, activities specifically concerned with personal relations, such as dancing, bathing, eating, and drinking together with Negroes, followed closely after intermarriage and interracial sexual relations as forbidden behavior.[10] Such practices are more characteristic of the South than elsewhere, but, in general, they characterize the relations between black and white persons throughout the United States. The caste system, which separates Negroes and whites, dictates that members of these two social categories should not associate in any relationships which imply social equality. This ban generally extends to marriage, dancing, eating together, and social visiting.

The traditional pattern of relations between black and white Americans has been slightly altered in recent years, but, in general, the pattern of almost total isolation of the black community from the white

[9] See, for example, E. Franklin Frazier, *Black Bourgeoisie* (Glencoe, Ill.: Free Press, 1957).

[10] Gunnar Myrdal, *An American Dilemma* (New York: Harper, 1944), p. 60.

community persists. As black people continue to settle in the central cities of the largest urban areas, the isolation is becoming more pronounced. Studies of black-white relations in the South show the pervasiveness of rigid segregation along racial lines insofar as the major social groups and institutions are concerned.[11] The tradition in the South is deeply rooted in the mores, and social change in this regard is slow. Indeed, it is unlikely that any significant change will occur in the near future.

Outside the South the isolation of the black community is only slightly less pronounced than in the South. Most white Americans live their lives with only the slightest awareness of the lives of their black fellow citizens, except during periods of racial unrest. A vast majority of the Negroes who live outside the South live in urban areas, but those who live in small towns live isolated lives compared to their urban counterparts. Two studies illustrate the dearth of interracial association between blacks and whites in smaller Northern cities. In Elmira, New York, it is reported that the Negro community is so isolated that its inhabitants think of themselves not as citizens of Elmira but as citizens of the black community. Such references as "all over town" or "the prettiest girl in town" do not refer to Elmira but to the specific section in which the Negroes are concentrated.[12] Given such conditions as these, it is clear that Negroes have not entered into social groups and activities with their white co-residents. Social contacts between the two groups are minimal.

In a small Connecticut town it is reported that, "while Negro-white neighborhood relations are friendly, they are characterized for the most part by lack of contact between the two races."[13] The Negroes maintained their own church, and in public social activities sponsored by other churches, discrimination against Negroes was evident. There were few adult interracial social contacts. Only two of the many formal organizations, the Chamber of Commerce and the town band, had black members. On the adolescent level a similar pattern was discerned. Social

[11] See, for example, Allison Davis, Burleigh Gardner, and Mary Gardner, *Deep South* (Chicago: The University of Chicago Press, 1941); John Dollard, *Caste and Class in a Southern Town* (New Haven, Conn.: Yale, 1937); Hylan Lewis, *Blackways of Kent* (Chapel Hill, N.C.: The University of North Carolina Press, 1955); Hortense Powdermaker, *After Freedom* (New York: The Viking Press, Inc., 1939).

[12] Robert B. Johnson, "Negro Reactions to Minority Group Status," in *American Minorities,* ed. Milton L. Barron (New York: Knopf, 1957), pp. 192–212; Robin M. Williams, Jr., *Strangers Next Door* (Englewood Cliffs, N.J.: Prentice-Hall, 1964), pp. 235–43.

[13] Frank F. Lee, "Race Relations Pattern in a Small Town," *American Sociological Review,* Vol. 19 (1954), 138–43.

contact between black and white persons was, in this case, limited to athletic and recreational activities. The school system was found to be the only institution in which black and white citizens participated with some degree of equality.

In large cities outside the South there is little social contact between blacks and whites. Black social life tends to be centered around their own social, civic, and religious organizations.[14] Recently, however, middle- and upper-class Negroes have often participated freely with whites in social groups. Nevertheless, the vast majority of Negroes continue to have only superficial social contact with white persons. The maintenance of rigid residential segregation is a strong deterrent against the structural assimilation of Negroes into the life of the larger society.

Structural assimilation may be subdivided into primary and secondary assimilation.[15] Those social institutions which are rooted in the black community (e.g., schools) are primary, and those either partially (e.g., schools) or totally (e.g., economic activities) located in the white community are secondary to the black community. When this dichotomy is made, it is clear that assimilation has progressed at a much more rapid pace in secondary institutions than in those which are primary. Inasmuch as primary institutions tend to be in the private sector of American life, and those which are secondary tend to be public, it appears that the interest of black people has been more in secondary assimilation than in primary assimilation.

MARITAL ASSIMILATION

The United States represents a society which has attempted to curb the process of racial amalgamation through legislation forbidding the marriage of Negroes and non-Negroes. Historically most states have enacted laws forbidding the marriage of black and white persons. Although these laws were disregarded in some states, they were rigidly enforced in others, thereby limiting the number of Negro-white interracial marriages. The penalties for violating these antimiscegenation

---

[14] St. Clair Drake and Horace Cayton, *Black Metropolis* (New York: Harcourt, Brace, 1945); Kenneth B. Clark, *Dark Ghetto* (New York: Harper & Row, 1965). Recent research conducted in a suburban community 13 miles from Detroit, Michigan, indicates that this pattern holds there. See Stanley Weiss, "The Contextual Effect: A Mosaic of Social Class Phenomena as Reflected Through Subcultural Life Within a Bi-Racial Metropolitan Community," Seminar in the Metropolitan Community (unpublished, University of Michigan, 1966).

[15] See E. Franklin Frazier, "The Negro Middle Class and Desegregation," *Social Problems,* Vol. 4 (April 1957), 291–301; Donald L. Noel, "Minority Responses to Intergroup Situations," (unpublished paper, Department of Sociology, Ohio State University).

laws varied by state, ranging up to $2,000 in fines and terms of imprisonment up to ten years.[16]

These antimiscegenation laws were gradually repealed in most non-Southern states, but when the Supreme Court declared them unconstitutional in 1967, 16 states still retained such laws. Even in those states where the laws had been repealed, social mores strongly forbidding intimate interpersonal association across racial lines served to limit the number of Negro-white intermarriages. The result has been that such marriages have occurred infrequently in the United States.

Data on the incidence of Negro-white intermarriages are somewhat limited, but sufficient evidence exists to give a reasonable picture of the extent to which this phenomenon occurs. One writer reports that, in 1956, some 1,137 Negro-white intermarriages were contracted, of which 90 percent involved Negro men and white women. This number represents 0.07 of 1 percent of the total of 1,569,000 marriages contracted in the United States during that year.[17] Another writer reports that, in 1939, Negro-white interracial marriages accounted for only eight out of every 10,000 marriages in the country.[18]

Data from states and municipalities confirm the relative infrequency of Negro-white intermarriage. In Connecticut, for the seven-year period from 1953 to 1959, there were a total of 285 marriages between Negro and white persons out of a total of 124,746 marriages, or 2.3 per 1,000 marriages.[19] The highest rate of interracial marriages was recorded for Los Angeles during the period from 1924 to 1933, when 1.2 per 100 marriages were reported. California then enacted a law forbidding interracial marriages. When this law was nullified by a state court in 1948, there was no significant increase in the number of interracial marriages involving black and white persons. During a 30-month period (November 1948 to April 1951) the rate of interracial marriages was 56 per 10,000. Of this number approximately 20.5 percent involved Negro men and 7.4 percent involved Negro women.[20]

From 1916 to 1937 the percentage of Negro-white marriages among all marriages involving Negroes varied from 1.7 percent to 4.8 percent. In Boston for the period from 1914 to 1938 Negro-white marriages con-

---

[16] See Brewton Berry, *Race and Ethnic Relations* (Boston: Houghton Mifflin, 1958), p. 250.

[17] See Louis Lomax, "Interracial Marriage—An American Dilemma," *Pageant*, November 1957, p. 6.

[18] Albert I. Gordon, *Intermarriage: Interfaith, Interracial, Interethnic* (Boston: Beacon Press, 1964), p. 2.

[19] *Ibid.*, p. 267.

[20] John H. Burma, "Research Note on the Measurement of Interracial Marriage," *American Journal of Sociology*, Vol. 57 (1952), 587–89.

stituted approximately 5.2 percent of all marriages involving Negroes.[21] In Chicago between 1925 and 1938 the percentage of Negro men married to white women was 2.1, while the figure for white men married to Negro women was 0.6 of 1 percent.[22] Data from Washington, D.C., show that between 1940 and 1948, of the 97,599 marriage licenses issued, only 26 involved Negro-white marriages.[23] From the foregoing data it is clear that Negro-white intermarriage in the United States is an uncommon phenomenon.

IDENTIFICATIONAL ASSIMILATION

The position of black people in the United States is a unique one. They form one of the largest and oldest minorities in the country. Racially distinct from the majority, they are highly visible as a minority group. They were enslaved for more than two and one-half centuries, and they continue to be rather widely regarded as racially inferior. Consequently they are responded to as Negroes rather than as Americans. The circumstances under which they live virtually preclude their development of a sense of peoplehood based exclusively on the host society. They are forced to think of themselves as a separate ethnic group rather than simply as Americans.

Despite the many difficulties black people have encountered, their allegiance to the United States is clear. Their interest appears to be in being accorded full citizenship. For example, in a nationwide survey conducted in 1963, an overwhelming majority (81 percent) of Negroes indicated that they thought the United States was worth fighting for in a war.[24] Similarly, when asked, in 1966, to rank Negro leaders, a nationwide sample of Negroes ranked integrationist leaders such as Martin Luther King, Jr., and Roy Wilkins higher than the more militant anti-integrationist leaders such as Stokely Carmichael and Elijah Muhammad.[25] In general, then, it appears that the main concern for a vast majority of America's Negroes *at the present time* is that they be accorded the same rights of citizenship as other Americans.

When legal slavery ended in the United States, black people were

---

[21] Gordon, *op. cit.*, p. 265.

[22] *Ibid.*, p. 267.

[23] Helen Schaffer, "Mixed Marriage," *Editorial Research Reports*, Vol. 1, May 1961.

[24] William Brink and Louis Harris, *The Negro Revolution in America* (New York: Simon and Schuster, 1964), p. 61.

[25] William Brink and Louis Harris, *Black and White* (New York: Simon and Schuster, 1967), p. 54.

not permitted to enter into the mainstream of society, as were their counterparts in Brazil and the Caribbean. Rather, a situation developed in which all Negroes, no matter what the extent of their achievement might have been, were regarded simply as Negroes; they could never expect to be accorded treatment comparable to that of a white American, regardless of his lack of achievement. A Negro is not just another public official, he is a *Negro* public official: the Negro Justice of the Supreme Court, the Negro mayor of Washington, D.C., the Negro Senator from Massachusetts, etc. When the official's position is known, he is accorded a certain amount of deference regardless of his race. However, if his position is not known, he is responded to by most Americans as "just another Negro," and he would be treated accordingly in most situations. White Americans do not see black people as individuals, distinguishable from one another; rather, they see them as an indistinguishable mass. Under such circumstances they are responded to indiscriminately. The black farm laborer and the Nobel Prize winner are both simply Negroes, with all that the word implies. One Negro respondent, in commenting on job relations with white fellow workers, said: "I don't care how a white person treats you. They have a feelin' in 'em that you're colored— I know my place, no matter where I am." [26] This respondent, in a Northern city, accurately defined the general attitude of white Americans toward Negroes.

Forced into such a position of a self-conscious minority, the tendency of members of that group to think of themselves collectively is inevitable. When a fellow Negro achieves a certain distinction, it becomes a source of pride for other Negroes. Conversely, when a fellow Negro is charged with some act which meets with social disapproval, it becomes a source of embarrassment for other Negroes.[27] In other words, to black Americans, as well as to white Americans, one is either black or white, and one responds in terms of these two categories. To a Negro "us" means Negroes and "them" means white persons.[28]

Because black people have occupied an oppressed and segregated status in the United States for centuries, the likelihood of their developing a sense of "peoplehood" with white Americans seems remote. Indeed, in recent years, although they have made some gains in the realm of integration, there appears to be a growing tendency for black people to develop a strong sense of identification with other blacks. That is, there

[26] Williams, *op. cit.*, p. 246.
[27] See Seymour Parker and Robert Kleiner, "Status Position, Mobility, and Ethnic Identification of the Negro," *The Journal of Social Issues*, Vol. 20 (April 1964), 85–102.
[28] Johnson, *op. cit.*, pp. 192–212.

appears to be an increasing pride on their part in being black. Such ingroup identification serves to militate against the development of a sense of identification with the host society.

ATTITUDE RECEPTIONAL ASSIMILATION

Studies of prejudice among white Americans generally indicate that anti-Negro prejudice is widespread in the United States. Intensity of attitudes vary, depending on the region of the country, social class level, age, religion, and other variables, but, in general, anti-Negro prejudice is the social norm among white Americans. There is some indication of change in attitudes, insofar as the more impersonal dimensions of prejudice are concerned, especially in recent years,[29] but in certain realms attitudes remain firmly anti-Negro.

The earliest studies of prejudice indicate that white Americans maintained strongly negative attitudes toward intimate association with nonwhite persons, especially black persons. In the 1920's an overwhelming majority of white Americans indicated that they would reject Negroes as relatives through marriage (98.6 percent), as personal friends in social clubs (90.9 percent), and as neighbors (88.2 percent).[30] In the 1960's the pattern still holds: 84 percent of white persons reported that they would object to a close friend or relative marrying a Negro, and 51 percent said they would object to Negro neighbors.[31]

The extent of anti-Negro prejudice in the United States has been reported in several other studies. In one nationwide study of prejudice it was found that only 5 percent of white persons interviewed received the lowest possible score on a four-point scale of prejudice; 48 percent received the highest possible score.[32] In a study of white veterans in Chicago, it is reported that only 8 percent expressed tolerant attitudes toward Negroes.[33] A recent (1966) nationwide survey of white attitudes toward Negroes provides data on the extent of anti-Negro prejudice in

[29] See Paul B. Sheatsley, "White Attitudes Toward the Negro," in *The Negro American*, eds. Talcott Parsons and Kenneth B. Clark (Boston: Houghton Mifflin, 1966), pp. 303–24.

[30] Emory S. Bogardus, *Immigration and Race Attitudes* (Boston: Heath, 1928), p. 25.

[31] Brink and Harris, *The Negro Revolution in America*, p. 148.

[32] Donald L. Noel and Alphonso Pinkney, "Correlates of Prejudice: Some Racial Differences and Similarities," *American Journal of Sociology*, Vol. 69 (1964), 610; see also Alphonso Pinkney, "The Anatomy of Prejudice" (unpublished Ph.D. thesis, Cornell University, 1961), Chap. 3.

[33] Bruno Bettelheim and Morris Janowitz, *Social Change and Prejudice* (New York: Free Press, 1964), p. 130.

the United States.[34] At least one-half of all respondents subscribed to stereotypes about Negroes, such as: Negroes are different (52 percent), and Negroes have looser morals (50 percent). Furthermore, significant proportions of white persons indicated that they would object to close associations with Negroes in a variety of situations—for example: having a Negro child to supper (42 percent), trying on clothes Negroes had tried on (31 percent), using the same rest-rooms as Negroes (22 percent), and sitting next to a Negro in a movie (21 percent).

The Cornell Studies in Intergroup Relations reported a significant degree of anti-Negro prejudice in communities throughout the United States in the 1950's.[35] In these studies prejudice was indicated by the acceptance of anti-Negro stereotypes, such as "Generally speaking, Negroes are lazy and ignorant," and the manifestations of social distance feelings, such as finding it distasteful (1) to eat at the same table with a Negro, (2) to dance with a Negro, (3) to go to a party and find that most of the people there are Negro, and (4) to have a Negro person marry someone in their family. Prejudiced responses on these items varied anywhere from virtually all respondents disapproving of the marriage of a relative to a Negro to more than one-third (34 percent) of all respondents on the West Coast endorsing the anti-Negro stereotype.

Opposition to integration in public schools and housing provides some indication of change in attitudes of white persons toward black persons. In 1942 only one-third (30 percent) of white Americans expressed the opinion that black and white children should go to the same school; by 1963 the percentage had more than doubled (63 percent). Slightly more than one-third (35 percent) of all white Americans approved of residential integration in 1942, and by 1963, 61 percent expressed approval.[36]

Anti-Negro prejudice, while on the decline, remains deeply rooted in society.[37] The daily newspaper accounts of resistance both to racial integration in public schools and to racial integration in housing

[34] Brink and Harris, *Black and White*, p. 136.
[35] Williams, *op. cit.*, Chap. 4.
[36] Sheatsley, *op. cit.*, pp. 305–8.
[37] In addition to the studies cited above, other recent studies include the following: Reva W. Allman, "A Study of the Social Attitudes of College Students," *Journal of Social Psychology*, Vol. 53 (1961), 33–51; Herbert Hyman and Paul B. Sheatsley, "Attitudes Toward Desegregation," *Scientific American*, Vol. 211 (July 1964), 16–23; Russell Middleton, "Ethnic Prejudice and Susceptibility to Persuasion," *American Sociological Review*, Vol. 25 (1960), 679–86; Harold A. Nelson, "Expressed and Unexpressed Prejudices Against Ethnic Groups in a College Community," *Journal of Negro Education*, Vol. 31 (1962), 125–31; Thomas F. Pettigrew, "Regional Differences in Anti-Negro Prejudice," *Journal of Abnormal and Social Psychology*, Vol. 59 (1959), 28–36; Alphonso Pinkney, "Prejudice Toward Mexican and Negro Americans: A Comparison," *Phylon*, Vol. 24 (1963), 353–59.

throughout the United States attest to the extent to which anti-Negro prejudice is institutionalized in American society. The likelihood that the situation for Negroes in the United States will ever reach the point that they do not encounter prejudiced attitudes is remote.

BEHAVIOR RECEPTIONAL ASSIMILATION

The prejudiced attitudes of white Americans are frequently translated into discriminatory behavior. Hence black Americans experience difficulty in securing employment, housing, and education; they are treated differentially in the administration of justice. In the South they experience discrimination in voting and in places of public accommodations. Indeed, discrimination against black people in the United States is so widespread that it is institutionalized.[38] Like prejudiced attitudes, discriminatory practices vary depending on the region of the country. Outside the South black people experience little difficulty in voting or gaining access to places of public accommodation, but in housing, employment, and education discrimination against black people is commonplace in all regions. Discriminatory practices serve to relegate black people to an inferior status in the United States. It affects each aspect of their lives. When they are forced into inferior schools, they receive inferior education, which relegates them to inferior employment, which in turn relegates them to inferior housing. The cycle is thus complete. Furthermore, their low status makes them "inferior," and their "inferiority" serves to justify acts of discrimination against them. The product of past discrimination is cited to justify continued discrimination.

Acts of discrimination are a manifestation of the legacy of slavery. Although these acts have been practiced since emancipation, they were intensified and extended in scope between 1890 and 1925. For example, Mississippi passed a statewide law requiring separate taxis for Negro and white persons as late as 1922.[39] Few attempts were made on the part of the federal government to deal with anti-Negro discrimination until the 1950's, although there had been executive orders which ostensibly dealt with discrimination as early as World War II. The most sweeping federal attempt to deal with these practices was the Civil Rights Act of 1964.

[38] See Wallace Mendelson, *Discrimination* (Englewood Cliffs, N.J.: Prentice-Hall, 1962).
[39] See C. Vann Woodward, *The Strange Career of Jim Crow* (New York: Oxford, 1957), p. 103.

Perhaps the area in which discrimination against black people is most widespread is housing. Throughout much of the present century the mere entry of a black family into a neighborhood inhabited by white Americans, when such was possible, has provided the stimulus for mob violence. Discrimination in housing is so widespread that virtually all Negro families that attempt to leave neighborhoods inhabited by Negroes are likely to experience acts of discrimination relating to housing.[40] Discrimination in housing is not limited to low-income Negroes. Many well-known, upper-class Negroes—baseball players, opera singers, popular entertainers, judges, and educators—have experienced difficulty in finding housing outside the black neighborhoods of large cities. For example, "The scientist Percy Julian, upon purchasing a fine home in Oak Park in 1951, encountered threats to his person, harassment of his children, and serious attempts to bomb and burn him out. But he stood his ground (hiring a private watchman for two years to guard the place) and finally won acceptance as a respected citizen of that upper-class Chicago suburb." [41] The pattern of widespread discrimination against black people in housing is nationwide. In every American city it is possible to tell the race of a citizen by his address. There is no large American city in which blacks and whites share the same neighborhoods to any great extent.[42]

Repeated attempts to prohibit discrimination in housing have met with little success. On November 20, 1962, the President of the United States issued an executive order barring discrimination by reason of race, color, religion, or national origin in the "sale or rental of residential property and related facilities owned by the federal government or aided or assisted by it." [43] Prior to that time several states and municipalities had enacted legislation barring racial discrimination, and the Supreme Court had ruled in 1948 that federal and state courts could not enforce restrictive covenants in housing. Most housing in the United States is privately owned and financed, and few municipal and state laws, and prior to 1968 no federal laws, covered such housing. Further-

---

[40] Eunice Grier and George Grier, *Discrimination in Housing* (New York: Anti-Defamation League, 1960); Eunice Grier and George Grier, "Equality and Beyond: Housing Segregation in the Great Society," in Parsons and Clark (eds.), *op. cit.,* pp. 525–54; Davis McEntire, *Residence and Race* (Berkeley: University of California Press, 1960); L. K. Northwood and Ernest A. T. Barth, *Urban Desegregation* (Seattle: University of Washington Press, 1965).

[41] Richard Bardolph, *The Negro Vanguard* (New York: Vintage Books, 1961), pp. 286–88. Copyright holder: Holt, Rinehart & Winston, Inc.

[42] Karl E. Taeuber and Alma F. Taeuber, *Negroes in Cities* (Chicago: Aldine, 1965).

[43] U.S. Commission on Civil Rights, *Civil Rights '63: 1963 Report of the United States Commission on Civil Rights* (Washington, D.C.: Government Printing Office, 1963), p. 99.

more, where laws forbid discrimination in housing, e. virtually nonexistent.

Feelings among white Americans against sharing hous. neighborhoods with black people are strongly negative, as is evi by the racist mobs gathered in Chicago in 1966 and in Milwaukee 1967 when civil rights activists demonstrated against discrimination in housing. In Milwaukee the demonstrations were led by a Roman Catholic priest, and during one of them a mob of angry white persons carried a simulated coffin which read, "God is White," and "Father Groppi Rest in Hell." Others carried a placard reading, "You no we're alright, uptight, Out of Sight, We no we're Right, Cause We're WHITE." [44] Because discrimination in housing is so deeply rooted, it is unlikely that black people will achieve equal opportunity in housing in the near future. In 1964 the citizens of California voted overwhelmingly (4.5 million to 2.4 million) in favor of an amendment providing that "Neither the state nor any subdivision or agency thereof shall deny, limit, or abridge, directly or indirectly, the right of any person, who is willing or desires to sell, lease, or rent any part or all of his real property, to decline to sell, lease, or rent such property to such a person or persons as he, in his absolute discretion, chooses." [45] A South African novelist, on a visit to the United States, summed up the situation in these words: ". . . school segregation is dying, but in housing the Negro's dilemma is grim. In most places they can either live quietly in the slums or dangerously elsewhere." [46]

In the United States the ability of the individual to earn a living is largely his responsibility. Federal, state, and municipal governments have, however, from time to time, enacted legislation to assure that black people would enjoy equal employment opportunities with other Americans. The first of these attempts was an executive order banning discrimination in war industries, government training programs, and government industries. It was issued by the President in 1941, after Negroes threatened a massive march on Washington to protest discrimination in the national defense program. Since that time many federal, state, and municipal laws ostensibly forbade racial discrimination in employment, the most recent being the Civil Rights Act of 1964. Nevertheless, discrimination against Negroes continues. Because of acts of discrimination, it is frequently difficult for black males to fulfill their potentials as

[44] *The New York Times,* September 17, 1967, p. 4E, cols. 4–6.
[45] Cited in Charles Abrams, "The Housing Problem and the Negro," in Parsons and Clark (eds.), *op. cit.,* p. 519. This act was subsequently voided by the U.S. Supreme Court.
[46] Alan Paton, "The Negro in America Today," *Collier's,* October 29, 1954, p. 70.

husbands and fathers. They are literally the last to be hired and the first to be fired.

Discrimination exists not only in securing employment but also in the type of employment to which black Americans are relegated. (See Chap. Four.) Because of discrimination against them in employment, the median income of black families in 1964 was only slightly more than one-half the white median family income. In the same occupational category and with comparable experience, black people can expect to earn anywhere from one-half to nine-tenths of what their white counterparts earn.[47] Some of the differential in income may be attributed to lack of training on the part of Negroes, but the major factor accounting for these differentials is discrimination in employment.[48]

Discrimination in securing employment continues on a wide scale. It is most clearly reflected in differential rates of unemployment for black and white workers, and it is one of the most cruel forms of discrimination. At no time between 1954 and 1965 was the unemployment rate for black workers less than twice the rate of white unemployment.[49] Some Negro unemployment must be attributed to structural changes in the economy, and black workers are likely to be less well trained than white workers, but high rates of black unemployment exist for black workers *at all levels of skill.* That is, black professional workers are just as likely to have significantly higher rates of unemployment than white professionals as are black unskilled workers compared to white unskilled workers. Furthermore, when Negroes are unemployed, it is likely to be for longer periods than their unemployed white counterparts.

All types of economic discrimination against black citizens are rooted in the tradition of economic exploitation, dating back to the slave era. Since it is no longer possible for white Americans to own Negroes as property, it is through discriminatory practices that the exploitation of black workers is maintained. Since such practices have become institutionalized throughout the years, the prospects for black workers are not promising.

Overt discrimination in education is much more prevalent in the

[47] U.S. Department of Labor, Bureau of Labor Statistics, *The Negroes in the United States, Their Economic and Social Situation* (Washington, D.C.: Government Printing Office, 1966), pp. 138, 147.

[48] See Ralph Turner, "Foci of Discrimination in the Employment of Non-Whites," *American Journal of Sociology,* Vol. 58 (November 1952), 247–56; Rashi Fein, "An Economic and Social Profile of the Negro American," in Parsons and Clark (eds.), *op. cit.,* p. 120.

[49] U.S. Department of Labor, Bureau of Labor Statistics, *The Negroes in the United States . . . ,* p. 80.

South than elsewhere in the United States. The major factor affecting the quality of education for Negroes outside the South is *de facto* segregation of public schools, which results in the overwhelming majority of Negro pupils attending schools which are either totally Negro or predominantly Negro. *De facto* segregation in public schools, of course, results from residential discrimination in most cases. As late as 1966 more than 65 percent of all Negroes in first grade in the United States attended schools that were between 90 and 100 percent Negro. Eighty-seven percent of first-grade pupils and 66 percent of 12th-grade pupils attended schools that were at least 50 percent Negro.[50] Within these all-Negro or predominantly Negro schools, the pupils are denied equality of educational opportunity. In virtually every school district, South and non-South, where the schools are racially segregated, facilities for Negro pupils are inferior. For example, there are more pupils per teacher, the buildings are older, and the schools are less well equipped.[51]

In the South, from elementary schools to universities, discrimination against Negroes is widely practiced. Ten years after the Supreme Court decision of 1954, only 8 percent of all black pupils were enrolled in desegregated schools. By 1967 the Southern Educational Reporting Service estimated that the figure had doubled.[52] There is some evidence that, as the federal government presses Southern school boards to comply with the Supreme Court decision of 1954 and the Civil Rights Act of 1964, the Northern pattern of *de facto* segregation results from the exodus of white families to the suburbs. And it seems likely that the practice of differential facilities in schools attended primarily by Negroes will continue.

Discrimination in the administraton of justice, at all levels, is as characteristically American as any other aspect of the culture. (See Chap. Six.) Probably the most prevalent form of discrimination in the administration of justice is police misconduct, which often takes the form of excessive use of force, sometimes culminating in the death of Negroes. Such police misconduct has been the stimulus for riots and uprisings in American cities in recent years. Within the context of American society the conviction of policemen for acts of brutality is rare. It is somehow felt that violence committed by law enforcement officials is invariably justified.

[50] U.S. Department of Health, Education, and Welfare, Office of Education, *Equality of Educational Opportunity* (Washington, D.C.: Government Printing Office, 1966), p. 3.

[51] *Ibid.,* pp. 10–11.

[52] *The New York Times,* September 24, 1967, p. 57, cols. 3–8.

In the South law enforcement officials are known to have co-operated with other racists in committing acts of violence against black people and their sympathizers.[53] In Neshoba County, Mississippi, the county sheriff, his deputy, and a policeman were among the 21 persons charged by the Federal Bureau of Investigation with the murder of three civil rights workers in June 1964. The U.S. Commission on Civil Rights listed various forms of police misconduct in Birmingham, Alabama; Cairo, Illinois; Baton Rouge, Louisiana; Jackson, Mississippi; and Memphis, Tennessee—all cities in which Negroes had held civil rights demonstrations in 1963. Police officials acted to curb the rights of citizens to speak freely, assemble peaceably, and petition the government for redress of grievances.[54]

Police misconduct is not limited to the South. As more and more black people settle in the centers of large cities, relations with police officials are being increasingly strained. Negro sections of cities are patrolled by an increasingly hostile police force. Their attitudes and behavior are closer to that of occupying forces than public servants who are responsible to the citizens in these communities.[55] Acts of police misconduct toward black people have been responsible for several of the outbreaks of violence which have become characteristic urban sum-mer phenomena.

Discrimination in the administration of justice is not limited to police misconduct. It is characteristic of law enforcement in general. Such a situation has led many Negroes to manifest little respect for the legal system of the United States. One civil rights leader recently issued a statement which contained the following:

> I am charged with inciting black people to commit an offense by way of protest against the law, a law which neither I nor any of my people have any say in preparing. . . .

> I consider myself neither morally nor legally bound to obey laws made by a body in which I have no representation. That the will of people is the basis of the authority of government is a principle universally acknowl-edged as sacred throughout the civilized world and constitutes a basic foundation of this country. It should be equally understandable that we, as black people, would adopt the attitude that we are neither morally nor

---

[53] Mendelson, *op. cit.*, Chap. 5; James W. Silver, *Mississippi: The Closed Society* (New York: Harcourt, Brace & World, 1964); Elizabeth Sutherland, *Letters from Mississippi* (New York: McGraw-Hill, 1965); Howard Zinn, *SNCC: The New Abolitionists* (Boston: Beacon Press, 1964).

[54] U.S. Commission on Civil Rights, *op. cit.*, pp. 107–25.

[55] See Robert Conot, *Rivers of Blood, Years of Darkness* (New York: Bantam, 1967); Tom Hayden, *Rebellion in Newark* (New York: Random House, 1967); Mendelson, *op. cit.*, Chap. 5.

legally bound to obey laws made without our consent and which seek to oppress us.[56]

Outside the South, where approximately one-half the black people in the United States live, there is little, if any, discrimination against Negroes in voting. Within the South, however, such discrimination is widespread. (See Chap. Five.) After several unsuccessful attempts to curb discrimination against Negroes attempting to vote, Congress passed the Civil Rights Act of 1964, the first title of which concerned Negro voting rights. Again in 1965 Congress passed a voting rights law specifically designed to ensure the franchise to Negroes. The enforcement of these laws has not yet served to assure Negroes in the Deep South that they can exercise their voting rights, but increasingly large numbers have voted in recent elections. Nevertheless, a variety of extralegal measures serve to perpetuate discriminatory practices in voting.

CIVIC ASSIMILATION

There appears to be a growing conflict between black and white persons concerning some fundamental "value and power" interests in the United States. Although such conflicts are not new, it is only in recent years that they are manifesting themselves openly. Inasmuch as Negroes share the same religion and other basic culture elements with white Americans, there are fewer conflicts than is the case with some other minority groups. Nevertheless, Negroes constitute one of the groups which has shared less than equally in the basic rewards of society, both in goods and services. They have faced discrimination in every aspect of American life, and today they are overrepresented among the country's poor. The result of such a set of circumstances has led to serious questions about the professed cultural values of society.

The major civic conflicts between black and white Americans appear to be in two areas: (1) the disproportionate distribution of power in society, and (2) the lack of responsibility on the part of government toward citizens. The former is clearly evident in the current Black Power movement and the latter in such organizations as Mothers for Adequate Welfare, the National Welfare Rights Organization, the Poor People's Campaign, and the New York Citywide Coordinating Committee of Welfare Recipients, a coalition of some 90 welfare action groups in New York City.

[56] This statement, issued by H. Rap Brown, chairman of the Student Nonviolent Coordinating Committee, is quoted in Staughton Lynd, "A Radical Speaks in Defense of S.N.C.C.," *The New York Times Magazine,* September 10, 1967, p. 148.

The Black Power movement first gained prominence in the spring of 1966 and has continued since that time. It is a direct result of the almost total lack of control by black people of the institutions and agencies which are responsible to them. As Stokely Carmichael, the man most responsible for the current interest in Black Power, views the concept, it refers to political, economic, and judicial control, by black people, in areas where they are in a majority. In areas where they are in a minority, it refers to a sharing of control. "It means the creation of power bases from which black people can work to change statewide and nationwide patterns of oppression through pressure from strength— instead of weakness." [57] In other words, Black Power means that blacks, like other minorities, should organize themselves into power blocs, a fundamental aspect of the pluralist pressure group process in American society.

Black Americans have always been, and continue to be, overrepresented among the nation's poor. They frequently find it impossible to secure employment during periods of general economic prosperity. When such a situation results, they are forced to partake in a dehumanizing system of social welfare whose meager allowances are provided grudgingly. They have organized to demand welfare payments adequate for a minimal standard of living. For example, in New York City thousands of welfare recipients have recently filed claims for welfare funds which they maintain the city owes them for such necessities as winter coats and beds. [58] Such a development in the United States represents the first time that a group of Americans is demanding a satisfactory standard of living *as a right*.

The Freedom Budget prepared by the A. Philip Randolph Institute has as its aim the achievement of freedom from want by 1975. The basic objectives include restoring full employment, assuring adequate income for those employed, guaranteeing maximum adequate level of income for those who cannot or should not be employed, providing a decent home for all Americans, and providing medical care and educational opportunity for all.[59] It is assumed by the authors of this report that the federal government should take primary responsibility for achieving these objectives.

In May 1968, the Southern Christian Leadership Conference (SCLC) organized the Poor People's Campaign. The idea for the cam-

[57] Stokely Carmichael, "What We Want," *The New York Review of Books,* September 22, 1966, p. 5.

[58] *The New York Times,* October 3, 1963, p. 1, cols. 5–6.

[59] *A Freedom Budget for All Americans* (New York: A. Philip Randolph Institute, 1966), pp. 2–3.

paign originated with the late Martin Luther King, Jr., founder and past president of this organization. It was led by the Rev. Ralph David Abernathy, his successor as president of SCLC. The objective of the Poor People's Campaign was to demonstrate the plight of America's poor and to demand government reforms necessary to eradicate poverty and racism in the United States. Several demands were made to government officials at all levels. These included the expansion of federal manpower programs to provide 1 million new jobs a year, the establishment of a guaranteed minimum income, the construction of millions of new low-rent housing units, the liberalizing of the surplus foods program, the repeal of punitive welfare legislation, and other benefits in education, health care, and human rights.

To dramatize its demands, the Poor People's Campaign erected a shantytown on the Mall at the Lincoln Memorial in Washington, D.C., to house the thousands of poor people—American Indians, Mexican Americans, Negroes, Puerto Ricans, white people—who had made the trip to Washington, D.C., from all parts of the country, traveling by bus, foot, mule train, and private automobile. Others were housed in local churches and schools.

The Poor People's Campaign was organized on the assumptions that poverty, illiteracy, disease, and destitution are unnecessary in the United States at the present time and that it is the responsibility of the government to establish a satisfactory standard of living for all of its citizens,

In general, there appears to be a growing awareness among black people in the United States that responsibilities between citizens and government are reciprocal. That is, the government has the right to make certain demands on citizens, and citizens have a similar right to make certain demands on their government. Throughout most of American history the former idea has been accepted, but the latter has not.

Although it must be said that, at the present time, there are few areas of value or power conflict between black and white Americans, they do exist in certain crucial areas, and in all likelihood these conflicts will intensify as demands are made by black people for greater sharing in society. As the conflicts intensify, their resolution is likely to become more difficult.

•　　•　　•

From the preceding analysis one must conclude that, among black people, assimilation has not been accomplished in most aspects of American life. They are, by and large, acculturated, for they share the culture of the larger society. However, there is minimal structural, marital, and identificational assimilation. They continue to experience widespread prejudice and discrimination; therefore, in terms of attitude receptional and behavior receptional assimilation, they lag behind many other minorities. On the civic assimilation variable, the process is uneven. Few conflicts exist at present, but, where there is conflict, it is fundamental, and the likelihood is that these conflicts will increase.

The prospects for the complete assimilation of black people into American life are extremely grim. Perhaps the single most important impediment to this process is the extent to which racism has become institutionalized in American life. White Americans refuse to accept black people as equals. Black Americans, on the other hand, have endeavored through the years to achieve assimilation into the larger society through peaceful and legal means. They have been constantly rebuffed. Consequently a small but growing number of black people are now questioning the desirability of total assimilation. Thus it seems fair to say that the likelihood of complete assimilation is indeed remote.

SELECTED BIBLIOGRAPHY

Bettelheim, Bruno, and Morris Janowitz, *Social Change and Prejudice*. New York: Free Press, 1964.

Brink, William, and Louis Harris, *Black and White*. New York: Simon and Schuster, Inc., 1967.

————, *The Negro Revolution in America*. New York: Simon and Schuster, Inc., 1964.

Clark, Kenneth B., *Dark Ghetto*. New York: Harper & Row, Publishers, 1965.

Conot, Robert, *Rivers of Blood, Years of Darkness*. New York: Bantam Books, Inc., 1967.

Cox, Oliver C., *Caste, Class and Race*. Garden City, N.Y.: Doubleday & Company, Inc., 1948.

Davis, Allison, Burleigh Gardner, and Mary Gardner, *Deep South*. Chicago: The University of Chicago Press, 1937.

Dollard, John, *Caste and Class in a Southern Town*. New Haven, Conn.: Yale University Press, 1937.

Drake, St. Clair, and Horace Cayton, *Black Metropolis*. New York: Harcourt, Brace and Co., 1945.

Frazier, E. Franklin, *Black Bourgeoisie*. Glencoe, Ill.: Free Press, 1957.

————, *The Negro in the United States*. New York: The Macmillan Company, 1957.

A Freedom Budget For All Americans. New York: A. Philip Randolph Institute, 1966.

Gordon, Albert I., *Intermarriage: Interfaith, Interracial, Interethnic.* Boston: Beacon Press, Inc., 1964.

Gordon, Milton M., *Assimilation in American Life.* New York: Oxford University Press, Inc. 1964.

Greenberg, Jack, *Race Relations and American Law.* New York: Columbia University Press, 1959.

Herskovits, Melville J., *The Myth of the Negro Past.* New York: Harper and Brothers, 1941.

Laurenti, Luigi, *Property Values and Race: Studies in Seven Cities.* Berkeley, Calif.: University of California Press, 1960.

Lewis, Hylan, *Blackways of Kent.* Chapel Hill, N.C.: The University of North Carolina Press, 1955.

McEntire, Davis, *Residence and Race.* Berkeley, Calif.: University of California Press, 1960.

Mendelson, Wallace, *Discrimination.* Englewood Cliffs, N.J.: Prentice-Hall, Inc., 1962.

Myrdal, Gunnar, *An American Dilemma: The Negro Problem and Modern Democracy.* New York: Harper and Brothers, 1944.

Northwood, L. K., and Ernest A. T. Barth, *Urban Desegregation.* Seattle, Wash.: University of Washington Press, 1965.

Powdermaker, Hortense, *After Freedom.* New York: The Viking Press, Inc., 1939.

Sheatslcy, Paul B., "White Attitudes Toward the Negro," in *The Negro American,* eds. Talcott Parsons and Kenneth Clark. Boston: Houghton Mifflin Company, 1966.

Silver, James W., *Mississippi: The Closed Society.* New York: Harcourt, Brace & World, Inc., 1964.

Simpson, George E., and J. Milton Yinger, *Racial and Cultural Minorities.* New York: Harper & Row, Publishers, 1965.

Sutherland, Elizabeth, ed., *Letters from Mississippi.* New York: McGraw-Hill Book Company, 1965.

Taeuber, Karl, and Alma Taeuber, *Negroes in Cities.* Chicago: Aldine Publishing Co., 1965.

U.S. Department of Health, Education, and Welfare, Office of Education, *Equality of Educational Opportunity.* Washington, D.C.: Government Printing Office, 1966.

Williams, Robin M., Jr., *Strangers Next Door: Ethnic Relations in American Communities.* Englewood Cliffs, N.J.: Prentice-Hall, Inc., 1964.

Woodward, C. Vann, *The Strange Career of Jim Crow.* New York: Oxford University Press, Inc., 1957.

The post-World War II era has been a period of rapid change in the United States and in the world. Although changes affecting the status of black Americans have been neither rapid nor widespread, they have occurred and they have generated greater expectations. The resistance of white Americans to change has served to make Negroes apprehensive about the willingness of society to accord them treatment equal to its white citizens. The caution with which public officials have moved to make amends for what are rather widely regarded as past injustices has made for greater militancy on the part of Negroes. The depth of anti-Negro sentiment in society has frequently been indicated by the negative response of white Americans to increased Negro militancy. Because white Americans insist upon determining the pace with which changes in race relations occur, a crisis has resulted. Negroes have learned from experience that positive changes affecting their status are more likely to result from political pressures than from altruism. Nevertheless, in the mid-1950's it appeared that increased civil rights for Negroes might become one of the major tasks to which American society might address itself for the first time in a century.

The Present and

the Future

BEGINNINGS OF THE REVOLT: BLACK PERSISTENCE AND WHITE RESISTANCE

The Supreme Court decision of May 1954 was welcomed by black Americans and their white supporters. It was felt that somehow this act might signal the beginning of a new era in the relations between black and white Americans. The decision outlawing segregation in public education had been expected, and black Americans felt that it would afford white Americans, especially those in the South, the opportunity to share in the worldwide movement for greater human rights. White Southerners responded to the desegregation ruling not with feelings of relief, but by establishing, during the summer, White Citizens Councils, which had as their primary function massive resistance to the ruling of the Supreme Court. Since the Supreme Court did not indicate how its ruling was to be implemented, school districts which had either required or permitted segregation reopened in September on a segregated basis (except those in Washington, D.C., and Baltimore, Maryland, where attempts were made to comply with the ruling of the Court). Throughout the South plans were made to do whatever became necessary to maintain the long-standing practice of racial segregation in schools. Statements by public officials in that region (governors, Senators, Representatives) served to lend support to the notion of massive resistance.

When the Supreme Court finally issued its implementation decree— that desegregation in public education should proceed "with all deliberate speed"—in May 1955, the forces opposing integration in public education had already organized themselves throughout the South.[1] Southerners were determined to maintain separate schools for black and white pupils, regardless of the ruling of the Supreme Court. The extent of their opposition came as a surprise to Negroes and their white supporters. It appeared that their hopes for a new era in race relations would not materialize. If a ruling of the highest court in the country could be met with such contempt by those responsible for maintaining the constitutional rights of citizens, how could black people ever expect to be accorded rights equal to those of white Americans?

Signs of growing unrest were evident among black Americans. African colonies were demanding and receiving independence from European colonial powers, and it appeared that all of Africa would achieve political freedom before black people in the United States would be able to assert the fundamental rights of service in places of public accommodation or attendance at schools supported by taxes imposed on them. Later in the summer of 1955, Emmett Till, a 14-year-old Negro boy from Chicago, visiting in Money, Mississippi, was kidnapped and lynched. He was accused of having whistled at a white woman, and, characteristically, those responsible for his murder were never apprehended. Feelings of disillusionment were widespread in black communities.

On December 1, 1955, a Negro seamstress, Mrs. Rosa Parks, boarded a public bus in Montgomery, Alabama. She took a seat in the section set aside for Negroes. Shortly thereafter she was ordered to vacate her seat so a white man could occupy it. She refused and was arrested. When word of the arrest spread through the black community, the Montgomery Bus Boycott was organized.[2] The bus boycott lasted for more than a year, ending in December 1956, when the Supreme Court upheld a lower court ruling outlawing racial segregation on buses in Montgomery.

This massive demonstration of solidarity among Negroes in opposition to long-standing practices of segregation and discrimination can be considered the first major act of resistance by Negroes in modern times

[1] See Anthony Lewis, *Portrait of a Decade* (New York: Random House, 1965), Chap. 3.
[2] See Martin Luther King, *Stride Toward Freedom* (New York: Harper, 1958).

and signals the birth of what might be called the Negro Revolt.[3] The story of the Montgomery Bus Boycott spread throughout black communities in the United States and served as an impetus for similar acts in other cities. Tallahassee, Florida, and Birmingham, Alabama, followed with bus boycotts. Nonviolent resistance to what was considered an "evil" system composed of "unjust" laws became the official means of dealing with the caste system of the South. The philosophy of nonviolence, according to its principal spokesman, contains the following elements: (1) active resistance to "evil," (2) attempts to win one's opponent through understanding, (3) directing one's attack against forces of "evil," rather than against persons performing such acts, (4) willingness to accept suffering without retaliation, (5) refusal to hate one's opponent, and (6) the conviction that the universe is on the side of justice.[4]

As the nonviolent resistance movement spread, massive opposition to social change in the realm of race relations was intensified by white Southerners. One hundred Southern members of Congress signed the Southern Manifesto, opposing the Supreme Court decision of 1954. They vowed "to use all lawful means to bring about a reversal of this decision which is contrary to the Constitution." Accordingly, laws implementing massive resistance to desegregation were enacted in Alabama, Georgia, Louisiana, Mississippi, South Carolina, and Virginia. While the Southern Manifesto did not explicitly call for the use of violence as a means of preventing Negro pupils from attending schools with white pupils, its impact served to generate violence.

A federal court ordered officials at the University of Alabama to admit a black student in February 1956. Her appearance on campus was met by mob violence from white students and others who were determined to maintain an all-white student enrollment.[5] She was removed from campus when the rioting flared and was forced to sue for readmission. The university officials responded with permanent expulsion on the grounds that she had made unfair statements about the University of Alabama.

On the elementary and secondary school levels, violence became the accepted means of preventing desegregation. In September 1956 a mob prevented Negro pupils from enrolling at the public high school in Mansfield, Texas. Mobs demonstrated against school integration in Clinton, Tennessee, and in Sturgis and Clay, Kentucky. In the latter cases it became necessary to deploy the National Guard to protect the

[3] See Louis Lomax, *The Negro Revolt* (New York: Harper, 1962), pp. 81–100.
[4] King, *op. cit.*, pp. 102–7.
[5] Charles Morgan, *A Time to Speak* (New York: Harper & Row, 1964), pp. 38–39.

Negro pupils. In the following years, when Negro parents attempted to enroll their children in schools with previously all-white enrollments, they were met with acts of violence, frequently directed at them by white women. One of the more highly publicized of these events occurred at Central High School in Little Rock, Arkansas, in 1957.[6] The courts had approved a desegregation plan, submitted by the Little Rock School Board, calling for the gradual desegregation of public schools beginning with the admission of nine Negro students to Central High School. The evening before they were scheduled to enroll, the governor announced that he would dispatch the National Guard to the school because of the possibility of violence. When the first Negro pupil appeared two days later, she was met by thousands of jeering white citizens who barred her from entering the building and by 270 National Guardsmen. Weeks later the National Guardsmen were withdrawn; nine Negro pupils entered the school, but local citizens forced them to withdraw. Mob violence in Little Rock continued to keep the Negro pupils from entering the school until the President ordered 1,000 paratroopers to Little Rock and federalized 10,000 members of the Arkansas National Guard to ensure their enrollment. This action represented the first time since Reconstruction that federal troops had been sent into the South to protect the rights of black people. Finally, on September 25, the nine Negro students entered Central High School. Federal troops remained at Central High School throughout the school year. At the beginning of the following school year the governor of Arkansas ordered all high schools in the city closed for the school year 1958–59. This was ostensibly done to prevent "impending violence and disorder." When the schools finally reopened in 1959, Negro pupils enrolled in both Central High School and another high school which had previously maintained a policy of admitting only white pupils.

Little Rock was not alone in its policy of massive resistance to integration through the closing of public schools. When desegregation was ordered for the Virginia cities of Norfolk, Charlottesville, and Front Royal, the governor responded by closing the schools involved. In Prince Edward County, Virginia, resistance to desegregation was so strong that the county's public schools were closed from 1959 to 1964.

In the years immediately following 1954, little desegregation of public schools was accomplished. Every September, at the beginning of the school year, one could expect the news releases to carry stories of violence directed toward Negro pupils. These pupils were frequently required to walk through racist mobs to get to class, and, once in the

6 Lewis, *op. cit.*, pp. 46–69.

classroom, they experienced a variety of insults and physical abuse from younger racists.[7]

On the college level desegregation was not achieved without violence. At both the University of Mississippi and the University of Alabama the admittance of Negroes triggered violence from white students. In fact, the admission of one black student to the University of Mississippi in 1962 triggered violence which ended in two deaths and 100 injuries. It was finally necessary to station 12,000 federal troops on the campus to assure the attendance of this student in classes. Federalized National Guardsmen were required to escort two black students to classes at the University of Alabama in 1963.

THE CIVIL RIGHTS
MOVEMENT

By 1960 desegregation of public education was proceding at a slow pace, and in the Deep South massive resistance remained an effective answer to the Supreme Court's ruling and to the demands of Negroes. Feelings of despair over the school segregation issue were widespread in the black community. The federal government assumed no responsibility for assuring enforcement of Negroes' declared constitutional rights. The responsibility for desegregating schools rested with Negroes themselves, and when they sought admission for their children to desegregated schools, it was frequently a long, costly, and complicated court procedure. Segregation and discrimination were still the social norms throughout the South, and all-white Southern juries continued to refuse to convict white persons responsible for lynching black people.

In February 1960 four black college students in North Carolina sought service at a lunch counter in a five-and-dime store. When they were denied service, they remained seated. The manager ordered the lunch counter closed, but they remained seated, reading their textbooks. The news of their actions quickly spread throughout the country, and within a few days the "sit-in" movement had spread to 15 cities in five Southern states. Whenever a group of black people appeared at a lunch counter, a mob of Southern whites appeared to heckle and jeer them. But the actions of the students inspired many others, black and white, to support them. Because of the determined resistance to desegregation of Southern white persons, and because of the strong determination of Negroes for social change in race relations, thousands of white Americans

[7] See Daisey Bates, *The Long Shadow of Little Rock* (New York: McKay, 1962); Robert Coles, *Children of Crisis: A Study of Courage and Fear* (Boston: Atlantic Monthly, 1967).

joined forces with the Negroes to give birth to the civil rights movement. Black college students organized the Student Nonviolent Coordinating Committee (SNCC) to coordinate activities aimed at desegregating places of public accommodation in the South. Peaceful demonstrations, led by college students, occurred in every major city where racial segregation was practiced openly. Thousands of Negroes and their white supporters were jailed for violating local segregation laws. The lunch counter demonstrations were accompanied by nationwide economic boycotts of the stores which maintained practices of segregation. Within a period of one and a half years it is reported that at least 70,000 black and white persons participated in the sit-in movement. More than 3,600 were arrested, and some 141 students and 58 faculty members were expelled by college authorities for their activities. Altogether, one or more establishments in each of 108 Southern and border cities had been desegregated because of the sit-ins.[8]

The combined effects of these demonstrations and boycotts served to force several of the larger chain stores to abandon practices of segregation in service and discrimination in employment. The example then spread to other areas: "wade-ins" were held at segregated public beaches, and "kneel-ins" were attempted in segregated churches. Always these demonstrators were peaceful, in keeping with the philosophy of non-violent direct action. However, in virtually all cases violence resulted from white persons determined to maintain white supremacy at all costs.

The Interstate Commerce Commission had ruled, in 1955, that racial segregation of passengers in buses, waiting rooms, and travel coaches involved in interstate travel violated these passengers' constitutional rights. Nevertheless, individual bus drivers and local law enforcement personnel continued to require Negroes to sit separated from white passengers. In February 1961 the director of the Congress of Racial Equality (CORE) announced that members of that organization would test the effectiveness of this ruling by staging a series of "freedom rides" throughout the South. Other civil rights organizations joined this effort, and in May a group of black and white activists started their journey from Washington, D.C., to New Orleans, Louisiana. When the bus reached Anniston, Alabama, it was bombed and burned by a mob of local white persons, and the group of freedom riders was beaten. In Montgomery, Alabama, the presence of the freedom riders met with such hostility that it was necessary to dispatch 400 U.S. marshals to keep order.

The freedom riders were jailed, beaten, or both in Alabama, Louisi-

[8] Lerone Bennett, Jr., *Before the Mayflower* (Baltimore, Md.: Penguin, 1966), p. 407.

ana, and Mississippi. There were more than a dozen freedom rides in the South, and these rides combined the efforts of the four major civil rights organizations. In addition to CORE and SNCC, the National Association for the Advancement of Colored People (NAACP) and the Southern Christian Leadership Conference (SCLC) participated. The freedom rides involved more than 1,000 persons, and the legal expenses they incurred exceeded $300,000.[9] As a result of these activities, the Interstate Commerce Commission issued an order outlawing segregation on all buses and in all terminal facilities.

The civil rights movement appealed to increasingly large numbers of white Americans. Demonstrations protesting all forms of segregation and discrimination were conducted throughout the United States, especially in the South. There were attacks on legally imposed segregation in the South and *de facto* segregation elsewhere and on discriminatory practices throughout the country. There were demonstrations at public libraries, swimming pools, public parks, and at seats of municipal government throughout the Deep South and Border South. Discrimination against black people in voting became a special target for civil rights activists, based on the assumption that, once armed with the franchise, Negroes would be in a position to elect public officials sympathetic to their demands. The Civil Rights Act of 1960 provided for the appointment of federal voting referees to receive applications to qualify voters if it could be proved that a person had been denied the right to vote because of race. Throughout the South voter registration schools were set up in churches. The response of many white Southerners was characteristic of their resistance to change in existing practices. Negro churches were bombed and burned. Churches had traditionally been exempt from the tyranny which Southern Negroes encountered daily, and now it appeared that they were not even safe in their houses of worship. Appeals to federal officials were in vain, and the reign of terror continued unabated. Arrests for these activities were rare, for local policemen often supported such activities. Black people and their white supporters remained nonviolent despite daily provocations and beatings.[10]

On occasion one city was selected to be a major target of civil rights demonstrations. SNCC selected Greenwood, Mississippi, as the site of its emancipation centennial campaign in response to an attempt to assassinate one of its field workers. They organized a massive voter

[9] Lomax, *op. cit.*, pp. 132–46.
[10] See Alphonso Pinkney, *The Committed: White Activists in the Civil Rights Movement* (New Haven, Conn.: College and University Press, 1968); Howard Zinn, *SNCC: The New Abolitionists* (Boston: Beacon Press, 1964).

registration campaign and were met by heavily armed policemen with police dogs. When they attempted to escort local Mississippi Negroes to register to vote, they were attacked by the police and their dogs.[11] The late Martin Luther King, Jr., selected Birmingham, Alabama, as SCLC's major site of antisegregation demonstrations during the centennial year. Birmingham was one of the most rigidly segregated larger cities in the South, and it was felt that if segregation barriers there could be penetrated, it would make for less difficulty elsewhere. The demonstrators were met in Birmingham by a force of policemen and firemen led by a well-known segregationist. Police and firemen were ordered to use a variety of techniques to curb the demonstrations, including fire hoses, cattle prods, and police dogs. For several days the demonstrators met greater brutality from law enforcement personnel than they had ever encountered previously, and the policemen and firemen were supported in their acts by an injunction from a local judge prohibiting protest marches. When the demonstrators defied this injunction, hundreds of them were jailed. The constitutional right of citizens to petition peacefully for redress of grievances was violated, and the Department of Justice issued a statement that it was watching the situation but that it was powerless to act. It was decided by the leaders of the demonstrations that schoolchildren should participate along with adults. They, too, were met by police clubs, dogs, and fire hoses. The pictures of the repressive measures used by the police and firemen served to alert the nation and the world to the extremes which segregationists would resort to in order to maintain white supremacy.

A turning point was reached in Birmingham when, following a meeting of the Ku Klux Klan, the home of the brother of the late Martin Luther King, Jr., and the motel which had served as King's headquarters and residence were bombed. Thousands of Negro demonstrators abandoned the philosophy of nonviolence and took to the streets with bottles and stones. They burned houses and stores and stoned policemen and passing cars. Before the uprising ended, they had burned a nine-block area of the city. When the demonstrators had requested federal protection from police dogs, fire hoses, and police clubs, the President announced that no federal agency could act. However, when the Negroes stoned white policemen and other citizens, federal troops were dispatched to Alabama within hours. Apparently the latter constituted acts of violence, while the former did not.

Demonstrations in many other Southern and border cities followed those in Birmingham. Danville, Virginia, and Cambridge, Maryland, were among the most prominent. During the summer of 1963 some 35

[11] Bennett, op. cit., pp. 329–40.

homes and churches were bombed or burned, at least ten people were killed, and more than 20,000 demonstrators were arrested. Thousands of others were shocked by cattle prods, set upon with high-pressure fire hoses, bitten by police dogs, and beaten by policemen. The summer demonstrations culminated in August, when some 250,000 Negroes and their white supporters participated in the March on Washington, the largest civil rights demonstration in history. As a direct outgrowth of these demonstrations Congress enacted the Civil Rights Act of 1964. The major provisions of this act are: (1) sixth-grade education was established as a presumption of literacy for voting purposes; (2) segregation and discrimination in places of public accommodation were outlawed; (3) public facilities (parks, playgrounds, libraries, etc.) were desegregated; (4) the Attorney General was authorized to file school desegregation suits; (5) discrimination was outlawed in all federally assisted activities; (6) discrimination by employers or unions with 100 or more employees or members was outlawed; (7) the Attorney General was authorized to intervene in private suits in which persons alleged denial of equal protection of the laws under the Fourteenth Amendment.

The leaders of several civil rights organizations, after achieving the victory which this act signaled, decided to concentrate their activities on voter registration and education. They had been urged by the Department of Justice to concentrate on these activities instead of street demonstrations. Consequently, in 1964 the Mississippi Summer Project was organized. Thousands of black and white activists journeyed to Mississippi to engage in activities aimed at improving the status of that state's nearly one million Negroes. They concentrated on voter education and registration and on "freedom schools." [12] The activists were subjected to a serious initial setback when three of their volunteers were abducted and murdered by a mob of local racists.[13] Throughout the summer they were subjected to a variety of harassments and abuse. The casualty list was high: by October 21 at least three persons had been killed, 80 were beaten, three were wounded by gunfire in 35 shootings, more than 35 churches were burned, 35 homes and other buildings were bombed, and more than 1,000 persons had been arrested. In addition, several unsolved murders of local Negroes were recorded.[14]

The Civil Rights Act of 1964 contained a provision ensuring Negroes the right to vote in all elections. However, when they attempted

[12] See Sally Belfrage, *Freedom Summer* (New York: Viking, 1965); Pinkney, *op. cit.*; Elizabeth Sutherland, *Letters from Mississippi* (New York: McGraw-Hill, 1965).
[13] See William Bradford Huie, *Three Lives for Mississippi* (New York: Trident Press, 1965).
[14] John Herbers, "Communique from the Mississippi Front," *The New York Times Magazine*, November 8, 1964, p. 34.

to register, a variety of techniques, especially intimidation, served to keep them from exercising this right. Consequently the major effort for 1965 was the campaign to ensure the right to vote. Resistance to Negro voting rights was strong. Several civil rights organizations decided to focus their attention on Alabama, which had been one of the most intransigent in this regard. Attempts to register Negroes failed, and a march from Selma to Montgomery was planned to dramatize the plight of that state's black citizens. Thousands of black activists and their white supporters gathered in Selma for the march. Several attempts to march were thwarted by the police, under orders from a local sheriff. Acts of excessive use of force by police were widespread, and these acts served to motivate additional thousands of citizens, including many clergymen, from all over the United States to join the activists in Selma. The march finally materialized but not without violence. Two white activists and one Negro were killed and scores of others were injured.

The Selma to Montgomery march served as a stimulus for the Voting Rights Act of 1965, which made it possible for Southern Negroes to register and vote with little difficulty. It was also the last mass demonstration of the civil rights movement. During the years of peak activity the civil rights movement enlisted the support of thousands of Americans, both black and white. Its nonviolent, direct action approach is responsible for many of the changes affecting the status of Southern Negroes. But its goals and methods were hardly applicable to the problems facing the many Negroes in urban slums throughout the country. Thousands of Negroes and their white supporters had combined for what was felt to be the most significant movement for social change in the United States.[15] The issues were clear, and, although there were differences on means toward achieving the goals, a coalition of many groups had united to work for a common end: the eradication of segregation and discrimination in American life. To a significant degree they were successful in achieving greater civil rights for Negroes, but black Americans remained a basically oppressed underclass of citizens.

DESPAIR IN THE SLUMS

By 1965 approximately half of all the Negroes in the United States lived outside what is generally regarded as the South (see Chap. Two), primarily in the slums of urban areas. For the most part, the lives of those in non-Southern urban areas have not been affected by the gains of the civil rights movement. A majority (three-fifths) of those remaining in the South are also crowded into the slums of urban areas, and, al-

[15] See Pinkney, *op. cit.*, Chap. 5.

though their lives have in some ways been affected by the civil rights movement, they too suffer from the gap between promise and performance. A vast majority of Negroes, then, live under conditions of hopelessness and despair. Little hope for change in their depressed status was apparent in 1965. At a time when the economy of the country was experiencing continued expansion, the median family income of black people was only slightly more than one-half (54 percent) of the white median family income. Eleven years after the Supreme Court outlawed segregation in public education, schools in the United States as a whole were more segregated than ever before. The unemployment rate for black people remained chronically high. Vast sums which had been allocated for public low-income housing had been diverted into middle-income housing which slum dwellers could not afford. At least 36 murders of civil rights workers in the South had been recorded, only three of which led to convictions, with no sentence of more than ten years imprisonment.

Many of the millions of recent Negro migrants from the South are from farms. Mechanization of agriculture and racist terror force them to leave the cotton fields. They packed their bags and boarded buses headed for New York City, Chicago, Detroit, Los Angeles, and other large cities. Many thought that these moves were into less hostile territory. Upon their arrival they were forced into slums in the centers of these cities. They arrived poorly educated and lacking in skills. They were in many ways similar to the great waves of European immigrants who entered the United States during the last decades of the 19th century and the first decades of the 20th century. However, no provision was made to ease the transition for these migrants, as has been done for recent white European refugees. As one observer has commented:

> Had Northern cities received hundreds of thousands of immigrants from Europe in the past few decades, no doubt all sorts of emergency provisions would have been made to help settle the newcomers, make them welcome, provide food, clothing, and shelter for them, and enable them to find work. Southern Negroes obtained no such courtesy, and what recognition they did get was calculated to remind them that white Americans may fight among themselves but in the clutch know how to stand together as a race.[16]

These migrants quickly learned that outside the South as well as within that region their place in the society had been clearly designated for them.

Federal measures ostensibly aimed at improving the standard of living for urban Negroes have either been inadequate or have not been

[16] Robert Coles, "When the Southern Negro Moves North," *The New York Times Magazine,* September 17, 1967, p. 25.

enacted by Congress. Many of the appropriations under the Economic Opportunity Act of 1964 never reach the persons they are designed to assist. For example, in some cases as much as half the money in anti-poverty programs is utilized for administrative purposes. The Congressional elections of 1966 saw conservatives elected in many states, and the administration virtually abandoned many of its civil rights proposals in response to what was interpreted as an upsurge of anti-Negro feeling among the electorate. Several cities had experienced violent Negro demonstrations in 1964 and 1965, and conservatives seeking public office based much of their campaign on curbing "crime in the streets" (i.e., black uprisings). In such a climate either proposed legislation was defeated (e.g., the rat control bill), or the requested appropriation was significantly reduced (e.g., the model cities bill). In the end, politics took precedence over the welfare of poor people, a significant proportion of whom are Negro.

The powerlessness of black Americans is clear. The communities in which they live are not significantly different from colonial territories in the underdeveloped world. They have no control over the institutions in their communities which are technically responsible to them. Virtually all black communities are among the major depressed areas in the country. The chief support for the communities comes from outside sources; the economy is dominated by people who do not and would not live in the communities. The inadequately maintained houses are often owned by affluent (and often politically powerful) suburban residents. The schools are staffed and controlled by outsiders. Law and order are maintained by suspicious and frightened policemen who frequently resort to the excessive use of force on the slightest provocation. When these residents are able to secure employment, they provide a cheap labor supply for the white community. Yet they are forced to pay prices far in excess of those paid by affluent suburban citizens for inferior products available in stores in slum neighborhoods. In many ways, then, the black community in the 1960's represents what might be called a form of internal colonialism. As one social scientist has written: "The dark ghetto's invisible walls have been erected by the white society, by those who have power, both to confine those who have *no* power and to perpetuate their powerlessness. The dark ghettos are social, political, and—above all—economic colonies. Their inhabitants are subject peoples, victims of the greed, cruelty, insensitivity, guilt, and fear of their masters." [17] Most white citizens are unaware of the conditions in these communities until the residents, as a result of their feelings of hopeless-

---

[17] Kenneth Clark, *Dark Ghetto* (New York: Harper & Row, 1965), p. 11.

ness and despair, rebel against conditions through what have come to be traditional summer uprisings.

One of the most articulate and perceptive leaders to address himself to the millions of poor blacks in the slums was Malcolm X. He was a product of slum life and had experienced virtually all aspects of destitution so common to poor black people in the United States.[18] Because of his abilities, he achieved an international reputation as a spokesman for the aspirations of poor black people. Malcolm X was feared and admired by both black and white Americans, and frequently the same individual shared both these sentiments. He was often misunderstood, although his speeches were clear. He urged black people to consolidate their efforts and to link their struggle with that of their African brothers as a means of achieving political, economic, and social equality. He did not feel that integration into the larger society was either likely or necessary in the near future. Therefore he advocated a policy of group solidarity. As a means of achieving this solidarity, he constantly advocated positive identification (i.e., pride in blackness). Malcolm X urged white Americans who sympathized with the aspirations of black people to organize themselves and work within the white community in an effort to rid it of its racist practices. He did not advocate the initiation of violence, but he was a strong proponent of armed self-defense as a means of meeting violent attacks by racists. Few leaders have been so misunderstood as was Malcolm X. As a social critic, his exegesis of American society was severe but meticulous. In many ways he was the inaugurator of the current Black Power movement.

BLACK POWER

For all practical purposes the civil rights movement ended in 1965. The following year civil rights organizations appeared to be searching for some cause around which to rally as a means of continuing their protest activities. Although implementation was lagging, they had won important victories: the Civil Rights Act of 1964, the Voting Rights Act of 1965, and, perhaps most important of all, the recognition by Americans that the low status of black people posed a serious social problem in a world where oppressed people were fighting for freedom and self-determination. The question "Where do we go from here?" was being asked by the leaders of the major civil rights organizations. In June 1966 James Meredith was shot as he started his freedom march through Mississippi. Immediately thereafter the leaders of several civil rights

18 Malcolm X, *The Autobiography of Malcolm X* (New York: Grove Press, Inc., 1964).

organizations gathered in Memphis, Tennessee, and made plans to turn the aborted march into a major civil rights campaign. During this march Stokely Carmichael, the chairman of SNCC, introduced a new and controversial slogan into the nomenclature of the movement to achieve greater civil rights for Negroes. The concept of Black Power was first used in this context when the marchers reached Greenwood, Mississippi.[19] Field workers from SNCC had worked in this community, and, at a mass rally, when Carmichael proclaimed, "What we need is black power," he was cheered by the crowd of poor Mississipians.

The introduction of the concept of Black Power was debated by the leaders of CORE, SCLC, and SNCC. Martin Luther King and his associates from SCLC disapproved of its use, but the leaders of CORE and SNCC supported its use. A compromise was reached—that the concept was not to be used as the official slogan of the march—but it gained worldwide usage and generated a heated debate among the major black organizations.

Somehow the combination of the words "black" and "power" seemed to offend and frighten white Americans, especially some "liberal" white persons who had contributed time and money to the civil rights movement. To them the concept implied black supremacy (or reverse racism) and black violence. Consequently they resigned from membership and withheld financial support from the more militant organizations. Similarly the more moderate civil rights organizations, such as the NAACP and the National Urban League, expressed their disapproval of Black Power. The organizations which had led the civil rights movement and which had cooperated in the major campaigns and demonstrations in the South were divided along ideological lines.

Those leaders advocating Black Power have attempted to define the concept, but such attempts have usually been lost in the growing debate in the mass media of communications. To Stokely Carmichael of SNCC the concept speaks to the needs of black people at the present time. It is a call to black Americans to liberate themselves from oppression by assuming control over their lives economically, politically, and socially. He has said:

> Black Power means black people coming together to form a political force and either electing representatives or forcing their representatives to speak to their needs. It's an economic and physical bloc that can exercise its strength in the black community instead of letting the job go to the Democratic or Republican parties or a white-controlled black man set up as a puppet to represent black people. *We* pick the brother and make sure he

[19] Martin Luther King, Jr., *Where Do We Go From Here?* (New York: Harper & Row, 1967), pp. 23–32.

fulfills *our* needs. Black Power doesn't mean antiwhite, violence, sepa-
ratism, or any other racist things the press says it means. It's saying, "Look,
buddy, we're not laying a vote on you unless you lay so many schools,
hospitals, playgrounds, and jobs on us." [20]

Later he and Charles Hamilton elaborate on the concept of Black Power:

It is a call for black people in this country to unite, to recognize their
heritage, to build a sense of community. It is a call for black people to
begin to define their own goals, to lead their own organizations, and to
support those organizations. It is a call to reject the racist institutions and
values of this society.

The concept of Black Power rests on a fundamental premise: *Before a
group can enter the open society, it must first close ranks.* By this we mean
that group solidarity is necessary before a group can operate effectively
from a bargaining position of strength in a pluralistic society.[21]

Floyd McKissick of CORE sees the following as elements of Black
Power: increased political and economic power for Negroes, improved
self-image, the development of young, militant black leadership, the
development of black consumer power, and strong resistance to police
brutality in black communities.[22]

Although Martin Luther King, Jr., opposed the use of the concept
of Black Power for a variety of reasons, he acknowledged that it had
what he called a "positive meaning." [23] He saw it as a "cry of disappointment" and of despair with the present state of black-white relations. He
also interpreted it as ". . . a call to black people to amass the political
and economic strength to achieve their legitimate goals." Finally, he saw
Black Power as "a psychological call to manhood." Despite its many
positive features, King felt that the concept had too many negative
values for it to serve as the basic strategy with which to meet the problems faced by black people at the present time.[24] He believed that it
embodied a philosophy of hopelessness about achieving basic changes in
the structure of American society. In addition, as an integrationist, King
saw the Black Power movement as one based on separation of the races
in the United States. He rejected the notion that any group within
the larger society could achieve equality through separation. Finally, as

[20] Quoted in Gordon Parks, "Stokely Carmichael: Young Man Behind an Angry
Message," *Life*, May 19, 1967, p. 82.

[21] Stokely Carmichael and Charles V. Hamilton, *Black Power: The Politics of
Liberation in America* (New York: Random House, Inc., copyright 1967), p. 44.

[22] See Fred C. Shapiro, "The Successor to Floyd McKissick May Not Be So Reasonable," *The New York Times Magazine,* October 1, 1967, p. 102.

[23] King, *Where Do We Go From Here?*, pp. 32–44.

[24] *Ibid.*, pp. 44–63.

a foremost exponent of nonviolence, he felt that the concept was often a call for retaliatory violence, which, he maintained, could only serve to impede progress in race relations.

The more moderate leaders of civil rights organizations have opposed the concept of Black Power from its inception. The leaders of the NAACP and the Urban League joined five other prominent black spokesmen and responded to the militant organizations by placing an advertisement entitled "Crisis and Commitment" in numerous newspapers.[25] In response to the advocates of Black Power they enumerated what they considered to be the "principles upon which the civil rights movement rests." They included four points: (1) a commitment to the principle of racial justice through the democratic process, (2) the repudiation of violence, (3) a commitment to the principle of integration, and (4) a commitment to the principle that the task of bringing about integration is the common responsibility of all Americans, both black and white.

One of the leading critics of Black Power rejects the concept in favor of coalition politics. Bayard Rustin feels that the concept is harmful to the movement for greater civil rights for America's Negroes because "It diverts the movement from a meaningful debate over strategy and tactics, it isolates the Negro community, and it encourages the growth of anti-Negro forces." As an alternative to Black Power, Rustin advocates a "liberal-labor-civil rights coalition which would work to make the Democratic Party truly responsive to the aspirations of the poor, and which would develop support for programs (specifically those outlined in A. Philip Randolph's $100 billion Freedom Budget) aimed at the reconstruction of American society in the interests of greater social justice." [26]

Supporters of Black Power reject the notion of forming coalitions with predominantly white liberal, labor, and religious organizations. They insist that those who advocate such coalitions proceed on the basis of three fallacious assumptions: (1) that at the present time the interests of black Americans are identical with the interests of these groups, (2) that a viable coalition can be established between groups with power and powerless Negroes, and (3) that it is possible to sustain political coalitions on a "moral, friendly, sentimental basis; by appeals to conscience." [27]

The debate over Black Power continues. The more militant organizations, CORE and SNCC, are its chief proponents; the more moderate

[25] *The New York Times,* October 14, 1966, p. 35.
[26] Bayard Rustin, " 'Black Power' and Coalition Politics," *Commentary,* Vol. 42 (September 1966), 35–40.
[27] Carmichael and Hamilton, *op. cit.,* Chap. 3.

organizations, the NAACP and the Urban League, are strongly opposed; and SCLC takes a middle position. In keeping with their position that Black Power means black consciousness and solidarity, the militant organizations have urged their white supporters to form parallel organizations and to work with the white community to rid it of the racism which is endemic to American life. A coalition between black and white Americans at the present time is seen as unworkable. The major impediment to equality for black people is seen as the resistance of the white community. Consequently, CORE and SNCC have urged their white supporters to work within their own communities.

Less than one year after the concept was first introduced, it had gained widespread prominence. In July 1967 the first National Conference on Black Power was held in Newark, New Jersey. This conference was attended by more than 1,000 black delegates from 42 cities in 36 states. They represented a broad cross section of black leaders, ranging from the militant black nationalists to employees of government agencies. One of the most significant aspects of the conference was its bringing together for the first time a wide assembly of black people who met in workshop sessions to define the concept of Black Power and who agreed to implement its components. When the conference ended, a series of resolutions had been passed, including the following: (1) the establishment of black financial institutions such as credit unions and nonprofit cooperatives, (2) the establishment of black universities, (3) selective purchasing and boycotting of white merchants in black communities, (4) the demand for a guaranteed annual income for all people, (5) a boycott by black athletes of international Olympic competition and professional boxing, in response to the stripping of the world heavyweight boxing title from Muhammad Ali, (6) boycotts of Negro churches which are not committed to the "black revolution," (7) boycotts of Negro publications accepting advertisements for hair straighteners and bleaching creams.

Meanwhile, Black Power gained wider acceptance among more radical white Americans. In November 1966 students at Oberlin College, in Oberlin, Ohio, held an intercollegiate conference entitled Black Power in the Urban Ghetto, in an effort to "eliminate the emotionalism which clouds the debate on Black Power and to try to point out the basic issues involved." At its annual meeting in August 1967 the National Student Association, the largest organization of college students in the United States, resolved to support the implementation of the concept of Black Power "through any means necessary." In September the delegates attending the National Conference for New Politics in Chicago voted by a margin of more than two to one to support all resolutions of the Newark Black Power Conference and to support "black control of the political, economic, and social institutions in black communities."

Current interest in the concept of Black Power is perhaps too recent in its origin to gain wide acceptance on its relevance to the problems faced by Negroes. It has emotional implications which white Americans fear, but, stripped of its emotional connotations, it appears to mean the amassing by black people of the economic, political, and social power necessary to deal effectively with the problems they face as a powerless people relegated to a life of poverty in an affluent society. Furthermore, it is a call to black people to reject the social values (especially racism) which are responsible for their low status in the United States and to replace them with an ideology which embraces dignity and pride in blackness. Black solidarity is seen as a precondition to the achievement of these ends. Integration, it is felt, is much more likely to be achieved from a position of strength than from one of weakness.

The concept of ethnic power is not alien to American society. Historically, many ethnic groups have managed to improve their status through the process of organizing themselves into power blocs. Indeed, historically, ethnic solidarity has been a fundamental aspect of American minority relations. One writer has defended Black Power as follows:

> . . . . to the extent that "Black Power" expresses a determination to build a Negro community which would be something more than euphemisms for the ghetto, it is a valid and necessary cry; to the extent that it expresses a despair of the one-by-one absorption of "deserving" Negroes into the general society and puts its faith instead in collective action aimed at dealing with collective fate, it is an intelligent response to the reality of American life.[28]

He sees the attempts to establish group loyalty among Negroes, which is a fundamental aspect of Black Power, as an essential means of dealing with a basically hostile society. Although other minority groups have effectively organized themselves along religious and ethnic lines into political and economic power blocs as a means of improving their status, once this goal has been achieved, they effectively combine forces and join what Negroes call the white power structure, which serves to perpetuate the low status of Negroes. They may be of Irish, Italian, Jewish, or Polish extraction, but in encounters with Negroes, racial homogeneity serves to solidify them. In short, black subordination was achieved and has been maintained by the unabashed use of "white power."

[28] David Danzig, "In Defense of 'Black Power,'" *Commentary*, Vol. 42 (September 1966), 46. Reprinted from *Commentary*, by permission; copyright © 1966, by the American Jewish Committee.

Another writer, who sees Black Power as "the acquisition of power by Negroes for their own use, both offensively and defensively," defends the concept, especially its emphasis on black nationalism and black consciousness, as follows:

> It *is* important to establish a positive black identity in a great many sectors of the black communities, both North and South, rural and urban, lower and middle class. Indeed, it is both important and legitimate to teach black people (or any other ethnic minority) about their history, placing special emphasis upon the positive contributions of other black people. This black consciousness has the potential to create unity and solidarity among black people and to give them hope and self-confidence.[29]

She reports that Black Power has achieved success among Mississippi Negroes because attempts at racial integration in that state have failed.

The use of black political power to achieve Negro rights is not new. In 1941 black leaders effectively forced the President to issue an executive order banning discrimination in employment in industry doing business with the federal government. Such organizations as the Negro American Labor Council of the American Federation of Labor–Congress of Industrial Organizations and the all-Negro organization within the New York City Police Department exist to protect the interests of their members. The idea underlying the concept of Black Power, then, is not a new one. It has, however, gained new strength within the last two years. In 1967 a nationwide organization of elected Negro public officials was formed to develop methods of utilizing their combined power to improve the status of black citizens. A nationwide group of Negro ministers met in November 1967 in an effort to make Black Power a force in American Protestant church policies. They are organizing to serve as a pressure group within the National Council of Churches in an effort to increase the number of Negroes in policy-making positions and to "bring the resources of white churches into urban ghettos in such a way as to enhance Negro leadership."[30]

The civil rights movement was basically reformist, aimed at changing some aspects of the structure of American society insofar as black people were denied some of the rights guaranteed citizens in the Constitution. It was directed toward establishing the principle of legal equality as public policy and toward the responsibility of the federal government in protecting the constitutional rights of citizens. To a degree these goals have been achieved, or, at least, they have been accepted as a matter of

[29] Joyce Ladner, "What 'Black Power' Means to Negroes in Mississippi," *Transaction*, Vol. 5 (November 1967), 14.

[30] *The New York Times*, November 2, 1967, p. 52, col. 2.

principle. The Black Power movement, on the other hand, goes beyond social reform. If the demands for political, economic, and social control by black people over the institutions which are responsible to them, along with the other changes necessary for the "liberation" of American Negroes, are achieved, American society will have undergone revolutionary changes. The civil rights movement did not address itself to the complex, deeply rooted problems facing black people in the slums of the United States. The Black Power movement does. In this sense, the Black Power movement might be said to be the logical extension of the civil rights movement. Where the civil rights movement ended, the Black Power movement begins, and it might be said that the death of the civil rights movement gave birth to the black liberation movement.

WHERE WE STAND

The passage of the Civil Rights Act of 1964 and the Voting Rights Act of 1965, both of which resulted from massive civil rights campaigns conducted by black and white Americans in such places as Birmingham and Selma, Alabama, brought about a measure of change in the lives of Southern Negroes. The daily indignities which had characterized their lives for centuries had been somewhat ameliorated. To a degree they could share public facilities—libraries, restaurants, parks, and hotels—with white Americans. To a lesser degree they could exercise their constitutional right to vote. Many white Americans rejoiced that significant progress had been achieved in these realms, and to them the civil rights "revolution" was accomplished. They had demonstrated, marched, and suffered with their black brothers, and they had won. With this sense of accomplishment, they abandoned the civil rights movement. As long as black people were marching and singing "We Shall Overcome," they were eager to lend support. But they were unaware that the eradication of overt practices of racial segregation in public places and discrimination at the polls signaled only the first step toward equality for black people. Rather, they saw it as an end. Black people, on the other hand, were aware that the lives of few Negroes outside the South had been affected by these changes. The Southern Negro was beginning to achieve the token degree of equality which his counterpart outside the South had already achieved.

Collectively black people represent a vast underclass of citizens in the United States, and little attempt has been made to deal with their many long-standing problems—poverty, discrimination in employment, inadequate housing, etc. Because of the expense involved, proposed remedies for these problems have not been taken seriously by many who

have worked in the civil rights movement. Little expense had been incurred in accomplishing the modest gains of the civil rights movement,
but to alter significantly the status of black people in the United States
in a fundamental sense would be expensive, both in money and in psychological readjustment. It would no doubt cost billions of dollars, and
in psychological readjustment, white Americans would be forced to
abandon one of America's longest-standing cultural myths—that of racial
inferiority of the black man. Taken collectively, the price is too high for
a vast majority of America's privileged class. Therefore the civil rights
movement has reached a deadlock: Black Americans demand equality,
while most white Americans continue to cling to the ideology of white
supremacy.

   The status of black people in the United States in 1967 indicates
how much remains to be accomplished before black Americans will have
achieved equality. Earnings and employment rates for Negroes lag far
behind those of white Americans. The average Negro earns approximately one-half of what the average white American earns, and the rate
of unemployment among Negroes is twice as high as among white Americans. Furthermore, when unemployed, they are likely to remain in that
state twice as long as white workers. A vast majority (three-fourths) of
Negroes hold menial jobs. They continue to do the low-paying, unskilled
jobs essential for contemporary society. At least one-half of all black
people live in substandard (slum) housing, for which they are forced to
pay more than their white counterparts who enjoy better-quality housing. These conditions contribute to low standards of health. For example, the infant mortality rate is twice as high for Negroes as for white
Americans. In education, most Negroes continue to attend segregated
public schools with inferior facilities. Consequently their achievement
level lags behind that of white pupils.

   Significant changes have been recorded in the lives of black Americans during the past decade, but they have affected mostly only the
small middle class. Today many Negroes are employed in positions which
heretofore had been reserved for white persons. However, the lives of
the black masses in the urban slums remain unaffected. The appointment of a Negro to the Supreme Court or as chief administrative officer
of Washington, D.C., hardly affects those persons living substandard lives
in the many cities throughout the country. Such appointments sym-
bolize a remote opportunity which mocks the plight of the members of
the underclass and reinforces their despair. It is among the black people
living in urban slums that despair is most pronounced. They have become acutely aware that officials of the federal government are willing to
commit annually ten times as much of the nation's resources to a war in

Asia as they are to programs ostensibly designed to eradicate poverty at home. Similarly, they are aware that, proportionately, twice as many blacks as whites are killed in action in Vietnam. These factors, coupled with the lack of change in race relations in the past decade, have contributed to the feelings of hopelessness which pervade Negro slums throughout the United States. Peaceful petition for redress of grievances has resulted in token change in the overt practices of segregation and discrimination. It has not secured effective action regarding the more fundamental problems which a vast majority of black people face.

One result of this lack of change in the realm of race relations has been the massive uprisings in black communities which have come to be a regular summer feature in the United States. Each summer hundreds of black people strike at the structure of society through these uprisings. In the summers of 1963–67 these phenomena occurred in hundreds of cities throughout the country, often taking on the character of urban guerrilla warfare, with the oppressed slum dwellers opposing the helmeted federal troops and local law enforcement personnel. Federal, state, and local officials have generally been insensitive to the real meaning of these uprisings, charging that they have been led by small bands of "extremists" directed from Havana, Cuba, or Peking, China. But for a significant proportion of black people, leaders as well as rank and file, the disturbances have had a more positive than negative impact. For example, approximately one-third (34 percent) of a sample of Negroes indicated that they felt that "riots" have helped their cause. Among a sample of leaders more than two-fifths (41 percent) gave a similar response. One-fifth of both categories of individuals (20 percent of rank and file and 19 percent of leaders) indicated their belief that the "riots" have hurt the cause of civil rights.[31]

The first of the major uprisings occurred in Watts, the black section of Los Angeles, California, in August 1965.[32] In 1966 it was Cleveland, Ohio, and in 1967, Newark, New Jersey,[33] and Detroit, Michigan.[34]

---

[31] William Brink and Louis Harris, *Black and White* (New York: Simon and Schuster, 1967), p. 67.

[32] See Robert Conot, *Rivers of Blood, Years of Darkness* (New York: Bantam, 1967); R. J. Murphy and James Watson, *The Structure of Discontent* (Los Angeles: Institute of Government and Public Affairs, University of California, 1967); T. M. Tomlinson and D. L. TenHouten, *Los Angeles Riot Study Method: Negro Reaction Survey* (Los Angeles: Institute of Government and Public Affairs, University of California, 1967).

[33] Tom Hayden, *Rebellion in Newark* (New York: Random House, 1967); report of the New Jersey Select Commission on Civil Disorder, *The New York Times*, February 11, 1968, p. 1, cols. 2–3.

[34] See Tom Parmenter, "Breakdown of Law and Order," *Transaction*, Vol. 9 (September 1967), 13–22.

In 1967 alone these uprisings occurred in some 56 cities in 31 states, resulting in at least 84 deaths, 3,828 injuries, 9,550 arrests, and hundreds of millions of dollars in property damage.[35]

The uprising in Watts lasted for five days. Thirty-four persons were killed, more than 1,000 were injured, some 4,000 arrests were made, and the estimated property damage was $40 million. More than 200 buildings were destroyed by fire, and another 400 were damaged. Of those persons killed, coroner's inquests indicated that 16 of the deaths of Negroes had been caused by the Los Angeles Police Department and seven had been caused by the National Guardsmen.[36] After the uprising many public officials appeared to be more concerned about the property losses than about the loss of human lives.

The Watts uprising signaled the end of the monopoly previously held by the advocates of nonviolence as a method of protest among Negroes. At the peak of the uprising some 10,000 black people took to the streets, and for more than five days they fought against a force of 15,500 policemen and National Guardsmen. The police seized more than 850 weapons from the demonstrators, and the uprising was finally suppressed.

Another major uprising occurred in Newark in July 1967. Some 26 persons were killed, more than 1,100 injured, and more than 1,600 jailed. Property damage was estimated at $15 million. The black community was occupied for several days by a force of 3,000 National Guardsmen, 1,400 local police, and 500 state troopers. A majority of the deaths resulted from gunfire from Newark policemen, who have been described as racists. It is reported that 100 Negro-owned stores were destroyed by the police.[37]

Immediately after Newark, Detroit experienced the bloodiest racial uprising in modern America. In this uprising 43 people were killed, more than 2,000 were injured, and more than 5,000 were arrested. Property damage exceeded $500 million. The Negro residents of Detroit engaged in a form of urban guerrilla warfare with heavily armed policemen and soldiers. Altogether 7,000 National Guardsmen and 4,700 paratroopers supplemented the 2,500 members of the city and state police forces. With the use of tanks and machine guns the uprising was finally brought to an end after seven days of fighting. As with preceding urban uprisings, there were evidences of police brutality motivated by racism. It is reported that three young black men were executed by white policemen who found them with three white women in a motel room several

[35] Figures compiled from news reports in *The New York Times* during August 1967.

[36] *Violence in the City—An End or A Beginning?* (Los Angeles: Governor's Commission on the Los Angeles Riots, 1965).

[37] Hayden, *op. cit.*, p. 38; *The New York Times*, February 11, 1968, p. 1, col. 3.

blocks from the scene of the fighting.[38] Other Negroes present insisted that the three men were unarmed and that the police were motivated by anti-Negro prejudice.

Each of these uprisings—Watts, Newark, and Detroit—was immediately triggered by what the black people involved considered unfair police action. Black people are often apprehended for minor infractions of the law for which white persons are rarely punished in similar circumstances. The police are seen as the society's enforcers of unfair standards of justice and as occupying forces, and many slum residents reject this legal authority. During uprisings police frequently shoot black people of all ages for such infractions of the law as looting stores. The assumption that property rights are more sacred than human life prevails. Black people, on the other hand, interpret the looting as a means of sharing in the material rewards of a society which has, through a variety of techniques, denied them their rightful share. Although seemingly trivial incidents involving law enforcement serve to kindle slum uprisings, these are not the underlying cause of such phenomena. In urban slums black people are forced to live in poverty and deprivation. They utilize the uprisings as a means of bringing their economic plight (unemployment and low earnings) maintained by white racism to the attention of public officials who have generally been insensitive to their status.[39] It is through the destruction caused by these uprisings that public officials in a highly materialistic society are made aware of the hopelessness and despair of these citizens.

The conditions under which black people live have improved somewhat in the last decade, but these changes have heightened their feelings of relative deprivation in relation to the status of white Americans. It is this feeling of relative deprivation that has led to the crisis in race relations which has brought American society to the point where, as the National Advisory Commission on Civil Disorders concludes: "Our nation is moving toward two societies, one black, one white—separate and unequal." [40] The commission, which investigated the black uprisings of 1967, reported that these disorders were caused by the attitudes of white Americans toward black Americans: "White racism is essentially responsible for the explosive mixture which has been accumulating in our cities since the end of World War II." [41] Elsewhere the commission reports:

[38] Parmenter, *op. cit.,* pp. 15–16.

[39] See Stanley Lieberson and Arnold R. Silverman, "The Precipitants and Underlying Conditions of Race Riots," *American Sociological Review,* Vol. 30 (December 1965), 887–98.

[40] *Report of the National Advisory Commission on Civil Disorders* (New York: Bantam, 1968), p. 1.

[41] *Ibid.,* p. 203.

"What white Americans have never fully understood—but what the Negro can never forget—is that white society is deeply implicated in the ghetto. White institutions created it, white institutions maintain it, and white society condones it." [42] Sociological studies of the causes of present Negro militance generally attribute this phenomenon to the feelings of relative deprivation which black people feel when compared to white Americans.[43]

White Americans frequently compare the socioeconomic status of black Americans with that of other people living outside the United States. Such comparisons are invalid because it is the relative status of black and white Americans which has precipitated the present crisis. Black people in the United States may enjoy a higher standard of living than do citizens of the so-called underdeveloped nations, but the gap between black and white Americans continues to be vast.

It is frequently maintained that the uprisings sweeping American cities impede the cause of Negro equality. Such phenomena may make for an increase in anti-Negro prejudice, but at the same time their long-term effect may serve to improve the status of Negroes insofar as decreased discrimination is concerned. In short, a reduction in discrimination is more important to the cause of Negro equality than an increase in prejudice. The so-called "riots" of 1967 resulted in the far-reaching report by the National Advisory Commission on Civil Disorders. If the recommendations of this report are put into effect, the result will be widespread change in the status of black people in the United States.

In the meantime, recent developments among black people are likely to alter the character of American race relations. One such development is the increasing political awareness of black college students. Since 1962 black students at the major colleges and universities throughout the United States have organized themselves into all-black clubs and are challenging established practices.[44] They question the content of courses and the hiring practices of these institutions, and they reject integration into the white middle-class social life of these schools. They read the works of black writers, most of whom rarely appear on reading lists for regular courses. They conduct discussions on topics such as black identity and publish newspapers and magazines. In short, they have introduced the concept of Black Power on the college campus.

[42] *Ibid.*, p. 2.

[43] James A. Geschwender, "Social Structure and the Negro Revolt: An Examination of Some Hypotheses," *Social Forces*, Vol. 43 (December 1964), 248–56; Ruth Searles and J. Allen Williams, Jr., "Negro College Students' Participation in Sit-Ins," *Social Forces*, Vol. 40 (March 1962), 215–20.

[44] Ernest Dunbar, "The Black Revolt Hits the White Campus," *Look*, Vol. 31 (October 1967), 27–31.

Students were among the earliest participants in the civil rights movement in the South, but black students at predominantly white colleges and universities outside the South were often more involved in fraternities, sororities, and other social activities than in questions of equality for black slum dwellers. In the South they were made aware of their status daily through the practice of rigid segregation, but outside the South the few black students could easily be absorbed into the life of the school or effectively isolated. Frequently their lives were such that it was possible for them to forget that they were black while they remained on campus. The transition from school to work, difficult at best, became increasingly so for black college students. They were not being prepared for the reality of what they would face as professionals in a racist society.

The response of black students to this situation has been an attempt to organize themselves. The first of these organizations outside the South was the Student's Afro-American Society at Columbia University. It was followed by Harvard University's African and Afro-American Students group, Yale University's Black Students Alliance, Princeton University's Association of Black Collegians, Dartmouth College's Afro-American Society, the University of California at Berkeley's Afro-American Student Union, Hunter College's Kubanbanya, City College's Onyx, and other similar organizations at colleges throughout the United States. In December 1966 a Northeastern regional conference of these groups met at Columbia University. It was attended by 300 delegates from 30 schools.

One of the primary functions of these organizations is to stress black consciousness and black pride. Through them, students come to identify with each other and with their less fortunate fellow Negroes. Frequently the students spend their free time working with black slum dwellers, especially in tutorial programs and other educational projects. This action provides a link between the politically sophisticated students and the powerless slum dwellers. Furthermore, these students are more likely than the others to understand the nature and functioning of the society in which they live. Consequently they provide an important source of black leadership at a crucial time.

Another recent development in the black movement is the attempt among leaders of the more militant organizations to link the movement for black equality in the United States with the movements of other oppressed peoples throughout the world, especially those in Africa, Asia, and Latin America. One of the first black leaders in recent years to see the struggle of black Americans in international terms was Malcolm X.

He traveled and consulted extensively in Africa and Asia.[45] It was an attempt to link the struggle of black people in the United States and that of Africans which led Malcolm X to establish the Organization of Afro-American Unity. Since his death several other black leaders have made contacts with revolutionary individuals and organizations throughout the world.

These leaders see the struggle of black Americans as being similar to those of other oppressed peoples, and they increasingly turn to what they call the Third World for support. In 1967 Stokely Carmichael was the guest of honor and a delegate at the meeting in Havana, Cuba, of the Organization of Latin American Solidarity, an organization of the leaders of revolutionary movements in Latin America. In his address to the conference he said:

> We greet you as comrades because it becomes increasingly clear to us each day that we share with you a common struggle; we have a common enemy. Our enemy is white Western imperialist society; and our struggle is to overthrow the system which feeds itself and expands itself through the economic and cultural exploitation of nonwhite, non-Western peoples. We speak to you, comrades, because we wish to make clear that we understand that our destinies are intertwined. We do not view our struggle as being contained within the boundaries of the United States, as they are defined by present-day maps. . . .[46]

At the first meeting of the National Conference for New Politics in Chicago in September 1967, black delegates insisted that the conference adopt a resolution pledging total and unquestionable support to all wars of national liberation in Africa, Latin America, and, particularly, Vietnam.

According to one reporter, "Negroes increasingly see Black Power as not confined to ghetto rebellions, but rather as part of a general fight of the oppressed against the oppressor all over the world." [47] He cites several instances in which black leaders in the United States have met with leaders of revolutionary movements around the world. Floyd McKissick of CORE joined a team of other Americans which traveled to Cambodia to investigate the claims by the U.S. Department of Defense that the area of Cambodia which borders on South Vietnam was used by the North Vietnamese forces as a sanctuary. While there, he reportedly conferred with the chief of state on "peace and racism." A black lawyer and

[45] Malcolm X, *op. cit.*, especially Chaps. 17–19.
[46] Reported in John Gerassi, "Havana: A New International Is Born," *Monthly Review,* Vol. 19 (October 1967), 27.
[47] William Worthy, "The American Negro Is Dead," *Esquire* (November 1967), p. 126.

other leaders went to North Vietnam to gather evidence for the International War Crimes Tribunal organized by Bertrand Russell, and representatives of SNCC served as judges on this tribunal. In addition, SNCC maintains an international affairs department through which contact is made with other revolutionary movements, principally in Africa. When the United Nations sponsored a seminar on racial discrimination and colonialism in southern Africa in the summer of 1967, both CORE and SNCC were represented.

Increasingly, the more militant black leaders are attempting to internationalize the movement for equality. Such events as the assassination of Patrice Lumumba in the Congo and that of Malcolm X in New York at a time when he was establishing contacts with African leaders, as well as the implication of the Central Intelligence Agency in antirevolutionary acts outside the United States, have forced some of the black leaders to see their fight for equality in global terms.

By the end of 1967 the status of the black American remained a domestic problem of considerable magnitude. Although greater changes have occurred in the last ten years than during the nearly 100 years since the Reconstruction, Negroes remained a large underclass of citizens. The movement responsible for these changes appears to have suffered an irreparable split over the introduction of the concept of Black Power. The militant leaders who favor the concept talk in terms of black liberation, while the more moderate leaders who oppose it cling to a belief in racial justice through the democratic process. In the meantime, black people throughout the United States are becoming increasingly politically aware of the society in which they live.

This increasing political awareness was recently manifested by the widespread support in black communities throughout the United States for a Negro state legislator from Georgia who was denied his seat because of his outspoken opposition to the war in Vietnam; by the support accorded the world's heavyweight champion when he was stripped of his title for refusing to permit himself to be inducted into the armed forces (again because of opposition to the war in Vietnam); and by the nationwide solidarity expressed by black people when a Congressman from New York, one of the most powerful elected Negro officials in American history, was denied his committee chairmanship and his seat in Congress. Such incidents as these were rather widely interpreted by Negroes as a continuing refusal on the part of white Americans to permit Negroes to share power in the society. That is, white persons in positions of power appear willing to resort to whatever tactics are necessary to perpetuate the low status of black people in the society. The 1967 mayoral elections in Cleveland, Ohio, and Gary, Indiana, illustrate the point. In both these cities Negro mayors were elected, primarily because of the heavy turnout of Negro voters. In both cities at least 90 percent of the traditionally Democratic white voters switched parties and cast their ballots for the white Republican candidates rather than vote for Negroes.[48]

In addition to increased political awareness, Negroes are now more aware of their own history and of the history of the United States than at any previous time. A continuous series of past injustices and the refusal of white Americans to discontinue such practices have made for increased impatience and bitterness throughout the black community. For their part, white Americans generally appear to be incapable of understanding this mood. Therefore, with few exceptions, there is little dialogue between the growing number of black militants and white Americans. Large numbers of black people are demanding control over the institutions in their communities as a means of dealing with the problems they face. Although the Black Power militants are in a minority at the present time, an increasingly large number of Negroes reject integration as necessary for the achievement of equality. Integration, they feel, fails to solve these problems. White Americans, for the most part, reject this notion and express satisfaction with the pace of civil rights in the United States. The result is that relations between black and white Americans have reached a point of greater strain than at any other time in the 20th century.

Finally, the strain in race relations in the United States has been intensified by systematic attempts to curb black militancy. Black Americans have learned through the years that increased militance in pursuing their goal of liberation is likely to be met by attempts to preserve white supremacy at all costs. At no time has this been more evident than at the present time. Attempts to control the pace of the movement frequently take the form of silencing the more militant leaders, either by assassinating them (e.g., Medgar Evers, Martin Luther King, Jr., Malcolm X) or by jailing them (e.g., H. Rap Brown, Eldridge Cleaver, LeRoi Jones). Black Americans see such acts as further manifestations of the racism which pervades the fabric of the society.

For the black community the murder of Martin Luther King, Jr., on April 4, 1968, clearly indicated the extent to which white bigots are willing to go to preserve the low status of the black man in the society. Although the bullet which killed King may have been fired by a single individual, he did not exist in isolation. His act must be understood within the larger context of the racism which has become institutionalized in American society.

[48] Jeffrey K. Hadden, Louis H. Masotti, and Victor Thiessen, "The Making of the Negro Mayors, 1967," *Transaction*, Vol. 5 (January–February 1968), 21–30.

Until his death, King remained the most widely respected leader in the black community. While many of the militants disapproved of his goals and tactics, his dedication and courage were unchallenged. He steadfastly maintained a faith in nonviolence as a means of achieving the liberation of black Americans. With his assassination many black people who shared his belief became disillusioned, as the widespread disorders which followed his murder showed.

In black communities throughout the United States the response to his assassination was immediate and angry. Altogether 125 cities were affected; serious outbursts occurred in Baltimore; Chicago; Kansas City, Missouri; Pittsburgh; and Washington, D.C. A total of 46 persons were killed, 2,600 were injured, and nearly 22,000 arrested. The rage of these black people was manifested by rioting, looting, and destroying buildings and other property. After nearly 10 days, 55,000 federal troops, working with local police, were able to restore order.

White Americans responded to the murder of Martin Luther King, Jr., with a massive outpouring of both genuine sentiment and sentimentality, and many of the individuals who had been the strongest opponents of his goals were among those who were most dramatic in their mourning. The results: one of the longest periods of mourning and one of the largest funerals in American history. For many in the black community the message of the assassination was clear: Any serious attempt to fundamentally alter the existing pattern of race relations in the United States would be met with whatever measures were necessary to curb it.

THE FUTURE

Predictions about the future of race relations in the United States must be tempered with caution. Changes are occurring at a rapid rate compared to the past, and one is frequently at a loss to explain these changes. An appraisal of the events of the past few years, however, indicates that what has been called the Negro Revolution was not a true social revolution. The status of black people as a group has not been significantly altered, despite the changes that have taken place. Because of constant domestic pressure and changing world conditions, black Americans have been granted some concessions, and these concessions have served to create greater expectations for social change in the realm of race relations. For the vast majority of black people, however, no significant change in their lives has resulted. Therefore what has been rather widely regarded as a revolution has really been only minor reforms on the part of the society in response to the "revolt" by Negroes, aided by their white supporters, and by increasing concern about the so-called underdeveloped nations of the world. Revolutionary change in the status of black Americans would require greater willingness on the part of white Americans to share the decision-making process and the rewards of the society proportionately with Negroes. Events of the past few years indicate that such basic changes are unlikely at the present time. The mood of increasing numbers of young black militants is that these changes must be granted without delay or else the society will face a protracted attempt on the part of black people to achieve their liberation through whatever means become necessary.

Based on the experience of the past decade, it seems fair to assume that in the immediate future black Americans will continue to make greater demands on the society and that resistance by white Americans to these demands is likely to intensify. The employment gap between black and white Americans is likely to increase. In both rates of employment and in earnings, Negroes will continue to lag behind white Americans. In housing, middle-class Negroes will find it easier to move from the slums, but the central cities are likely to become more segregated and the black community will probably expand with the increasing influx of low-income rural Negroes and their continued high birth rate. Negro pupils will experience greater segregation in education as *de facto* segregation keeps pace with segregated housing. It is perhaps in the realm of politics that the greatest changes are likely. Throughout the country black people are likely to participate in the electoral process in greater and greater numbers, electing an increasing number of black people to municipal and state offices.

The black population is becoming increasingly urbanized. White Americans are vacating the centers of the largest cities for the "safety" of the suburbs, and black people are replacing them in these core areas. These central cities are major depressed areas with widespread unemployment and underemployment. Their inhabitants, both black and white, are becoming increasingly alienated from social institutions which perpetuate their status rather than respond to their needs. In periods of major unrest these citizens have already demonstrated the ability to create a crisis which local and state officials are unable to control. Federal intervention has been necessary to bring each of the major black uprisings under control. Inasmuch as the governmental agencies responsible to citizens in these areas are ineffective in dealing with the problems they face, the likelihood is that these problems will continue and that the uprisings will intensify and spread.

Militant young blacks, Black Power advocates and other black nationalists, appear to be gaining strength among Negroes in urban areas. They speak a language which is directed to the problems faced by these citizens. The more moderate Negro leaders maintain strength among middle-class Negroes and white "liberals," but they are frequently alienated from the poor Negroes in the slums. They advocate a policy of integration of Negroes into the society as a means of achieving equality, while the militants regard integration as irrelevant in dealing with long-standing problems. The militants feel that integration is unlikely at the present time and that the problems faced by black people are of such a magnitude that more radical measures are necessary than those proposed by the moderates.

Black militants are called "racists" by the moderates who see the concept of Black Power as "reverse racism." The militant young blacks are said to be inexperienced, self-seeking activists who lack a concrete program for social change. Most of them however are products of the major civil rights campaigns of the South and of the urban Northeast. From them they have learned of the many difficulties encountered in dealing with the established political and social realities of these areas. From such experience they have gained an understanding of problems involved in effecting concrete change through established procedures. This activism has served an educational function which the more moderate leaders who disagree with them lack. It seems likely that the militants will increase in number and influence among poor Negroes, whose problems continue to intensify. Black militants see the concept of Black Power as a reasonable approach to these problems, one that stops short of a protracted black-white guerrilla war in the United States, the first manifestations of which were evidenced in the recent urban black uprisings. Nevertheless, after Watts, Newark, and Detroit, urban guerrilla warfare looms as a possible response on the part of the urban black poor to their status.

The United States is basically a reformist society. Social change comes slowly, especially when it involves changes in black-white relations. It is a society more concerned with order and stability than with minority rights. Hence problems involving black people were permitted to compound themselves throughout the long period between the Reconstruction and the end of World War II. Rather than move to alleviate the problems of segregation and discrimination, the federal government either supported white supremacy or remained aloof while states and other political subdivisions perpetuated these practices. Hence the present crisis is a result of these problems having been compounded through the decades. That the status of black Americans represents a major social problem in the United States is a function of long-standing indifference on the part of public officials, at all levels, to their status as citizens. The status of black people as a problem is, then, social in origin. It is a product of segregation and discrimination fostered by the ideology of white supremacy.

A typical American approach to social problems is that they are permitted to go unattended until they reach crisis proportions in the hope that they will somehow disappear. Once the problems have reached a crisis state, attempts are made to deal with them without changing the basic institutions which are responsible for creating them. Again, this is especially true of problems stemming from black-white relations. Whether the racial crisis in the United States deteriorates or improves depends on the willingness of white Americans (especially those in positions of leadership) to face the problems with candor and to deal with them boldly. The demand by black Americans for equality is in no sense an unreasonable one; indeed, it is long overdue. The likelihood is that this demand will intensify with time. The mood and power of black Americans at the present time are such that this demand can no longer be ignored. The longer the delay, the greater the physical and social destruction which is likely to result.

Black Americans have never been an integral part of society. Their status is such that they have been excluded from the major institutions of society, and, as a result, they view society from a vantage point different from that of white Americans. Because of this rejection, they have maintained a detachment from society which is difficult for those who have been accepted by society and who identify with it to understand. This detachment has led to greater insight into society's contradictions and a greater receptivity to social change. Few of them have any vested interest in maintaining the status quo. Consequently black Americans are likely to view the racial crisis in the United States with greater urgency than white Americans. The extent to which the society is able to avoid increased racial conflict depends upon the willingness of white Americans to come to terms with the reality of the Negro's status and the requirements for improving this status. Past experience indicates that the prognosis is not favorable.

SELECTED BIBLIOGRAPHY

Barbour, Floyd B., *The Black Power Revolt*. Boston: Porter Sargent, Inc., 1968.
Bates, Daisey, *The Long Shadow of Little Rock*. New York: David McKay Co., Inc., 1962.
Belfrage, Sally, *Freedom Summer*. New York: The Viking Press, Inc., 1965.

Bennett, Lerone, *Before the Mayflower*. Baltimore, Md.: Penguin Books, Inc., 1966.

Burns, W. Haywood, *The Voices of Negro Protest in America*. New York: Oxford University Press, Inc., 1963.

Carmichael, Stokely, "What We Want," *The New York Review of Books,* September 22, 1966.

————, and Charles Hamilton, *Black Power: The Politics of Liberation in America*. New York: Random House, Inc., 1967.

Clark, Kenneth, *Dark Ghetto*. New York: Harper & Row, Publishers, 1965.

Coles, Robert, *Children of Crisis: A Study of Courage and Fear*. Boston: Atlantic Monthly Press, 1967.

Conot, Robert, *Rivers of Blood, Years of Darkness*. New York: Bantam Books, Inc., 1967.

Cruse, Harold, *The Crisis of the Negro Intellectual*. New York: William Morrow & Co., Inc., 1967.

Danzig, David, "In Defense of 'Black Power,'" *Commentary,* Vol. 42 (September 1966), 41–46.

Fager, Charles E., *White Reflections on Black Power*. Grand Rapids, Mich.: Wm. B. Eerdmans Publishing Co., 1967.

Grier, William H., and Price M. Cobbs, *Black Rage*. New York: Basic Books, Inc., 1968.

Hayden, Tom, *Rebellion in Newark*. New York: Random House, Inc., 1967.

Holt, Len, *The Summer That Didn't End*. New York: William Morrow & Co., Inc., 1965.

Hughes, Langston, *Fight for Freedom: The Story of the NAACP*. New York: Berkley Publishing Corp., 1962.

Huie, William Bradford, *Three Lives for Mississippi*. New York: Trident Press, 1965.

Jones, LeRoi, *Home: Social Essays*. New York: William Morrow & Co., Inc., 1966.

Killens, John O., *Black Man's Burden*. New York: Trident Press, 1965.

Killian, Lewis M., *The Impossible Revolution? Black Power and the American Dream*. New York: Random House, Inc., 1968.

————, and Charles Grigg, *Racial Crisis in America: Leadership in Conflict*. Englewood Cliffs, N.J.: Prentice-Hall, Inc., 1964.

King, Martin Luther, Jr., *Stride Toward Freedom*. New York: Harper and Brothers, 1958.

————, *Where Do We Go From Here: Chaos or Community?* New York: Harper & Row, Publishers, 1967.

Lewis, Anthony, *Portrait of a Decade*. New York: Random House, Inc., 1965.

Lomax, Louis, *The Negro Revolt*. New York: Harper & Row, Publishers, 1962.

Morgan, Charles, *A Time to Speak*. New York: Harper & Row, Publishers, 1964.

Muhammad, Elijah, *Message to the Black Man in America*. Chicago: Muhammad Mosque of Islam No. 2, 1965.

Pinkney, Alphonso, *The Committed: White Activists in the Civil Rights Movement*. New Haven, Conn.: College and University Press, 1968.

Powledge, Fred, *Black Power, White Resistance: Notes on the New Civil War*. Cleveland, Ohio: World Publishing Co., 1967.

Report of the National Advisory Commission on Civil Disorders. New York: Bantam Books, Inc., 1968.

Thompson, Daniel C., *The Negro Leadership Class*. Englewood Cliffs, N.J.:
    Prentice-Hall, Inc., 1963.
Williams, Robert F., *Negroes with Guns*. New York: Marzani & Munsell, Inc.,
    1962.
Wright, Nathan, Jr., *Black Power and Urban Unrest*. New York: Hawthorn
    Books, Inc., 1967.
X, Malcolm, *The Autobiography of Malcolm X*. New York: Grove Press, Inc.,
    1964.
Zinn, Howard, *SNCC: The New Abolitionists*. Boston: Beacon Press, Inc., 1964.

Index